PUPPIES FOR SALE

and Other Inspirational Tales

A "Litter" of Stories & Anecdotes
That Hug the Heart
& Snuggle the Soul

DAN CLARK

with
Michael Gale

Health Communications, Inc.
Deerfield Beach, Florida
www.hci-online.com

Library of Congress Cataloging-in-Publication Data

Clark, Dan
    Puppies for sale, and other inspirational tales : a "litter" of
stories & anecdotes that hug the heart & snuggle the soul /
Dan Clark ; with Michael Gale.
       p.   cm.
    ISBN 1-55874-469-X. — ISBN 1-55874-452-5 (pbk.)
    1. Conduct of life—Anecdotes.   I. Gale, Michael.   II. Title.
BJ1597.C57   1997
814'.54—dc21   97-36047
                                           CIP

Publisher: Health Communications, Inc.
             3201 S.W. 15th Street
             Deerfield Beach, Florida 33442-8190

Cover design by Andrea Perrine Brower.

To sweet K.C. for living her life as a picture
perfect story of unconditional love and peacemaking,
with unbridled support and devotion to all that is good.
I could not do what I do without you, Kelly.
To Danny, Nikola, McCall and Alexandrea for your storybook
lives of childlike wonderment. I love each of you for
reminding me of what really matters most.

Contents

5. TEACHING IS THE PROFESSION THAT MAKES ALL OTHER PROFESSIONS POSSIBLE

6. TELL THEM HOW YOU FEEL

7. LOOK BEYOND IT

11. FOR A MOST UNUSUAL PERSON

12. COMMUNICATION CONCERNS

13. AMERICA THE BEAUTIFUL

14. GREATER SENSITIVITY

15. LEADERSHIP

16. IT'S NOT WHAT'S ON THE OUTSIDE

Acknowledgments

To Dad, the special man who taught me there are two ways to look at everything: eyesight and insight. I admire you, Dad, for instilling in me a constant curiosity to internally excavate the stories and lessons out of every day of living. I miss you.

To my dear, sweet mother, who taught me that life is a story. She collects stories, observes stories and shares stories with all who will listen. I appreciate you, Mother Dear. You have always been my emotional and spiritual connection to reality. I need you.

To Zig Ziglar, my hero, my good friend, my sponsor into the National Speakers Association. You have always encouraged and supported my dreams to be a storyteller, motivational teacher and effective human being. God bless you for the positive example you set for all of humanity.

To Jim and Karen Elias Koeninger for believing in me and giving me my first break in the national public speaking arena. I wouldn't be where I am today without your direction, kindness, caring and keeping. Thanks for teaching me "The Best Is Yet to Be!"

To Sue Davis Purcell for always going beyond the call of duty, typing the manuscript and putting up with my constant changes. Your exceptional business savvy is truly amazing.

To Dr. Donald and Barbara Sansom, Normand Gibbons,

Royden Derrick, and Stephen Munn—for your extraordinary lives, inspiration and constant encouragement. Your are my heroes, my mentors. I thank God you are in my life!

To Mike Hassel, one of the greatest teachers and leadership trainers in the world. Thanks for validating that my writing makes a difference. I cherish our friendship.

To Charles Reed, Todd Petersen, Blain Hope, Bob Boothby, Brent Bowen, Steve Cosgrove, Patricia Mutch, Keith Harrell, Todd Morgan, Kirk Butler, Sam Clark, Debbie Clark and Paul Clark. You believed in me when I didn't. You inspire me and deeply bless my life. I think about each of you every day.

And to Michael Gale for writing some of the one-page stories in this book. Your special friendship from the good old days as "Butch and Sundance" up until today keeps me smiling.

To all of you, I give my endless love. We have shared at least one significant emotional experience together and the subsequent story of my life is what it is because of you. Thanks!

Introduction

Life is a story. The goal of every human being is to live in such a way that his or her story becomes a source of inspiration and emotional empowerment to others.

Stories have a magical power. They allow us to look at ourselves in relation to other people. They act as mirrors—reflecting our own actions through the actions of others. They make us aware of our own talents and idiosyncrasies, and serve as constant reminders of the forms of behavior that are appropriate.

Stories pump us up and help us do what it takes to make our dreams come true. They ignite our imagination and set our plans in motion.

Life is a collection of the various things people do and say. When we hear facts and figures based on data, we don't remember the information, we remember the interpretation of the information. When we hear a tale, our interpretation says, "If it happened to them, one day it could happen to me." Reading an inspirational story fills us with hope for humanity. It teaches us that dreams can come true, so I think I'll give it a try.

Inspirational stories spark creativity and unleash our imaginations to see beyond our limitations. History is our proof: Two Wright brother who sold bicycles one day decided that they could fly. Sure enough, Orville and Wilbur did. In 1903 there were no automobiles, houses didn't have running water, electricity was still a dream, nobody knew what an interstate freeway was, natural gas did not heat homes, and the mere mention of television, personal computers and radios would have made you the laughing stock at school. Much has happened since then. And the only explanation is that certain individuals were inspired!

I give the following principle-centered stories to you with only one purpose in mind: to inspire and rekindle your spirit and uplift your everyday sights. I have written most of them. As an honest disclosure, some of the stories were told to me years ago. While the lessons remain vivid, the names of the tellers of those tales have, unfortunately, been lost to time. If any of you recognize your stories, please let me know. Good deeds—and good yarns—should not go unacknowledged.

I have selected each of these stories as a special gift to you. Together, we wordsmiths of the world—known and unknown—are just trying to make a difference.

Thanks for giving us a chance!

1
UNDERSTANDING

Everybody can
find strength to take
just one more step.

Everybody can
climb the highest
mountain
one step at
a time!

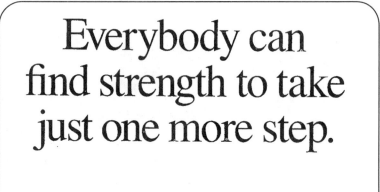

Puppies for Sale

A store owner was tacking a sign in his store window which read PUPPIES FOR SALE, when a little boy appeared.

"How much are you selling the puppies for?" he asked.

The man told the lad he didn't expect to let any of them go for less than $50.

The boy reached in his pocket, pulled out some change, looked up at the store owner and said, "I have two dollars and thirty-seven cents. Can I look at them?"

The store owner smiled and whistled. From the kennel, a dog named Lady came running down the aisle, followed by five tiny balls of fur. One puppy lagged behind. Immediately, the little boy asked about the limping puppy.

"What's wrong with that doggie?"

"The veterinarian told us the dog is missing a hip socket," said the store owner. "He'll always limp like that."

"That's the one I want to buy," the lad said quickly.

The store owner replied, "No, you don't want to buy that dog. If you really want him, I'll just give him to you."

The boy came close to the store owner's face and said angrily, "I don't want you to just *give* him to me. That doggie is worth just as much as all the other puppies and I'll pay the full price. In fact, I'll give you $2.37 now and 50¢ a month until I have him paid for!"

The store owner replied, "No, no, no. You don't want that dog. He's never going to be able to run and jump and play like the other dogs."

In response, the little boy pulled up his pant leg to reveal a badly twisted left leg, supported by two steel braces.

"Well, sir," he said, "I don't run so well myself and the puppy will need someone who understands."

Puppy Love

The young boy who had been wearing a steel brace on his left leg for the last four months walked through the front door of his home with a newly purchased puppy in his arms. The dog didn't have a hip socket and, when placed on the floor, it walked with a serious limp. The boy's selection of a physically challenged puppy intrigued his parents, for he had been down-and-out. But with his new companion at his side, they sensed a newly revitalized spirit of hope and enthusiasm emerging from his soul.

The next day the young boy and his mom went to see a veterinarian to find out how he could best help his little dog. The doctor explained that if he stretched and massaged his puppy's leg every morning and then walked with him at least one mile per day, the muscles around his missing hip would eventually strengthen to the point of no pain and less of a limp.

Although the dog whimpered and barked out his discomfort, and the boy winced and hassled with his own leg brace, for the next two months they religiously kept to their rehabilitation regimen. By the third month they were walking three miles every morning before school began and they were both walking without pain.

One Saturday morning when returning from their workout, a cat leaped out of the bushes and startled the dog. Breaking loose of the leash, the dog darted into oncoming traffic. With a speeding truck only seconds away, the boy ran into the street, dove for his dog, and rolled into the gutter. He was too late. The dog was hit and bleeding profusely from the mouth. As the boy lay there crying and hugging his dying dog, he noticed that his own leg brace had broken off. With no time to worry about himself, he sprang to his feet, picked up his dog, cuddled it close to him and started for home. The dog quietly barked, giving him hope and turning the boy's jog into an all-out, adrenaline sprint.

His mother rushed him and his suffering pup to the pet hospital. As they anxiously waited to see if his dog would survive the surgery, he asked his mother why he could now walk and run.

"You had osteomyelitis, which is a disease of the bone," she said. "It weakened and crippled your leg, which caused you to limp in severe pain. Your brace was for support. It wasn't necessarily a permanent condition if you were willing to fight through the pain and hours of therapy. You responded well to the medication, but you always resisted our encouragement for physical therapy, and your father and I didn't know what to do. The doctors told us you were about to lose your leg. Then you brought home your puppy and you seemed to understand his needs. Ironically, as you were helping him, you were actually helping yourself to strengthen and grow."

Just then the operating room door slowly opened. Out walked the veterinarian with a smile on his face. "Your dog is going to make it," he said.

And, the boy learned that when you lose yourself, you find yourself. It is more blessed to give, *then* receive.

Stay

A young girl was leaving for school, and her mother reminded her to come straight home when her last class ended. Thirty minutes late, she finally walked through the front door. Her mother scolded her. "Where have you been?" she asked. "I've been worried sick."

With a concerned face the daughter sweetly replied, "I walked home with my friend, Sally, and she dropped her doll and it broke all to pieces. It was just awful!"

"So you were late because you stayed to help her pick up the doll and put it back together again?" her mother asked.

"Oh, no, Mommy," she explained. "I didn't know how to fix the doll. I just stayed to help her cry!"

Support

John McMaster became a superstar basketball player in high school. For each of his three years on the team he was All-Conference, All-State. In his final season he was named the Most Valuable Player of the league. John's mother never missed a game—home or away—regardless of the travel distance or weather conditions. His mom was always in the bleachers cheering her son to victory.

Interestingly, John's mother was totally blind! What's the message? Although the mother could not see her son, he could see her. Support makes the special difference!

One Moment in Time

One day Henry Winkler, the actor best known for his portrayal of Fonzie on the television series *Happy Days*, decided to take some time off and treat himself to a matinee movie. To avoid fans making a fuss over him, Winkler entered the theater from the side exit door. He shuffled his way into an aisle and found himself a vacant seat.

As Henry turned around to sit down, the little girl sitting in the row behind him smiled broadly, pointed her finger and slowly said, "Fonzie." Winkler immediately snapped into the Fonzie character, flipping his hair, swiveling his hips and glancing left and right.

In his signature pose he then pointed his finger at the girl and said, "Whoa!" To everyone's surprise, the lady sitting next to the little girl passed out!

The theater manager came out to assist the woman. Lying in the aisle with a cold pack on her forehead, she was asked one question: "Why did you pass out?"

Pointing to the same little girl, she replied, "My daughter is autistic and that's the very first word she has ever spoken in her entire life!"

Promises

A young Japanese boy was spending the weekend with his elderly grandfather. The rendezvous would take place at the train station, for the grandfather lived in a village on the other side of the mountain. The boy's parents dropped him off, hugged both of them good-bye and drove away.

As the two of them waited in line to buy their tickets, the grandfather discovered that he had left his wallet on the previous train. He didn't have any money. It was cold and blizzardy, and he asked the ticket lady if she would loan him yen valuing $50. The grandfather promised he would pay her back later that night.

Because of the Japanese culture's deep and abiding respect for its elders, the ticket lady believed the grandfather and paid for their tickets.

An hour later, they arrived in the village. They walked 15 minutes through the horrible weather and finally entered the cottage. Hungry, tired and soaking wet, the grandfather went to his drawer and retrieved some money. "Let's go," he said. His grandson rebutted, "But Grandfather, I'm starving and we're going back to the train station in three days. Why can't you just pay her back then? It will cost you the price of two more round-trip tickets to go now, just to pay back two one-way passes."

Putting on a dry overcoat and handing his grandson a wool blanket for his comfort, the 80-year-old grandfather put his arm around his grandson's shoulders and taught him the lesson of the ages. "Son, we must get there tonight before the counter closes and she goes home. This is not about money. This is about honor. I gave her my word, and we must always keep our promises!"

Stride to Be Better

I was in Maui, Hawaii, on vacation when Naomi Rhode, a professional speaker who was in Hawaii doing some seminars, related this experience to me:

"My husband and I had been walking along the beach for several hundred yards when I paused to look back to see how far we had come. I noticed our footprints in the sand and immediately filled with pride. I pointed them out to my husband and commented, 'Wow, think about how many times we have left our footprints in the lives of others.'

"Suddenly the ocean interrupted by sweeping in and washing away our footprints, leaving no sign of them ever having been there. I was puzzled and almost hurt, and asked my husband, 'How can we leave a more lasting impression on people that will not be washed away with time?'

"He wisely replied, 'Just walk on higher ground.'"

Each of us should evaluate our daily lives and commit to reaching a higher level of living by striving and striding to walk on higher ground.

What Goes Around Comes Around

A unique directive was initiated at a high school in northern Utah, where students with a physical or mental challenge were fully integrated into the mainstream classes and curriculum. To make it work, the administration organized a mentor program that teamed up one special-needs student with a mainstream student who would help him or her along.

The athletic director presented the idea to the captain of the football team. John was a tall, strong, intense young man—not the patient, caring type needed for this kind of program. He made it clear this "wasn't his thing" and he didn't have time to be a mentor. But, the athletic director knew it would be good for him and insisted that John volunteer.

John was matched up with Randy—a young man with Down's syndrome. The minute they were introduced they became inseparable. Reluctant and irritated at first, John literally tried to "lose" Randy, but soon John welcomed the constant company. Randy not only attended every one of John's classes and ate with him at lunchtime, he also came to football practice. After a few days John asked the coach to make Randy the official manager responsible for the balls, tape and water bottles. At the end of the football season, the team won the state championship and John was awarded with the gold medal as the Most Valuable Player in the state. Randy was presented with a school letter jacket. The team cheered as Randy put it on. It was the coolest thing that had ever happened to him; from that day forward Randy never took it off. He slept in his jacket and wore it throughout each weekend.

Basketball season started and John was also the captain and star of that team. At John's request, Randy was again named the manager. During the basketball season they were still inseparable. Not only did John take Randy to special occasions—like dances as a joint escort for his girlfriend—but he also took Randy to the library to tutor him in his classes. As he tutored Randy, John became a much better student and made the honor roll for the first time in more than a year. The mentor program was unveiling itself as the most rewarding year of John's life.

Then tragedy struck in the middle of the state basketball tournament. Randy caught a virus and suddenly died of pneumonia. The funeral was held the day before the final championship game. John was asked to be one of the speakers. In his talk John shared his deep abiding friendship and respect for Randy. He told how Randy had been the one who had taught him about real courage, self-esteem, unconditional love and the importance of giving 100 percent in everything he did. John dedicated the upcoming state finals game to Randy and concluded his remarks by stating that he was honored to have received the MVP award in football and the leadership plaque for being the captain of the basketball team.

"But," John added, "the real leader of both the football and basketball teams was Randy, for he accomplished more with what he had than anyone I've ever met. Randy inspired all who knew him."

John walked from behind the podium, took off the irreplaceable 24-carat-gold state football MVP medallion that hung around his neck, leaned into the open casket, and placed it on Randy's chest. He placed his captain's plaque next to it.

Randy was buried in his letter jacket, surrounded by John's cherished awards, as well as pictures and letters left by others who admired him.

But this is not the end.

The next day John's team won the championship and presented the game ball to Randy's family. John went to college on a full athletic scholarship and graduated with a master's degree in education. Today John is a special education teacher; he also volunteers 10 hours a week for the Special Olympics.

Tree Talk

The heroine of this story is an eight-year-old girl in a Pennsylvania orphanage. She was painfully shy and had such annoying mannerisms that she was shunned by the other children and regarded as a problem child by the teachers. Two other orphanages had managed to have her transferred. Now, once again, the director was seeking some pretext for getting rid of her.

One afternoon it appeared that an opportunity had arrived. An ironclad rule held that any letter from a child in the institution had to be approved by the director or a house mistress before it could be mailed. The little girl had been observed sneaking down to the main gate and carefully securing a letter in the branches of a tree that overhung the wall of the orphanage. The director could scarcely conceal her elation.

She hurried down to the brick wall. Sure enough, the note was visible through the branches of the tree.

The director pounced on it and tore open the envelope. She pulled out the note and quickly read it. Stunned, she stood staring at the piece of paper, then hung her head. It read:

To anybody who finds this: I love you.

Take It to the Max

Take Relationships to a Deeper Level

The other night I had to take my four-year-old daughter to the hospital. Sitting in the emergency room, I just wanted to fit in and look like and be like everyone else. A macho man came in with his son, and the physician asked about the problem. "My boy fell down and broke three bones in his leg. Didn't even cry!" I thought, *Oh, perfect.* A mother came in with her little girl. The physician inquired about her daughter. "My daughter fell off the beam at the gymnastics meet and badly twisted her knee." I thought, *Oh, perfect!* The doctor finally asked me why I was there with my daughter. I said, "She has a raisin stuck in her nose!" Everybody laughed. I just wanted to fit in, but my little girl taught me that it's okay to be outside the lines!

A father came home from work and his five-year-old son met him in the driveway. "Daddy, welcome home, Daddy. Will you play baseball with me?" His father flippantly responded, "I have too much work to do. I don't have time. But I want you to know that I love you." His little boy replied, "Dad, I don't want you to love me, I want you to play ball with me!"

Take Competition to Its Highest Fulfillment

A young girl with a serious mental handicap ran in the 50-yard dash competition of the national Special Olympics track-and-field meet. When she lost the race, she sighed, "I just needed faster shoes!" With an IQ of 42, she then turned to all the timers, track personnel, meet officials and fellow athletes, and taught them all one of the greatest, most profound lessons of competition. "I finished at my best, and you have to give it your all and finish best before you can ever finish first!"

Take Mistakes to Their Sweetest Solutions

A little boy spilled cranberry juice on the new carpet in his living room. Shaking with fear and sobbing giant tears of pain, he humbly walked into the kitchen to confess. "Mom, I am so sorry. I just spilled my big glass of juice on your new carpet. I feel very, very bad." His mother hugged him and said, "It's okay. Don't be sad. We can get you another glass of cranberry juice."

Take Work to Its Greatest Enjoyment

As we were coming in for a landing at the Dallas/Fort Worth airport, our Delta Airlines jet hit heavy turbulence and bounced all over the sky. When we finally touched down, the flight attendant spoke over the cabin public-address system. "Welcome to Dallas, Texas. If you enjoyed your flight, tell your friends you flew Delta. If you did not enjoy your flight, tell your friends you flew Southwest."

Take Embarrassment Out of Play

One afternoon at a sales convention, the closing speaker, an 82-year-old man, made us fall out of our chairs laughing, as he wittily responded to several faux pas at the podium. He accidentally dropped his speech, and the stack of three-by-five cards scattered everywhere. He responded by saying, "I'm sorry I'm a bit jittery. I gave up beer for Lent and this whiskey is killing me!" The microphone went out and he yelled, "Some days you're the bug, some days the windshield!" He spoke from the heart for a few minutes, and then apologized for having to leave early. He said, "I've got to go. Tonight my wife and I are sharing our wedding anniversary with you. Yep. Me and my wife have enjoyed 17 great years of marriage—17 out of 55 ain't bad!"

Take Private Victories Way Beyond Public Victories

At a gala fund-raiser, I was sitting next to the distinguished actor, Mr. Gregory Peck. Throughout the evening, every other celebrity had been acknowledged and introduced—all except Mr. Peck. A journalist finally approached him to apologize. He simply replied, "No apology necessary. If you have to tell them that you are, then you aren't."

A Swimmer's Glory

Michael Swenson loved to swim. In fact, every night after school he would go to the community pool and swim lap after lap just for pure enjoyment. As time went on, Michael reached the age when he really needed some attention and recognition. And how do we get recognition? Usually by doing something we are good at.

In Michael's case, he decided to enter a swimming race. Ironically, the following day an ad appeared in the newspaper announcing a local meet. Michael entered and continued to practice. It was a ten-mile race across a lake. With only four weeks to prepare, Michael intensified his workouts.

Race day finally came, and to Michael's astonishment, hundreds of contestants had entered. On top of this pressure, thousands of people showed up to cheer for their favorite contender.

Instructions were given, the swimmers were lined up, and the gun went off to start the race. Michael's preparation and hard work paid off. At the five-mile mark he had a commanding lead. But then fatigue struck, and fatigue makes cowards of us all. Negative thoughts began flooding Michael's head. *What am I trying to prove? I can't make it,* Michael rationalized. *I'll quit now but learn from this so I can win next time.*

As Michael slowed down, the second-place swimmer started to make his move. He swam to within one hundred yards of Michael at the eight-mile mark. But Michael fought back. His second wind kicked in and he was able to put the negative thoughts aside and push himself to greatness. He decided that he wanted this victory, this glory. At the nine-mile mark, the second-place swimmer was now only thirty yards behind him. Michael knew it and pushed himself even harder.

With only five yards to go, the second-place contestant passed Michael and won the race. Both swimmers collapsed and lay in the sand gasping for breath. Then something interesting happened. All the spectators congratulated the winner for his excellence but immediately turned their attention to Michael. Why? he wondered. After all, he hadn't won. A lady passing by who didn't see the race and couldn't see the contestants was also confused.

She tapped a man on the shoulder and asked, "Why are they making such a big deal of this guy? He didn't win!"

The man turned to her and replied, "Because Michael would have easily won had he had two arms!"

The Circus

Once, as a teenager, my father and I were standing in line to buy tickets for the circus. Finally, there was only one family between us and the ticket counter. There were eight children, all under the age of 12. I could tell they didn't have a lot of money. Their clothes were frayed but clean, and the children were well-behaved—all of them standing in line, two-by-two holding hands in back of the parents. They were jabbering about the clowns, elephants and other acts they would see that night. I sensed they had never been to the circus before. This promised to be a highlight of their young lives.

The father and mother were at the head of the pack standing proud as could be, the mother looking at her husband as if to say, "You're my knight in shining armor." He was smiling and basking in pride, as if to reply, "You got that right."

The ticket lady asked the father how many tickets he wanted. He proudly responded, "Please let me buy eight childrens' tickets and two adult tickets."

As the ticket lady quoted the price, the wife let go of her husband's hand, her head dropped, the man's lip began to quiver. The father leaned a little closer and asked, "How much did you say?"

The ticket lady again quoted the price.

The man didn't have enough money.

How was he supposed to turn and tell his children that he couldn't afford to take them to the circus?

Seeing what was going on, my dad put his hand into his pocket, pulled out a $20 bill and dropped it on the ground. We were not wealthy in any sense of the word. Then my dad reached down, picked up the bill, tapped the man on the shoulder and said, "Excuse me, sir, this fell out of your pocket."

The man knew what was going on. He wasn't begging for a handout but he certainly appreciated the help in a desperate, heartbreaking, embarrassing situation. He looked straight into my dad's eyes, took my dad's hand in both of his and squeezed it tightly. With a tear streaming down his cheek, he replied, "Thank you, thank you, sir. This really means the world to me and my little family."

My father and I went back to our car and drove home. We didn't go to the circus that night, but we didn't go without.

Understanding that *who* is right is not as important as *what* is right—this is the secret to effective leadership, management, parenting, teaching and coaching. It's amazing how much we can accomplish if we simply focus on leaving everyone we meet in better shape than we found them.

Making Memories

It was the holiday season, with the "big three"—Halloween, Thanksgiving and Christmas—just ahead. My father was battling cancer at that time; he was very ill. Afraid that he wouldn't be around for Christmas, I wanted to make that year extra special. I thought the perfect gift was a grandfather clock, handbuilt by me. It was one of the things he had always wanted but could never afford. Although I had not built anything of that complexity, I felt it would not only make my dad proud of me, but it would give him something from me that he could treasure.

I purchased a magnificent self-assembly kit and immediately devoted my time to the overwhelming task of putting it together.

Every day after work I went to my brother's house to secretly work on the clock. Three hours a day, six days a week I labored all alone, trying to figure out those complicated instructions. As it started to take form, the anticipation and internal excitement were almost too much to bear. I was really proud and couldn't help visualizing how surprised, appreciative and amazed my dad would surely be when he unwrapped the masterpiece. On October 10, I finally finished the clock and wrapped it up with a big red bow, ready to be delivered in a couple of months on Christmas Eve. The next morning I left on a trip to Washington.

Two days later at 7:00 A.M., the phone rang in my hotel room. It was my brother. "Dad just died," he cried.

That was a sad and brutal Christmas for me. Mom had a gorgeous Christmas tree, there were gifts galore. And there in the corner of my mother's living room stood the tall, solid oak grandfather clock that I had spent 63 hours building. But there was no Dad! The presents meant nothing and the clock meant nothing in comparison to the loss of my dad.

Not a day goes by that I don't regret the time I spent on that clock, now knowing that I should have spent those final, most sacred hours—all 63 of them—at my father's side. What a fool I was to think a "thing" would make him happy. Things don't make people happy. Time spent together with loved ones does!

Pay Attention

Jason came from a good family with two loving parents, two brothers and a sister. They were all successful academically and socially. They lived in a posh neighborhood. Jason had everything a boy could desire. But he was always into some kind of mischief. He wasn't a bad kid who caused trouble, but he always wound up in the thick of things.

In first grade Jason was labeled Special Ed. They tried to keep him out of the regular classes. In middle school he was the "misfit troublemaker." In high school, although never officially tested, Jason was tagged with having attention deficit disorder (ADD). More often than not, his teachers kicked him out of class. His first report card had one C and all Ds.

One Sunday the family was enjoying brunch at the country club when a teacher stopped and said, "Jason is doing so well these days. We're pleased and delighted."

"You must be mixing us up with another family," said the father. "Our Jason is worthless. He is always in trouble. We are so embarrassed and just can't figure out why."

As the teacher walked away, the mother remarked, "You know, honey, come to think of it, Jason hasn't been in trouble for a month. He's even been going to school early and staying late. I wonder what's up?"

The second nine-week grading period was finally up. As usual, Jason's mom and dad expected low grades and unsatisfactory marks in behavior. Instead, he achieved four As and three Bs and honors in citizenship. His parents were baffled.

"Who did you sit by to get these grades?" the dad asked sarcastically.

"I did it all myself," Jason humbly answered.

Perplexed, and still not satisfied, the parents took Jason back to school to meet with the principal. He assured them that Jason was doing very well.

"We have a new guidance counselor and she seems to have touched your son in a special way," he said. "His self-esteem is much better and he's doing great this term. I think you should meet her."

When the trio approached, the woman had her head down. It took a moment for her to notice she had visitors. When she did, she leaped to her feet and began gesturing with her hands.

"What's this?" asked Jason's father indignantly. "Sign language? Why, she can't even hear."

"That's why she's so great," said Jason, jumping in between them. "She does more than hear, Dad. She listens!"

See

It was a hot, sunny day and a man was lounging at the hotel pool. Clad in a bright orange swimsuit and sleek wrap-around sunglasses, the man casually sipped a frozen drink. Soon a woman lay down on the chaise to the right of him and commented, "What a drag. There are clouds in the sky and one of them is going to cover the sun. It's even getting windy."

The man in the sunglasses replied, "No, it's a wonderful day. Can't you see the birds chirping in the trees? Can't you see that the clouds and breeze will cool down the blistering heat?"

In a moment, it started to sprinkle. The woman complained, "What did I tell you? This rain ruins everything." The man in the sunglasses said, "No it doesn't. Can't you see that the magnificent, fragrant flowers blossoming all around us and the freshly cut grass need the rain?"

Soon a couple pulled up chairs and sat down to the left of him. "You idiot. I can't believe you locked the key in the room," the man yelled at his wife. "Yeah, but you big imbecile, you forgot to bring the suntan lotion," she replied.

The man in the sunglasses interrupted, "Can't you see there is another key at the front desk and probably lots of lotion in the gift shop? Can't you see that fighting over shallow things is a waste of precious life?"

A mother sitting two seats away asked her son if he would please pick up a heavy box and take it to the car. He complained, "Oh, Mom, my back hurts, I'm tired, and ouch! I just got something in my eye!"

The man in the sunglasses turned to the lad. "Can't you see there are people in this world who would give anything just to be able to bend over and lift something?"

Just then, a woman came from behind the wall with a wheelchair. She helped hoist the paralyzed, blind man into the seat, rearranged his sunglasses, carefully wheeled him out the gate and extended his telescopic white cane so that he could tap his way back to the positive environment of his hotel room.

Paul's Best Day

In the middle of his 11th-grade school year, Paul's father was transferred from his job. Paul was forced to leave his spot on the varsity basketball team, his guitar teacher, his circle of best friends and his sweetheart whom he had been dating for two years. He was devastated to say the least.

Then one morning Paul woke up with a plan. It was his birthday, but he was convinced it wouldn't be much of a birthday because he didn't have any friends. His plan would solve that.

His father reassured Paul. "It'll be okay. You and your mother can have cake and ice cream this afternoon." But Paul still was not happy.

As he was leaving for work, the father saw a young man in the neighborhood he barely knew. He asked the teenager to drop by that afternoon for cake and ice cream. "It's my son's birthday," he said.

Later that day, the father had a phone call at work. His wife said, "I don't know what you did, but ten kids from the high school and two basketball coaches showed up here this afternoon for Paul's birthday party—with gifts."

It seems the neighbor boy told his mother he had been invited to a birthday party. She called others in the small Texas neighborhood to make sure Paul would have a real party. She had occasionally seen Paul shooting baskets in the driveway, so she also phoned the basketball coaches to tell them he was a pretty good player and they should probably take a look.

When Paul's father arrived home that evening, he was greeted by an excited son who said, "Dad, this has been one of the best days of my whole life. A girl even asked me to the girl's choice spring dance."

The point is it doesn't take much to make every day a best day for someone. All it takes is an invitation, a phone call, a thank-you note, a compliment or a word of encouragement.

Make today a best day for someone new in your neighborhood, or a relative who may be ill, or an acquaintance. How much time and effort does it take on your part to let someone know you care?

Amazingly, Paul's plan for that day was to kill himself after school. The weeks of loneliness had come to a head and he had been overwhelmed with despair. Luckily, things turned out the way they did.

It has been many years since then and Paul is now married with four beautiful children of his own. All of them are certainly glad he didn't give up in high school!

You Never Know

Leathy was an elderly woman who lived in our neighborhood. Her home was small and humble. Her reputation was one of grouchy seclusion, as she seldom ventured outside her home. When we moved into the neighborhood, we were told to keep away because Leathy was a witch. They said she walked slowly and always carried a broom. The children were not even allowed to trick-or-treat there on Halloween.

About a year after we moved into the area, a young, newly married couple moved into a house on our street. They moved next door to the "old scrooge woman," as we called her, and we felt we should warn them. But, by the time we went to visit the newlyweds, it was too late to explain their odd neighbor. They had already paid Leathy a visit, bringing with them a basket of fruit, some warm bread and friendship.

Over the next few months, it became a weekly occurrence to see the young newlyweds coming and going from Leathy's home. One evening, my wife and I were eating at a nice restaurant with our children, when two ladies entered the room. One was the young woman; the other she introduced as Leathy. Much to our surprise, Leathy was not a decrepit, unkempt, witchy woman, as we had been led to believe when we moved into the neighborhood. Instead, she was a dignified, elegant lady with a sparkle in her eye and a big, warm smile. She walked with a limp and used not a broom, but a cane, to support her. She explained that her sweet husband and two children had been killed an in automobile accident 15 years before. She had never remarried, and this day was the anniversary of their death. She briefly cried as she hugged our children and thanked the young woman for taking the time from her busy schedule to spend the afternoon with her. "It's tough," she said. "Sometimes I get so lonely. These beautiful children remind me of the good old days."

We left the restaurant and verbally committed as a family to visit Leathy during the next few days. Our busy schedule turned days into weeks, and a month later we finally got our act together. We walked the two blocks to Leathy's home as a family. As we approached the front door, a big, black hearse was just pulling away. Leathy had suffered a heart attack and passed away early that morning. We had waited too long to be kind, caring and considerate. It was too late to meet this "walking time machine" who had seen every major invention, dealt with the Great Depression and survived the concentration camps of the Holocaust.

Two weeks after the simple, quiet funeral service that only a few people attended, Leathy's will was read. To the young newlyweds who had befriended her and spruced up her yard, Leathy wrote, "For making me feel special, beautiful and needed again, I leave you $1 million and my house and property, with a guarantee that you will enlarge, update and remodel this small home, turning the property into the magnificent estate that I always dreamed of but didn't have the strength to create after my husband died. I leave you a second $1 million to set up your family, so you won't have to work outside your home and can help another elderly lady feel pretty and important like you did me." The will then left a young, single mother, who was Leathy's regular waitress at her favorite restaurant, $125,000. Since the young couple moved in, Leathy and her neighbors ate there three times a week. During the course of conversation, she discovered that the waitress had a new baby and was working two jobs so that she could go back to college and get the job she dreamed of, instead of just settling. The money Leathy willed her was earmarked for her education. Unbeknownst to most, Leathy served on the board of directors of three national foundations and a children's hospital. She left the rest of her fortune to them.

The attorney reading the will then concluded, "Leathy's husband made his millions as an inventor. He conceived the idea of recycling paper, aluminum and plastic. He based his process formula on two things: Leathy's life motto and the meaning of her name. Her motto was 'What Goes Around Comes Around.' Her name, Leathy, means 'Always remember, never forget.'"

In life and in death Leathy made a difference. We will always remember her and never forget her life of love and leadership. You never know whose life you touch when you unselfishly and unconditionally serve.

The Art of Being Alive

Pain can be a signal to grow, not necessarily to suffer. Once we learn the lesson that the pain teaches us, the pain goes away.

I played football for 13 years. My dreams of being an NFL star were on the horizon when I was hit in a practice tackling drill. My eye drooped, I experienced speech loss, my right side was numb and my right arm dangled at my side. My arm stayed numb and hung helplessly at my side for well over a year. It was a physical injury but it affected my whole life. Being right-handed, I couldn't write, and the constant pain made concentration on work impossible. I didn't have control over my muscle spasms, and every now and then my nerves would unexpectedly twinge and contract my shoulder, which whipped my arm out! One night, I knocked a bowl of dressing off the dinner table, and my younger brother showed up to the next meal wearing a batting helmet and goggles! I went to 16 of the best doctors in North America and they all concluded I would never recover. My dreams were shattered, my heart was broken and my life slowly fell apart.

Although I kept playing ball, I had to play with my arm strapped to my side. Eventually I had to give it up and I hit rock bottom. Totally confused and depressed, I decided to take my life. Obviously I didn't and today I enjoy a 95 percent recovery. So what three things did I learn from this experience and how does it relate to you?

1) I kept playing football—even though there was a chance for total paralysis—because I was unable to let go of the past. We've all been raised to believe that what we've been in the past makes us who we are. This is not totally true. It's what we hope to become in the future that makes us who we are. No matter what our past has been, we have a spotless future. Only when I let go of the past did I become emotionally available to embrace change, dream a new dream and get on with my life. I learned that we cannot and should not cling to the past—especially if it no longer sustains us. Lesson: When your horse dies, dismount!

2) Why would I want to quit or kill myself? I was somebody because I was an athlete. When I was injured, suddenly I was a nobody. Why? When we identify ourselves in terms of what we do, instead of who we are, we become a human doing instead of a human being. If lasting happiness is what we seek, we must realize we are not our bodies, our sports cars, our houses or our country club memberships. Lesson: We must be more than those superficial things!

3) Why didn't I quit? I stopped focusing on having fame and started focusing on being whole. I started focusing on purposes instead of just setting goals. I listened to a Zig Ziglar tape on motivation which inspired me to start dreaming again. He taught "If you don't have a dream, how are you going to make a dream come true?" That fired me up to do whatever it took to get better physically.

This significant awakening taught me a philosophy that affects my life each and every day. Lesson: It is summarized by J. Stone, who says:

The most visible creators are those artists whose medium is life itself. The ones who express the inexpressible without brush, hammer, clay, or guitar. Their medium is being. Whatever their presence touches has increased life. They see and don't have to draw. They are the artists of being alive.

2

PARENTING

No other success can compensate
for failure in the home.

—DAVID O. MCKAY

A broken clock
is right twice a day.

Never give up
on anyone—
especially yourself!
Make peace with
what you're not!

Secret Love

"May I see my baby?" asked the happy new mother.

When the little bundle was nestled in her arms and she moved the fold of clothes to look upon the tiny face, she gasped. The doctor turned away quickly to avoid seeing the mother's heartache. The baby had been born without ears.

Time proved that the boy's hearing was perfect, it was only his appearance that was marred. One day he rushed home from school and flung himself into his mother's arms.

"The kids are making fun of me," he sobbed. "They say I'm a freak. I don't want to go to school anymore!"

The boy's father asked the family physician if he could graft a pair of outer ears, if they could be procured. The doctor agreed but a donor was needed first.

Two years went by before a match was made.

The operation was successful and a new person emerged. The boy's talents blossomed; school and college became an unbroken series of triumphs. Later he married and entered the diplomatic service.

Although he urged his father to tell him who the donor was, the dad would not give away the secret.

Over the years the boy never knew, until the darkest day a son ever passed through arrived. He stood with his father, bowed over his mother's casket. He leaned in and kissed her forehead, whispering one last time how much he loved her. Slowly, tenderly, the father stretched forth a hand and raised her thick, red-brown hair to show him.

With tears streaming down their cheeks, they closed the casket on their special secret.

A Mother's Example

There were four clergymen who were discussing the merits of the various translations of the Bible. One liked the King James Version best because of its simple, beautiful English.

Another liked the American Revised Version best because it is more literal and came nearer to the original Hebrew and Greek.

Still another liked Moffat's translation because of its up-to-date vocabulary.

The fourth minister was silent. When asked to express his opinion, he replied, "I like my mother's translation best."

The other three expressed surprise. They did not know that his mother had translated the Bible.

But he assured them. "She translated it into life, every day of her life, and it was the most convincing translation I ever saw."

Special Man

A little boy wants to be like his dad
So he watches us night and day.
He mimics our moves and weighs our words,
He steps in our steps all the way.

He's sculpting a life we're the model for.
He'll follow us happy or sad.
And his future depends on example set
'Cause the little boy wants to be just like his dad.

A special man talks by example,
Takes the time to play and hug his lad,
A special man walks by example,
The very best friend a growing boy ever had.
Any male can be a father—
But it takes a special man to be a dad.

He needs a hero to emulate.
He breathes 'I believe in you.'
Would we have him see everything we see
And have him do what we do?
When we see the reverence that sparkles and shines
In the worshipping eyes of our lad,
Will we be at peace if his dreams come true
And he grows up to be just like his dad?

Yes, a special man talks by example,
Takes the time to play and hug his lad.
A special man walks by example,
The very best friend a growing boy ever had.
Any male can be a father—
But it takes a special man to be a dad!

I love you, Dad. You're my hero.

The Spanish Lesson

A wealthy couple arrived at a resort in Mexico wearing their finest and most expensive jewels and clothes. The man headed to the golf course to play a round with his buddies. The woman had an invitation to an exclusive auction held only one day each year, one that was sure to have the estate antiques she was looking for.

She hailed a taxi to take her to the auction house. On the way, the driver lost control of the car and slammed into a horse-drawn cart. Animals and produce flew everywhere. Two 10-year-old boys were thrown from the cart into the bushes.

Even though the woman had hurt her head, she scampered to see if they were all right. She found them dazed and bleeding. They pulled back in fright as she came close.

To gain their trust, she pulled out a photograph of her with her four small children. As they inched closer to see, one of the boys asked in broken English, "You mommy?"

She smiled. "Yes, me mommy."

They immediately snuggled in on her lap and hugged her until they stopped shaking. She noticed that one was bleeding from a deep wound on his leg. Since there was no cloth around, she ripped a piece of her expensive dress to bind the gash.

The taxi was demolished and the driver went to get help. While they were waiting an old jalopy pulled up. The driver said he would take them to safety—if she paid. "Gladly," she said. But the boys didn't want to leave the produce. They were on their way to sell it at the market and if they arrived at home empty-handed, they would be in trouble. The woman gave them each $25, which was much more than enough.

When they arrived at the hospital, they could not be admitted—until she paid. Which she did.

Two hours later she faced the dilemma of getting the boys back home. Not wanting to risk another cab ride, she called for a limousine.

Delighted with their luck, the boys climbed in and began

jabbering in Spanish. The woman didn't understand a word, but she enjoyed their enthusiasm. Along the way, they told the driver to stop. They stepped out and helped a little girl right her fallen wagon. They invited her and her two little girlfriends in for a ride. The five of them talked nonstop.

Before they reached the village, the boys had the driver stop a few more times to pick up more little girls. And when they finally arrived, the boys had a car full.

The children scampered out and disappeared. But before the woman could leave, they all reappeared, each with ice cream cones.

"Why have the boys spent their precious money buying ice cream for all these strangers?" the woman asked the driver. "And why are they being so nice just to the young ladies?"

The driver inquired of the boys. Their smiles lit up their faces like Christmas trees. Hugging the woman tightly, they proudly answered, "Tenemos que cuidarles a ellas especialmente, porque algun dia ellas van a ser una madra para alguien."

"What did they say?" she asked the driver.

"We must take extra special care of them, because someday—like you, lady—they're going to be somebody's mommy!"

The Last Game

Let's say it was the last football game of your senior year and a message came that your father had died. That's what happened to a fellow named Brian. When the coach found out, he decided to tell Brian before the game, knowing he probably would elect not to play. But instead of reacting sorrowfully, Brian just took it all in stride and said, "I'll leave right after the game."

The coach had heard Brian speak highly of his father and expected him to grieve. When he didn't the coach said, "Brian, you don't have to play. This game isn't that important."

Brian ignored him and played the game anyway. And play he did. Brian was the star, winning the game as a man possessed.

In the locker room, the other players showered with Brian and some offered condolences, but most were appalled at his lack of sorrow. Brian was casual and happy as if nothing had gone wrong. The coach was mad and thought he had taught too much devotion to sports and not enough compassion.

He scolded Brian, "Why did you play the game? Your father is dead. I'm ashamed of you and of myself."

Brian replied, "Coach, this was our last game. I am a senior. I had to play. This was the first time my dad has ever seen me play and I had to play like I never played before."

"But your father's dead," the coach replied.

Brian choked back the tears and smiled at the coach. "I guess you didn't know my father was blind, did you?"

Dad Held the Rope

A group of English botanists spent their vacation in the Swiss Alps collecting specimens and rare flowers. One morning they walked from a small village and came to a precipice. As they looked over a green valley, they spotted through their field glasses a peculiar flower which they thought was unusual. From the cliff upon which they stood, to the valley floor, was a sheer drop of several hundred feet. To descend would be impossible, and to reach the valley from another approach would mean a delay of several hours.

During the latter part of their climb a small boy had joined the party and watched with interest as the botanists discussed the situation for several minutes.

One of the men turned to the boy and said, "Young fellow, if you will let us tie a rope around your waist and lower you over a cliff so that you can dig up one of those plants for us, we'll pull you back up and give you $50."

The boy looked dazed for an instant, then ran off—apparently frightened at the prospect of being lowered over the cliff by a rope. But within a short time he returned, bringing with him an old man, bent and gray, with hands gnarled and callused by hard labor. Upon reaching the party of botanists the boy turned to the man who had made the offer and said, "This is my dad. I'll go down in the valley if you'll let him hold the rope."

Wouldn't it be nice if every young man had that kind of confidence in his father's abilities? I did. This is the way that a special relationship works best: when the father has faith in his son's abilities and the son trusts his father with his life.

The Way It Was and Still Should Be

There was a special lady that lived on a farm in Grace, Idaho. With every challenge or endeavor that came her way, she always went far beyond the call of duty. She was a widow with nine children—the youngest age 7, the oldest 22. Instead of complaining of her hard life, she accepted her fate and changed the ordinary into the extraordinary.

No matter how bleak or serious things seemed to be, she found the positive side and a ray of hope. She taught her family the value of hard work and the importance of education, although she only went as far as fourth grade.

Once a week she picked up supplies in town. Otherwise her days were full milking the cows; making butter, cottage cheese and ice cream; and raising pigs, sheep, and chickens. She had a large vegetable garden, as well as gooseberry and raspberry bushes, strawberry vines and apple trees. She was an excellent cook and neighbors often dropped in at mealtime.

Once, when unexpected company arrived, she took her .22 rifle and went outside to shoot a chicken. As the gun went off another chicken stepped in the line of fire. The bullet went through both chickens and grazed the back of a pig. It became a family joke—one shot to kill two chickens and skin the pig.

Her children didn't have material wealth, but they certainly received the necessary and important things in life: love, spiritual guidance, concern for others, appreciation for a table filled with food and respect for the law. She was truly an example of all that is good.

As a young man I remember sitting at her feet while she taught me. "If you can't say something nice, don't say anything at all." And, "I'll never throw upon the floor a crust I cannot eat, for many a little hungry one would think it quite a treat. Willful waste brings willful want and I may live to say, Oh, I wish I had that crust that once I threw away."

This incredibly strong and courageous woman is my

maternal grandmother, Alice Maughan. My mother is a lot like her mother. Many times my mother went without a new dress just so we could buy some great football cleats for me. Many times my mother insisted that we stay home, instead of going on a summer vacation, just so I could stay and play on a baseball all-star team. My mother is the greatest cook on earth, a spiritual giant, a church and community servant, and the very best mom who ever lived. She taught me right from wrong and, as far as I know, has never told a lie. I've never heard her swear or complain about her trials, heartache and pain. My dear sweet mother, Ruby Maughan Clark, truly is the epitome of service above self. It's the way it was and still should be.

Honor Our Parents

Honor your father and mother. That bit of counsel and wisdom has been passed down for a few thousand years, so it must be good advice. Here's how it works.

Leon White was an all-conference linebacker for the Brigham Young University Cougars, a team that won the national championship in 1985. In the Holiday Bowl that year, Leon White was a one-man wrecking crew, making bone-jarring tackles, sacking the quarterback and intercepting passes. Leon played better than he had ever played before. The crowd went wild.

But Leon White wasn't playing for the crowds or the glory. He was playing for his dad who was watching the game from the sidelines on a stretcher. Both of them knew this was the last game he would ever watch Leon play.

Between defensive sets Leon would hustle over and ask, "Dad, are you having a good time?" And was he ever.

His dad never stopped talking about that game or about his son right up until the moment he died from cancer a few days later.

Leon played a great game, but his father wasn't proud of him because he was a great linebacker. He was proud because Leon was a great man and son who made his parents proud. If we could all be like Leon, many of the problems that exist in society today would disappear.

If the relationship between you and your parents, or you and your offspring, needs some fixing, work on it. It's a worthwhile investment of time and energy.

Will I See You Again?

(dedicated to my dad, S. Wayne Clark)

There's a feeling stuck inside me
About a leader of life's band,
You're the one who showed me how to play
And whispered, "Yes, you can."
You taught me life and living love,
Your wisdom was my friend—
Will I see you again?

There's a memory making motion
About a beacon burning bright,
You're the one who turned my troubled times
From darkness into light.
Your guiding ray unveiled the way,
You counseled till the end—
Will I see you again?

You always cautioned at the door,
"Remember who you are."
'Cause I guess you saw in me what I could be.
I needed you to need me, and you stretched a helping hand,
Unselfishly, so tenderly, left footprints in my sand.
You let me understand.

There's a notion nestled in me
About the rules of the Master Man.
Even though you lost the battle here,
You won the war in his plan.
I'll miss your hugs and eyes that grin;
But we'll meet once more, so long till then,
When I see you again.
Yes, I'm going to see you again!

A Real Champion

I was one of the lucky ones, even though I was getting a little older and my dreams of athletic glory were behind me. I was still given the opportunity of watching the 1988 Summer Olympic Games with my parents. My dad was battling cancer at the time. My supportive mom served brownies and milk as we watched brawny athletes shatter world records. It was a very exciting and emotional time for me.

While I sat with my parents watching the track-and-field competition, cheering for the American athletes, my father asked, "Know what's wrong with the world? They don't give gold medals to the best parents."

It was a very casual comment, but I could tell my father was serious.

Since my dad's death in 1990, I've often wondered why our society doesn't give prizes to the people who play the most important roles. Being a great parent isn't a competition that can be translated into a dash, a dive or a contest. Like the training of Olympic athletes, the very nature of the task takes years and years of effort, sacrifice and commitment. But it cannot be condensed into a 10-second dash, a four-lap swim or a pole vault.

Judges don't raise scorecards into the air every time parents give perfect counsel or make another sacrifice for a child they love. If they did give out awards for parenting, I know one father and one mother I'd nominate for the gold medal. I'd put mine on the stand with medals around their necks.

How about you? Would you qualify?

If not, maybe it's time to start training and get into shape. It's a marathon race, and only the strong survive and thrive.

A Son's Letter

Dear Dad,

I am writing this to you although you have been dead for many years. If you can see these lines, I feel I must say some things I didn't know when I was a boy in your home—things I was too immature to say.

It's only after passing through the long, hard school of hard knocks—now, when my own hair is graying—that I understand how you felt.

I must have been a bitter trial to you. I was such a fool! I believed my own petty wisdom, and I now know how ridiculous it was compared to that calm, ripe, wholesome experience of yours. I now know that wisdom truly is the gift of the elderly. I realize there are two ways to see things: with eyesight and insight. And your insight was right on the mark.

Most of all I want to confess my worst sin to you: I was convinced that you didn't understand. When I look back, I know that you did—perhaps better than I did myself. Your wisdom flowed around mine like an ocean surrounding an island. How patient you were with me. How full of long-suffering and kindness, filled with unconditional love. How constant were your efforts to get close to me—to win my confidence, to be my pal.

I wouldn't let you. I couldn't. What was it that held me aloof? I was too hard, too macho, too self-centered. I believed in the tough image: I wanted to be a big boy and not cry.

I wish you were here across the table from me just for an hour, so I could tell you there's no wall between us any more. I understand you now, Dad, and God knows how I love you; how I needed you to remind me to remember who I am.

I now know what I could have done to make you happy. I know how you felt.

It won't be long, Dad, until I am over on your side of the veil. I believe you'll be the first to greet me, to take me by the hand and help me comprehend the new life after death that awaits me. When I see you again, I'll spend the first thousand years making you realize that not one moment of your

concern and yearning for me was wasted. It took a good
many years for this prodigal son to come to know himself
and his ultimate destiny. But I've come now. I see it all.

I know that the richest, most precious thing on Earth,
and the thing least understood, is the mighty love, tender-
ness and craving to help that a father feels toward his boy.
For I have a boy of my own. And it is he that makes me
want to go back to you and get down on my knees to beg
your forgiveness.

Up there somewhere in the stillness, hear me, Dad, and
believe me. I did need you and still do. The ultimate compliment I ever receive is when somebody says, "You're a lot like
your dad." I'm lucky to be your son.

Family Friendship

My wife and I were in our front yard when the newspaper boy came down the street on his bicycle, loaded with papers. About 20 yards behind him was another boy, following on his bicycle. I was not sure at that time what their relationship was, but I did notice they were coming down the street at a pretty good clip.

When the newspaper boy reached our sidewalk, he was traveling too fast to make the approach to our home. He went one way, the bicycle went another; the newspapers went everywhere. Noticing the boy had fallen on the lawn and was not hurt, but realizing he would undoubtedly be embarrassed from falling in front of his friend, we moved toward him.

At the sight of this perfect three-point landing, his companion shouted his pleasure and laughed heartily at his friend's misfortune.

Trying to relieve the embarrassment of the paperboy, knowing he didn't want help, but might need a Band-Aid on his pride, I took a few steps toward him and said, "It's a low blow to have your friend laugh when you've had a bad spill, isn't it?"

He went on picking up the papers without even looking up, hopped on his wheels and started to pedal away from us.

"He isn't my friend," he shouted over his shoulder. "He's my brother."

His words have been ringing through my ears ever since. Shouldn't a family teach siblings to be friends?

Wouldn't it be nice to build a home so that the members of this very special unit are friends as well as relatives? It is important to realize that parents and siblings can and should be more than merely blood relations. We should be buddies.

Friendships are important for maintaining and enjoying a lifetime of happiness and joy. The interesting thing is that we can always find new friends, but we are stuck with the members of our immediate family. Therefore, it's in our best interest to like, love, respect, trust, understand and befriend our fellow family members.

As the song says, "If families aren't forever, then what's forever for? If friendship's not forever, then what's forever for?"

Forever will be hell if we have to spend it with family members who are not our friends!

3

LAUGHTER IS THE BEST MEDICINE

Humor simultaneously wounds and heals, indicts and
pardons, diminishes and enlarges; it constitutes inner growth
at the expense of outer gain, and those who possess
and honestly practice it make themselves more through a
willingness to make themselves less.

—LOUIS KRONENBERGER

We've got to loosen up. Even God has a sense of humor.
If you don't believe it, look at the person sitting next to you!

Plane Perception

I was flying from San Francisco to Los Angeles. By the time we took off, there had been a 45-minute delay and everybody onboard was ticked. Unexpectedly, we stopped in Sacramento on the way. The flight attendant explained that there would be another 45-minute delay, and if we wanted to get off the aircraft, we would reboard in 30 minutes.

Everybody got off the plane except one gentleman who was blind. I noticed him as I walked by and could tell he had flown before because his Seeing Eye dog lay quietly underneath the seats in front of him throughout the entire flight. I could also tell he had flown this very flight before because the pilot approached him and, calling him by name, said, "Keith, we're here in Sacramento for almost an hour. Would you like to get off and stretch your legs?" Keith replied, "No thanks, but maybe my dog would like to stretch his legs."

Picture this: All the people in the gate area came to a completely quiet standstill when they looked up and saw the pilot walk off the plane with the Seeing Eye dog! The pilot was even wearing sunglasses. People scattered. They not only tried to change planes, they also were trying to change airlines!

The Cover-Up

Two ladies, who didn't know the meaning of being neighborly, had been feuding for months. One day they finally reconciled their differences and rekindled their friendship. They hugged and retired to their respective homes.

Thirty minutes later one of the women was looking out her patio window and discovered her dog with something white in its mouth. It was her neighbor's pet rabbit.

"Oh, no," she said to herself. "I've just glued our relationship back together and my dog kills her rabbit!" She quickly took the dead animal into her home, washed it and blow-dried its fur into a beautiful fluff. She tiptoed into her neighbor's backyard and secretly placed the dead rabbit in its hutch and locked the door. She thought all was well until she heard a blood-curdling scream.

She ran outside to greet her neighbor.

"What's wrong?" she asked.

"Five days ago my rabbit died and we buried it in the garden. Now it's back in its cage!"

Unexpected Laughs

A married couple came to Utah for a ski holiday. It was a beautiful spring day with perfect snow conditions and perfect weather, but long lines at the lifts. Midway through the day the wife needed to use the restroom, but because the slopes were crowded and she wanted to make the most of the day, she kept skiing. Run after run she put it off until eventually she gave in and headed for the facilities.

Her overzealous husband pleaded, "Just one more trip up. You can go when we get to the top of the mountain." But at the top, they discovered there was no lodge. As they skied to the bottom, she was unable to hold it any longer. The woman told her husband to stand guard while she went into the trees. With her skis still on and her pants down, the woman lost her balance and came shooting out of the trees going backward. Picking up speed, she flew across the ski run, hit the ski lift tower and broke her leg. Her husband flagged down the ski patrol, escorted them down the mountain and took her to the hospital.

Sitting in the emergency room trying to take her mind off the pain, she engaged another patient in conversation.

"Why are you here?" she asked.

"Lady," he responded, "You wouldn't believe what happened today. I was skiing and riding up the ski lift, when a woman came scooting out of the trees going backward with her drawers down around her ankles. She hit the tower and broke her leg. I started laughing so hard that I fell off the ski lift and broke my arm!"

Humor with Family and Friends

It's easy to verify the necessity for humor in our everyday lives—and the power it has to keep our spirits up.

Once I came home from school with a report card that had four Fs and one D. My dad said, "Son, looks like you're spending too much time on one subject!"

We were eating one evening when my five-year-old daughter stood on her chair and reached for the bread. Attempting to teach her some etiquette, I said, "Why don't you sit down and ask your brother to pass it?" She sweetly replied, "Okay, Daddy."

Then she yelled across the table, "Give me the bread!"

"What's the magic word?" I asked.

"Now!" she replied.

A father promised his son that if he practiced all day he'd play baseball with him after work. The father arrived home and they went into the backyard.

"Show me what you can do," the father said. The little boy shuffled his feet, threw the ball up in the air, took a swing and missed. "Strike one," said the dad.

The son repositioned his feet, threw the ball up again, took a second swing and missed again. His father said, "Strike two."

More determined than ever the kid dug in deeper, threw the ball higher and took a third mighty swing. He missed again, spun completely around and fell on the ground. His father said, "Strike three, you're out. What do you think about that?"

The youngster stood up, brushed himself off and said, "Man, am I a good pitcher!"

My friend's 13-year-old son said to his dad, "I'm starting to like girls and I hate it!"

A three-year-old found his dad's military identification tag and asked his mother what it was. His mother replied, "It's your father's dog tag."

The child then asked, "When was daddy a dog?"

The same three-year-old gained an interesting perspective on birth. His mother was pregnant and so was the family dog. So my friend thought it would be a good time to explain where babies come from. The boy stood wide-eyed and watched the birth of the puppies. Months later, on the day of delivery, the same child went to the hospital to visit his mother. As he looked at the row of babies through the nursery window, he asked, "Are these all ours?"

I have an older aunt who has been married four times— first to a banker, then an entertainer, a preacher and a funeral director. When asked why she had married that many times and to such a diverse mix of men she had a great reply. "One for the money, two for the show, three to get ready, and four to go!"

Sporting "Ha-Ha's"

A lot of the guys I played football with were true "dumb jocks." As steroid poster children whose cholesterol counts were higher than their SAT scores, they easily perpetuated the "meathead" stereotype. Richard, a big, strong, articulate lineman, appeared on television as a participant in the game show *Wheel of Fortune*. He was ahead by $300 when he interrupted by asking, "Pat, may I buy a vowel, please? Can you give me a *K*?"

One summer I worked as a Little League umpire. During one game a nine-year-old rookie came up to bat against an all-star pitcher who was twelve. The pitcher took a mighty wind up, reared back and threw a fast ball.

"Strike," I called.

The young batter said, "C'mon ump, that wasn't a strike."

I said, "Why? Did you see it?"

He replied, "No, but it sounded high."

One time our football coach was asked by news reporters why our team lost the game. Not one of our running plays went for any yardage all day. Coach answered, "We were tipping off our plays. They knew exactly where we were going to run. Every time we broke from the huddle, two of our running backs were laughing and the other one was as pale as a ghost!"

Once on a college recruiting trip I was with a young player who had never flown on a plane and had no idea about time zone changes. We were going from Atlanta, Georgia, to Knoxville, Tennessee. The clerk at the counter said, "The plane leaves at 4:00 P.M. and you arrive in Knoxville at 3:45. Would you like to buy a ticket?"

The astonished player replied, "No, I don't want a ticket. But I sure want to see the plane take off!"

Golf is a tough sport. I even lose balls in the ball washer! My friend Todd is a wild golfer. He has to tee off before he knows what course he's playing. He turns it into a contact sport. The other day he finally hit a ball 250 yards dead straight. It was great except it hit a man right in the head. The part that ticked off Todd the most was when the man pulled off the highway and came and found him!

The Things People Say

I was flying on an airplane when it suddenly dipped to the right. The pilot announced on the public address system, "We've just lost the right engine. We're going to have to gain more altitude. There will be a 15-minute delay."

Ten minutes went by and the plane dipped severely to the left. The pilot came on again and said, "I'm sorry, we've now lost the left engine. We'll have to gain more altitude and there will be another 15-minute delay."

The guy sitting next to me leaned over and said, "I sure hope we don't lose that last engine or we're going to be up here all day!"

A police officer pulled over an older couple and said, "You were speeding and you weren't wearing your seat belts."

The elderly man scoffed and replied, "Prove it. I just took the belt off to talk to you!"

Nonplussed, the officer turned to the wife. "Ma'am, your husband was speeding and he didn't have his seat belt on, now did he?"

"Officer," she replied. "After 40 years of marriage I've learned never to argue with my husband when he's been drinking!"

One day I was sitting on a bench on a folded newspaper. A man strolled by and asked, "Are you reading that?" A few minutes later the same thing happened but this time I was ready. I stood up, turned the page, sat back down and answered, "Yes, but I'll be done in a minute!"

Another time I was sitting in a restaurant when the man in the booth next to me asked what the special of the day was. The waitress replied, "Cow's tongue."

"Yuck," he said. "How could anyone eat anything that had been in a cow's mouth? I'll have two eggs over easy."

Have you ever wondered, "When cows laugh, does milk come out of their noses, too?"

Religion Isn't Always Serious

Although religion is a serious subject, there is a way to see humor in it.

Two nuns were driving down a country road when they ran out of gas. They walked to a farmhouse and a farmer gave them some gasoline, but the only container he had was an old bedpan. The nuns were happy to take whatever they were offered and returned to their car.

As they were pouring the gasoline from the bedpan into the tank of their car, a Protestant minister drove by. He stopped, rolled down his window and said, "Excuse me, sisters. I'm not of your religion, but I couldn't help admiring your faith!"

A man went to confess his sins. In the confessional he admitted that for years he had been stealing building supplies from the wood shop where he worked.

"What did you take?" the priest asked.

"Enough to build my house and three mountain cottages."

"This is very serious," the priest said. "I'll have to give you a stiff penance. Have you ever done a retreat?"

"No, Father, I haven't," the man replied. "But if you can get the plans, I can get the lumber!"

When I was playing football, before every game the coach would call on a player to offer the pregame prayer. On one occasion, a player who was not very religious was asked to lead the service. Unexpectedly he stopped in the middle of the prayer. Dead silence filled the room and seemed to last for an eternity. Finally, a guy in the back row yelled out, "Amen."

The praying player answered, "Thanks, man. I've been trying to think of that word for five minutes!"

Even God has a sense of humor. If you don't believe it, just look at the person sitting next to you right now!

He Who Laughs, Lasts

Have you noticed that the things we hate to hear the most are usually the things we need to hear the most? So how can we accept constructive criticism? Through humor.

"He who laughs, lasts."

The words are credited to Mary Poole, who would be scolded these days for not being gender sensitive and politically correct by saying "He or she who laughs, lasts."

It's a medical fact that if you keep your sense of humor, you'll probably live longer. Even large corporations realize the truth in it. Monsanto, the chemical giant, hired a humor consultant to work with research scientists. Productivity increased 50 percent. Digital Equipment designed a "Grouch Patrol" to make funny faces at grumpy workers. Productivity went up; absenteeism went down.

Bertrand Russell said, "One of the symptoms of an approaching nervous breakdown is the belief that one's work is terribly important." So lighten up!

Laugh, laugh, laugh. My friend T. Bubba Bechtol is a large man. On his internationally acclaimed comedy album, *Bill Ain't No Bubba*, he says, "I haven't always been fat. My doctor put me on a dehydrated food diet for six months, then one day I got caught in the rain. I gained 102 pounds in five minutes!"

Bubba weighs a few hundred pounds and claims he has beaten anorexia. He says he has it in permanent remission. "It ain't coming back!"

Another large friend was having some chest pains so he went in to have a physical examination.

"It must be a medical problem," he told the doctor.

The doc replied, "The only medical problem you have is that you retain too much chocolate-fudge cake!"

But, my friend insisted, "Obesity runs in my family."

With a grin and an honest sense of humor the doctor replied, "No, no one runs in your family!"

Bonus
(Just for Public Speaking)

Every great speech has an attention-grabbing opening, at least one middle qualifier and a memorable close. From a humorous perspective, here are three of my favorites:

Opening

When they were trying to find someone to give this speech, they phoned the best looking, most dashing, debonair man they knew. He turned them down. So they phoned the most intelligent, educated, brilliant genius they knew. He turned them down, too. So, they asked the sweetest, most humble, sincere guy they had ever met. Hey, I couldn't turn them down three times in a row, so here I am!

Middle Qualifier

I heard a speaker say, "We become what we think about." This is not true. If it were true, I would have been a woman by the time I was 12 years old!

Close

I challenge you to drink, steal, swear and lie.

- Drink from the fountain of truth; knowledge and wisdom constantly flow in our libraries and schools.
- Steal a little time each day to do something special for someone when you know you won't get the credit.
- Swear to make this the best day of your life so far. It may be your last.
- When you lie down tonight, thank God above that you are free and have the ability to dream mighty dreams and make them come true!

Best Lines

Best Bumper Stickers:
- Forget about world peace, use your turn signal!
- Consciousness is that annoying time between naps.
- You're unique—just like everybody else.

Best Signs:
- There are three kinds of people: those who can count and those who can't.
- i souport publik edekasion.
- Out of my mind—back in five minutes.
- Don't even think about crossing this field unless you can run it in nine seconds. The bull does it in nine and a half!

Best Headlines:
- Something Went Wrong in Jet Crash, Expert Says.
- Shot Off Woman's Leg Helps Nicklaus to 66.
- Iraqi Head Seeks Arms.
- Panda Mating Fails; Veterinarian Takes Over.
- Man Steals Clock, Faces Time.
- Squad Helps Dog Bite Victim.
- Man Struck by Lightning, Faces Battery Charge.
- Killer Sentenced to Die for Second Time in 10 Years.
- Typhoon Rips Through Cemetery: Hundreds Dead.
- Kids Make Nutritious Snacks.
- Hospitals Are Sued by Seven Foot Doctors.
- Sex Education Delayed, Teachers Request Training.

Best Drunk Driver Statements at Accidents:
- I'm not drunk and I didn't see that house.
- We were only trying to take a shortcut by jumping the stream.
- After hitting two cement posts, a bridge abutment, a dirt mound and a sizeable oak tree, the driver said, "Can't I just back out?"
- "What tree?"

- "Oops!"
- After hitting a telephone pole: "It was his fault."

Best Country Song:
- My Wife Ran Off with My Best Friend and I'm Going to Miss Him Dearly.

Best Pickup Lines:
- Wink, I'll do the rest!
- May I buy you a drink so I look better?

Best Body Image Lines:
- I'm losing hair on top of my head and growing it in my nose and ears.
- My only hope is that the hair in my right ear will grow long enough so I can comb it up over my head and fake everybody out.

The Best Sport is bowling.
You take a big heavy ball, cram two fingers and a thumb in it, take four Fred Flintstone twinkle-toes steps, roll the ball, sit down, eat a hot dog, have something to drink, and for this you need special shoes? And because they think we're going to steal the shoes, they make us leave a cash deposit. Now I don't know about you, but I don't own a green and purple shirt that's going to match those goofy shoes, and I definitely don't want to be seen walking around town with an 11½ on the back of my foot!

Why a Dog Is a Spouse's Best Friend

Dogs love it when your friends come over.
Dogs openly express their emotions and feelings.
Dogs think you sing great.
A dog's time in the bathroom is limited to a quick drink.
Dogs don't expect you to call if you're running late.
The later you are, the more excited dogs are to see you.
Dogs will forgive you for everything.
Work excites dogs.
Dogs don't mind if you give their offspring away.
Dogs can appreciate excessive body hair.
Anyone can get a good-looking dog.
If a dog is gorgeous, other dogs don't hate it.
Dogs like it when you leave lots of things on the floor.
Dogs never need to examine the relationship.
A dog's parents never visit.
Dogs love long car trips.
Dogs understand that instinct is better than asking for directions.
When a dog gets old and snaps at you incessantly, you can shoot it.
Dogs never criticize.
Dogs never expect gifts.
Dogs don't worry about germs.
Dogs don't want to know about every other dog you ever went out with.
You never have to wait for a dog—they're ready to go 24 hours a day.
Dogs have no use for flowers, cards or jewelry.
Dogs won't borrow your shirts.
Dogs never want foot rubs.
Dogs don't talk too much.
Dogs give unconditional love.

4

HEROES

Though thou art able to tear the scalp off an elephant,
if deficient in humanity, thou art no hero. The hero is
distinguished by his achievement; the celebrity by his image.
The hero is a big man; the celebrity is a big name. The hero
created himself; the celebrity is created by the media.
A hero is a man or woman who does what he or she can.

—DANIEL J. BOORSTIN

Dreams always come one or two sizes too big —

so you can grow into them!

Tribute to Preparation

Wayne Gretzky is clearly the greatest hockey player to ever play the game. He has influenced the lives of many young hockey players. The greatest single influence in Wayne's life, however, is his father, Walter. Walt was his coach, his mentor, and has always been and will always be his best friend. Wayne's greatest honor and most respected identity come when he is introduced as Walter Gretzky's son.

I had the honor of talking with Wayne, but the greatest thrill was spending two days with Walter in his home in Brantford, Ontario, Canada. We played golf, laughed, toured his famous basement full of Wayne's MVP Awards, trophies, autographed sticks, skates and jerseys, laughed some more and swapped countless inspirational stories. Walt is extremely smart and very intense, yet warm and engaging. He is a deeply committed family man, yet community oriented in his tireless efforts to help charitable organizations. Even today he still coaches junior hockey teams and touches hundreds of young people's lives each year. With Walt as his dad, it is obvious why Wayne is such a good, clean, pure, powerful, positive role model and elegant gentleman.

Walt is famous for saying, "You miss 100 percent of the shots you don't take." Wayne is famous for answering the question, "Why are you the greatest player?" with the highly quoted response, "Most players go to where the puck is. I go to where the puck is going to be." Yes, Wayne Gretzky teaches us about anticipation, but, according to his dad, Wayne teaches us even more about preparation.

If you want to discover why Wayne is the greatest hockey player who ever lived, you don't watch him on the ice: you watch him when he is on the bench. He studies every player to see where they go, how they pass, to whom they pass, do they favor their left side or right side, are they better skaters to the left or right, can they defend going backwards, and who their favorite partner is in certain playmaking situations. By the time Wayne hits the ice, he knows exactly where to go to intercept a pass, where to block a shot, and when to skate into the spacing lanes of the other team to get the competitive advantage to shoot and score. Preparation is why Wayne Gretzky is hockey's all-time leading scorer. Walt told me Wayne was also an exceptional baseball player. Wayne was named to the all-star team every year since he was nine years old. He was an extraordinary pitcher. Wayne wanted to practice every day, but most of his friends were out doing the playful things little guys like to do—i.e., riding bikes, hiking, catching lizards. So Wayne would bribe them away by paying them a quarter to play goalie while he took 100 shots and another quarter to catch while he threw 100 pitches. These kids would oftentimes go home with sore hands, black eyes and bloody noses from their inability to stop his extremely hard, fast shots and pitches. By the time Wayne was a teenager, he had a 90-mile-an-hour fastball. Walt told me it was amazing to watch Wayne pitch. Even if the batters hit against him in the first couple of innings, by the time Wayne had faced each of them once he remembered their strengths and weaknesses and struck them out from then on.

Walt told me Wayne is a perfectionist and used to practice the same shot from the same place on the ice hundreds of times in an afternoon. When most kids lost interest and concentration, Wayne would somehow kick it into a higher gear and endure until he succeeded at what he was trying to accomplish. He even practiced hitting the puck off certain places in the hockey rink baseboards so he would know exactly where the puck was going to be when it ricocheted. Wayne's desire to prepare was to intense that he convinced his dad to build a hockey rink in the backyard and flood it in the winter, which allowed Wayne to start practicing at the crack of dawn and continue until the neighbors complained late at night about the noise. The only thing that took Wayne off the ice was his dad's reminder that he needed to go to bed and rest so he could wake up refreshed, alert and ready to do it again.

Having met Wayne, I can say that his preparation philosophy of "leave no regrets" paid its greatest dividend when his dear sweet dad had a brain aneurysm at the age of 54.

When Wayne received the late-night emergency phone call in Los Angeles, he rushed on a private jet to be at his dying father's bedside. When he arrived, the doctors told Wayne there was very little hope.

Wayne ignored the prognosis and sat for hours and hours talking to his dad and stroking his arm. He found strength in the knowledge that he had no regrets. He had said all the things he needed to say to his hero many times before this tragedy occurred. He had spent more time with his dad than most children spend with their dads in an entire lifetime. Clearly Wayne was prepared for the worst, which allowed him to be strong for others and focus his energy on praying, hoping and coaxing his dad to hang tough and pull through. Even more important than Wayne's preparation, however, was the fact that the nurses were prepared, and the hospital staff was prepared, and a specialist doctor—who was one of the only physicians in the world prepared to perform the intricate surgery—was willing to come out of retirement because he was prepared.

Walter Gretzky miraculously recovered and remains the number one influence in Wayne's life today. And the message? Preparation not only gave Wayne his life, it also saved Walter from death. Gretzky is not the greatest hockey player who every lived simply because he can anticipate. Wayne is the Great One because his dad taught him to relentlessly pursue perfection through preparation.

"I Am the Greatest"

Cassius Marcellus Clay Jr., as Muhammad Ali was once known, was born in Louisville, Kentucky, January 17, 1942. During Ali's youth, Louisville was a city of segregated public facilities, the Kentucky Derby and other symbols of the Southern white aristocracy. African-Americans were the servants and poor working class. The grandest dreams available to them were being a preacher or a teacher in an all-Black church or school.

Young Cassius was intense and full of dreams, which in this environment brought frustration. He knew he was somebody and needed to somehow vent his societal suppression. That's when he discovered boxing. At 12 years of age and 89 pounds, young Cassius had his first official boxing match. He won by a split decision and immediately started jumping up and down yelling, "I am the greatest. I will be the greatest fighter who ever lived."

Years later, a childhood classmate remembered, "We were in elementary school together and Cassius was just another one of the kids. You push and you shove each other, and get into the normal fights. There were days he lost and days he won. So when he beat Sonny Liston to win the heavyweight championship, we all started laughing, saying, "He's not even undefeated in the neighborhood. How can he be champion of the world?"

I can't exactly explain why, but probably the most prestigious award, accomplishment or title in all of sports is to win the heavyweight boxing championship of the world. Cassius Clay won the championship, converted to the Muslim faith, changed his name to Muhammad Ali, was stripped of his title for refusing induction into the U.S. Army on religious grounds, and won the championship two more times. He truly is the greatest. He is not only the most famous fighter who ever lived, but the most famous athlete and most recognized face in the world.

As a teenager, I had been a Golden Gloves boxer, and Ali had been my idol. I emulated everything he did from tassels on my boots to the Ali Shuffle, rope-a-dope and taunting jab. With fairly quick hands and a desire to beat everybody, I was known as the "Great White Hope." Each time I fought, instead of chanting, "Danny, Danny," my friends chanted, "Dali, Dali!" Muhammad Ali truly was my hero and I would have given anything to meet him.

Years later, in 1988, I had just finished speaking to the students of Andrews University in Berrien Springs, Michigan. I was in the Union Building signing books when I overheard some students talking about seeing Muhammad Ali on campus. I was so excited I could hardly ask where. They informed me that he was gone, but it was no big deal because he lived there and visited the school often. I immediately excused myself and asked the two gentlemen who were driving me around to grab a camera and take me to Ali's home. They told me I was fooling myself if I thought I could meet him. They stopped at the big white wall and giant iron gate at the edge of a long curving driveway. I got out and walked the hundred yards to his beautiful home. His 88 acres had previously belonged to the Chicago gangster Al Capone and "Muhammad Ali Farms," as Ali called it, was an amazing sight.

With my heart pounding, I took a deep breath and knocked on the front door. A beautiful woman answered. I knew from photographs that she was his lovely wife. She asked, "May I help you?" I said, "Yes, ma'am. Is Muhammad in?" She asked, "May I tell him who is calling?" Sheepishly, I replied, "Sure, Dan Clark." She walked away, and within seconds an imposing six feet, three inch, 225-pound world champion, world peace ambassador, advocate of human rights, living legend and idol filled the entire doorway. Muhammad simply smiled his famous smile and in his quiet breathy voice invited me in. I excused myself for a minute, sprinted to the garden to where my friends could see me and wildly waved my arms and whistled for them to come in.

In 1988, Muhammad's Parkinson's disease had not yet taken away his speech. Although he was a little slow, he talked up a storm. The next four and a half hours we sat in his living room and watched his greatest fights: the Thrilla-in-Manilla, the Rumble-in-the-Jungle and more. With his own personal commentary, jokes and stories, he made every move come alive. Later he even performed some of his favorite magic tricks. The most incredible thing for me was when he asked me, "Did you ever fight?" I nodded yes and he said, "Let me see your left hook." We both put our hands up and started to playfully spar and dance around. I broke into the Ali Shuffle, and he kidded me, "That's not the shuffle, that's the Clark Scuffle!" He then got right in my face and said, "Everybody knows I'm the greatest, but so are you. Repeat with me, 'I am the greatest.' I repeated it and he said, "Louder, with more heart." I repeated it, and he said, "No, like your man Rocky. Mean it man, mean it. Say it like you want to beat Joe Frazier. Say it like you want to punch George Foreman. Say it to me like I'm Howard Cosell!" One more time he yelled, "I am the greatest," and again had me mimic him. He then put his arm around me, gave me a big hug, looked me square in the eyes and whispered, "How do you feel? Do you believe it? I do."

It's been many years since that wonderful day, but I remember it every time I walk past the photos of us hung on my basement "Wall of Fame." Even more important than the photos, whenever I am discouraged and feel that I can't go on anymore, I visualize Ali looking me square in the eyes and convincing me that, "I am the greatest." Muhammad Ali surely was and still is the greatest, and he wants each of us to believe that we can be, too.

Serve

On February 14, 1965, at 11:30 P.M., an older African-American lady was standing on the side of an Alabama highway, caught in a lashing rain storm. Her car had broken down and she desperately needed a ride. Soaking wet, she decided to flag down the next car. A young white man stopped to help her, an act that was generally unheard of in the Deep South during the conflict-filled 1960s. The man took her to safety, helped her get assistance and put her into a taxi cab to the airport so she could catch her flight to Los Angeles. She was in a hurry, but she managed to jot down his address and thank him before the cab pulled away.

Seven days later there was a knock on the man's door. To his surprise, a large combination console color TV and stereo record player was delivered to his home. The attached note read:

Dear Mr. James:

Thank you so much for assisting me on the highway the other night. The rain drenched not only my clothes but my spirits. Then you came along. Because of you, I was able to make it to my dying husband's bedside just before he passed away. God bless you for helping me and unselfishly serving others.

Sincerely,
Mrs. Nat King Cole

Nat King Cole died of lung cancer in Santa Monica, California on February 15, 1965.

The most important thing we can give others is our unselfish service to our fellow men and women. It supersedes weather conditions, educational background, time commitments, financial statements, political and religious preference, and especially skin color! Serve, Serve, Serve!

Kentucky Thoroughbreds

Recently I attended a most magnificent weekend extravaganza during the Kentucky Derby. Through the graciousness of my "host," while I was there I came to understand the secrets of optimal performance, success and what it takes to be a champion.

When a Thoroughbred race horse dies they bury only three of its body parts: the head, symbolic of wisdom and will; the heart, symbolic of spirit and courage; and the hooves, symbolic of speed and efficiency. Only two champion race horses have ever been buried "whole and upright"—Man o' War, one of the greatest Thoroughbreds of all time with 21 wins and only a single loss; and my favorite, Secretariat, who is the greatest race horse that ever lived.

There is also a human thoroughbred in Kentucky who epitomizes winning and also thrives on setting track records. He clearly possesses the qualities of a champion racehorse and instills them in both organizations and people! This human thoroughbred is the "host" to whom I refer.

Imagine a man who is always early and can't sleep for a short enough amount of time. He has vision and a genius's flair for invention. He conceives, believes and achieves success that is far ahead of that of the competition. He has played 18 holes of golf on a private golf course in Pennsylvania with Arnold Palmer. He loves country music yet dreams of conducting the *1812* Overture because it embodies everything he feels about business: "There is the beginning, creating the basis for the rest of the piece, then crescendos as the parts and instruments keep building toward the climax."

This human thoroughbred is a proud "life scout" with deep conviction regarding perfect honesty, unwavering discipline and commitment to community awareness, as taught to him by the Boy Scouts of America. He passionately believes in the utopian ideal of true equality—that everyone in America should have the same opportunities regardless of race, creed, socioeconomic status or background—and true to his conviction, he donated $25,000 to the Urban League for use in greater outreach to Lexington, Kentucky's African-American community. Over the last 10 years he has contributed more than $100,000 to the United Way through employee and corporate giving. He hails from Ashland, Kentucky and attended the University of Kentucky on one of the first full baseball scholarships the school ever offered. He then parlayed that scholarship into a professional baseball contract as a pitcher with the Chicago White Sox's Class B farm team. He graduated with a university degree in Radio Arts. By the time he was 21 he was working as a big-time radio disc jockey, a play-by-play football sportscaster, a color analyst for the Kentucky Central Football Network and the head of the powerful University of Kentucky Basketball Network.

At the age of 30 he was the youngest government cabinet member, serving as the Kentucky State Commissioner of the Department of Public Information and responsible for travel and tourism, as well as commerce promotion. He conceptualized, built and promoted Kentucky's first official Horse Park. When the state cabinet released him he started and ran a successful insurance and real estate agency.

You may be asking yourself whether this is a man with the Midas touch—one who has never suffered heartache, had his dreams shattered or seen his star fall. Quite the contrary. In 1971 he ran for Lieutenant Governor of Kentucky. Confident that he would win, he accepted no campaign contributions. Losing the election left him in financial ruin, with only $107.00 in the bank, a campaign debt, no job, payments for two cars, and a wife and children who didn't know just how dire the family's circumstances were. Metaphorically speaking, all he had left were his "head, heart and hooves"—his dream and his burning desire to succeed. In 1972 he returned to the vacant building where his agency had been located. He sat down at an old desk, above which a bare lightbulb dangled from the ceiling, and started his business. With no money to pay for the installation of a telephone system, he used the pay phone in the barbershop located next to his building to make all his calls.

I first met and worked with this champion in the late 1980s, and in 1997 I was honored to participate in the 25th anniversary celebration of his multimillion-dollar business. The business is called Host Communications, Inc.—a conglomerate of over nine separate companies and divisions that sets the standard of excellence in communications for college sports marketing, publishing, printing, audiovisual services, broadcasting and management services. With over 450 employees and 24 offices nationwide, Host Communications, synonymous with the National Tour Association and the NCAA, is more than a business—it's an institution.

Mr. W. Jim Host is the man behind this institution. Jim and Pat, his gorgeous, sustaining, supportive wife who is his counselor and the constant partner at his side, positively touch the lives of all who know them. Given all his accomplishments and his strong belief that at the end of the day what really matters are your children and your family, it is no secret why W. Jim Host is my hero.

In the words of one of his directors: "Jim Host is a man with many dreams and hard-earned insights. A man who loves what he does and appreciates how he got there. A man who will always be early . . . early enough to be part of the future before it happens."

Jim and Pat show the world two things, just as they showed me during that Kentucky Derby weekend. First, what it takes to be a champion thoroughbred—horse or human being. Second, what it takes to be an incredible "host."

The Loving Lady

A young teenage girl is discovered living in the back seat of a Volkswagen Beetle. A woman rescues her and, without qualification, gives her a place to live. A young boy is so physically abused by his father that he is afraid to even go outside his home. A woman rescues him and gives him unconditional love and safety. A young girl is sexually abused to the point where she is so afraid of male adults that she can't even stand to be hugged. A woman rescues her and gives her security. Several young male and female teenagers are involved in crime, violence and drugs. A woman rescues them and teaches them respect for themselves and others, responsibility and forgiveness, and gives them love. The list of tragedies is in the hundreds, but so are the success stories of rescue and recovery.

And who is this "Lone Ranger-Knight in Shining Armor"? I call her the "loving lady." Her name is Mrs. Lila B. Bjorklund. She is a leader among leaders who has dedicated her entire life and living to making a better life for others.

Her achievements are many and varied. They express her commitment to fairness, compassion, and real and practical assistance. It was not enough for Lila to be concerned about troubled children; she put a roof over their heads and taught them responsible behavior. It was not enough to found a program for troubled girls; she managed it, working 40-50 hours a week, without financial compensation for 25 years. It was not enough to build one group home; she built four. It was not enough to build 4 group homes; she opened 40 foster homes to care for younger victims of abuse and neglect. It wasn't enough to provide a safe home for over 300 children a year; she instituted a program to teach their parents to help the children so the families could remain together, could heal, and could learn to live with mutual respect and caring.

Lila founded Utah Girls' Village, which later became Utah Youth Village. She worked for better detention facilities and juvenile courts as chair of the Salt Lake Council of Women. She is a member of their Hall of Fame. Lila chaired the Utah

State Board of Education, where she worked with Title IX and its effect on girls in elementary and secondary education. She served as state president of the PTA, where she pioneered their Critical Issues Conference. She initiated legislation mandating testing of all newborns for PKU, enabling thousands of children to lead full, healthy lives. Lila influenced legislation on child abuse and neglect, driver's education, school lunches and educational funding. She cofounded the Intermountain Specialized Abuse Treatment Clinic for victims of sexual abuse.

Lila has served on over 40 organizations, task forces and committees, including the Governor's Committee on Children and Youth. She has also faithfully served at the national level as a: delegate to the National Judicial Conference for Trouble Children; member of the International Year of the Child Advisory Committee; board of directors member of the National Association of Homes for Children and the National Teaching Family Association; member of the National School Board Association Government Affairs Committee and their Special Committee on the Prevention of Delinquency in Teenage Girls. In 1997, Lila was honored as the national recipient of the prestigious J. C. Penny Golden Rule Award.

Lila has received numerous honors, but her greatest satisfaction in life is the genuine love the children at Utah Youth Village feel for her. Even in her wheelchair, Lila attends each graduation from the Village, and gives each child a handmade quilt. Lila has given her furniture, money, books, goodies, gifts, clothes and anything else she has to youth in need. She ruined two cars hauling building materials to that first group home. For many years, Utah Youth Village's offices were in Lila's home. One Village youth whose family had abandoned her held her wedding reception in Lila's home. Long after the youths leave the Village, Lila keeps in touch with them and gives them support.

In loving tribute to the "loving lady," it is appropriate to use her own words. Lila Bjorklund believes, "Help one child, help generations to come." Perhaps more than any independent single woman in the world, she has, she does and, in the loving lady legacy she will leave behind, she always will.

Show Me the Munny

In 1984 my window on the world widened "from sea to shining sea." I had been to California, but never to New York, and this night in Syracuse would drastically alter my concept of real success and change my understanding of "munny" forever. "Munny" is a respectful play on words in honor of Stephen P. Munn, who is the epitome of visionary leadership, parental guidance, compassionate service, financial wizardry and thinking in terms of limitless possibility. This kind of "munny" makes anybody wealthy and rich in the aspects of life that really matter the most.

The night we met I was the guest speaker at a regional Explorer Scouting awards dinner where Steve was to be honored with that organization's most prestigious service award, the Silver Beaver. Trying to pick him out in the crowd, I looked around the room for a man surely at least in his 60s, by virtue of the outstanding credentials contained in his résumé, which the awards host read aloud. The list included: graduate of Saint Lawrence University; star quarterback inducted into the university's athletic hall of fame; veteran of the Vietnam War who had served one year as a second lieutenant; M.B.A. from the State University of New York at Buffalo (a two-year program that he completed in one-and-a-half years, having sat for the GMAT graduate business school admissions test while still serving in Vietnam); territorial manager at Shell Oil; executive vice president of the petroleum division of Agway, Inc.; and the following three positions within divisions of the international conglomerate United Technologies Carrier—executive vice president of Carrier International, president of Carrier International Corporation (whose offices span the globe from England to Greece to Florida to Singapore plus ten other manufacturing sites worldwide) and senior vice president and chief financial officer of Carrier Corporation.

I couldn't believe my ears when I heard that Stephen P. Munn was born July 1, 1942 on Long Island and had already accomplished all this by the ripe old age of 42. One

year after the awards dinner he became president of Carrier
Transicold, another division of United Technologies Carrier,
where he served until 1988. At that point he accepted a new
position—truly the job of his dreams—as director, chairman
and chief executive officer of Carlisle Companies, Inc. His
hiring prompted a feature article in the *Wall Street Journal*
and he remains the leader of Carlisle Companies today.

"Amazing," you may say, "but probably a workaholic."

No way! In the process of achieving all this international
high-finance fame and corporate success, Steve has
remained a down-to-earth, well-balanced family man. He
has never forgotten his roots. When Steve was three years
old his father was killed in an automobile accident. His
sweet and devoted mother Catherine immediately moved
Steve and his brother, who was three years older than Steve,
to her hometown of Ogdensburg, New York. Catherine's
seven brothers and sisters tried to take the boys away from
her, but she refused to give in to them and raised them
entirely on her own until she remarried. As a result of his
tough relationship with a stereotypical stepfather, Steve
grew up learning to fend for himself. With the Saint
Lawrence Seaway in his backyard, he escaped through
water sports—boating, swimming and fishing. He also
became an outstanding athlete, excelling in football, basketball, baseball and everything else he played. His stepfather
died when Steve was a sophomore in college and he then
took care of his mother until she passed away in 1989.

This public Steve is obviously amazing, yet he is so
humble that most people never get the inside scoop. For this
reason let me "show you the munny."

Steve married the beautiful and intelligent Kathryn Ann
Powers in 1964. They are the proud parents of lovely daughters—two of the most incredible, bright, witty, athletic, well-
rounded, gorgeous women in our world. When I first met
Michelle and Robyn they were playing the stock market,
reading the newspaper's financial page, balancing their own
checking accounts and starring on their school's athletic
teams—all before they were 12 years old!

The aspect of his life of which Steve is the most proud is
his wonderful family. He is proud not just of his wife and

daughters, but of the good name passed on to him by his magnificent parents. His love for and loyalty to his mother inspired me, as I learned that he often drove to her home to bring her a favorite milkshake, then sat with her while she enjoyed the treat and the two of them talked for hours. To this day he glows with pride and his eyes well up with tears at the mention of his beloved mom.

Family is so important to Steve that he even treats his employees like family and all who work for him—from custodians to secretaries to blue-collar workers in the plants to other executives—affectionately call him "Steve." His greatest asset is his genuine compassion for people. His selfless volunteer efforts for the community include raising many thousands of dollars for such charities as: INROADS (a national collegiate program for minorities), AAU sports, the Special Olympics, the Boy Scouts and countless other charities. While still at Carrier, Steve established the "Carrier Dome" donation for Syracuse University. He has also served as a community leader in the following capacities: seven years of service as a member of the Board of Directors of Syracuse Symphony Orchestra and as its treasurer, nearly 10 years of service as a member of the Board of Trustees of Saint Lawrence University and as a member of the Board of Trustees of Georgetown University's business school from 1991-1994.

Stephen P. Munn is a true American hero. Every young man should want to be like him. I do. Every CEO should emulate his example. I love him like a brother and take great pride in calling him my friend. Steve is always there to help me learn, laugh, lead and line up my fifth putt! He truly is the "munny player" everyone dreams of having on his or her team!

The Company We Keep

It is said that we are judged by the company we keep. This applies to both our personal and professional relationships. Today's company cultures create official "vision statements" that quantify who they are and what they are about. One of the most interesting statements I've been professionally exposed to comes from the international, Oklahoma-based company Express Personnel Services. They are is business "to help as many people as possible find good jobs by helping as many clients as possible find good people, and help clients make those jobs and those people even better."

Clearly, Express Personnel Services is in the people-building business because of a belief that when the water in the lake goes up, all the boats rise with it. Founded in 1983, the company today boasts over 300 franchised offices throughout the U.S., Canada, Great Britain, Russia and the Ukraine. It employs more than 250,000 people annually while providing a full range of temporary and full-time staffing services. In every sense of the word, this billion dollar organization is "every company's company."

To conceive, believe and achieve such professional success obviously requires a personal touch. What kind of leadership "company" does this company keep? In February of 1983, Mr. Robert Funk, the founder, chairman and president of Express Personnel, was working for a different company. The man for whom he had been working died of a brain tumor. The company immediately hit hard times, and Bob's job was eliminated. At the same time Bob was having his crisis, there was an economic downturn that devastated Oklahoma's oil industry and financial institution. Thousands of people lost their jobs, and the positive climate for achieving success that had existed was suddenly dead. Dead to everyone except Bob Funk, that is.

Bob had a belief that through adversity comes opportunity, and an understanding that becoming successful and achieving continuous quality is directly related to the caliber of people with whom your surround yourself. Oklahoma City's banks were in bad shape in 1983 and no one wanted to lend him money, so Bob took a mortgage on his house and farm to secure credit. He partnered with two men he knew he could trust and with whom he could work, William Stoller and James Gray. Bob took advantage of the rich and deep talent pool sitting stagnate as a result of the enormous corporate down-sizing. He hired quality workers anxious to make a company go despite hard times, and started his own company—Express Personnel.

Mr. Funk recalls, "Things were so bad that everyone in the company gave whatever it took. That's how we survived." And how did they thrive? They kept giving more than they took. In 1997, they gave $258,000 to the Children's Miracle Network charity. Look around them. Mr. Stoller was a regional recipient of *Inc. Magazine*'s Entrepreneur of the Year, and Bob Funk was a national finalist three times. They are listed in *Inc. Magazine*'s 500 fastest-growing, privately held companies, and were part of *Success Magazine*'s "Gold 100 List" that evaluates and recognizes a company's staying power. Express Personnel's printed and published, principle-centered organizational values of people first, integrity, professionalism, positive attitude, teamwork, continuous improvement, ease of doing business, perseverance and partnership for profitability are a direct reflection of its leader. As an Oklahoman, Bob understands that a person is judged by the people he shares the spotlight with: in his case, the late, great baseball legend Mickey Mantle, humorist Will Rogers, and country crooners Garth Brooks, Reba McEntire and Vince Gill. Yes, Bob Funk understands a person is judged by the company he keeps. Personally, I am a much better man for having kept his company, and it is a feather in my cap to have spoken several times for his people.

Cowboy Constitution

I recently spoke for two and a half hours at a retreat for the Dallas Cowboys Cheerleaders. My topic was a combination of effective television and radio interviewing, media control and personal development. I arrived at the famous South Fork Ranch with a mindset to teach and inspire them. Ironically, these 33 beautiful, intelligent, articulate, sensitive, polished professional women—the epitome of sophisticated elegance and total class—reminded me about seven important things I needed to know and remember:

1. Perception is not always reality. Although picture perfect on the outside, some of the cheerleaders had dealt with broken hearts and broken bodies, and had overcome challenges. Stereotypes are not fair. All cheerleaders are not ditzy girls who can only cheer, any more than all athletes are dumb jocks who can only lift weights or all CEOs are insensitive power- and money-maniacs who can only work. Let us not judge one another only by our outward appearance, gender, occupation, interests, or by the color of our skin, but by the content of our character.

2. We are not our bodies, our cars, our clothes or our titles and positions. We can and deserve to have all of that, but we must be *more* than that. These cheerleaders are mothers and teachers and PTAers and corporate managers.

3. Work hard to have influence, and then use your influence to unselfishly serve and uplift others. In addition to their hectic practice and performance schedule cheering on the Cowboys, the cheerleaders spend hours cheering on Make-A-Wish kids, visiting hospitals and schools, and making personal appearances to promote worthwhile products and causes.

4. Live your own dreams. Be yourself. You will make a lousy somebody else. The cheerleaders are part of a 33 person cohesive team, but each cheerleader has her own unique look, personality and burning desire to be

all she can be. Being a whole, well-rounded, complete human being should be enough cause to stay highly motivated, focused on excellence and committed to self-fulfillment. We cannot effectively compete against somebody else in our competitive world until we first compete against ourselves.

5. Think big. If best is possible, good is not good enough. Don't settle for a subpar dream, a subpar job or a subpar relationship. Shoot for the stars! Go for it! Every one of the cheerleaders grew up in somebody's neighborhood and went to somebody's high school. Each is one of only 33, and the 33 in the squad are only a fraction of the millions of women in the world. Yet they are Dallas Cowboys Cheerleaders, and so many are not. Why? They set a goal, worked extra hard and never quit. The good news is if it happened to them, it can happen to you and me!

6. Take charge of your time and talents. Get a life. When we say we are bored, we are admitting we are boring. We can't expect society to make our lives exciting and rewarding. We can't expect others to infuse our lives with passion, meaning, emotion and fulfillment. It is our responsibility to use our imagination and be assertive about what we are doing, where we are going, why we are going there and when we will get there.

7. It's okay to show emotion in public, at home and at work. Cheering is about emotion and it's not just for football games. It's okay to laugh and cry together and connect at a deeper heart-to-heart level. We did for two and a half hours. It's not a sign of weakness to show vulnerability, but a demonstration of strength. Real, authentic, strong women want and need real, authentic sensitive men who open up and openly express their feelings.

The next time you see the Dallas Cowboys Cheerleaders, remember their unwritten constitution. Their cheers are not just for football. Their cheers are about life, love excellence, determination, class and having it all.

Being a Good Kidd

When you think of a kid, what comes to mind: dreams, never-ending energy, positive optimism, "can-do" spirit, a love for life and a genuine desire to play games? Add another *d*—for determination—to *kid* and what do you get? The clues are in Richmond, Kentucky.

A football stadium bears his name, and his name is engraved in the record books alongside the sport's legendary characters—Bear Bryant, Joe Paterno, Bobby Bowden and Pop Warner. With his 272 coaching victories (as of 1997), he ranks sixth all-time in the nation, and he still has time left in his coaching career to climb further up the ladder. Given this information, you might think this coach is some old superstar.

Actually, he is a Kidd—the Kidd. His name is Roy Kidd, and he is one of the most successful and respected coaches in the history of the sport. As of the 1997 season, coach Kidd has been a football coach for 42 years. He coached at Madison High School for six years with a record of 54 wins and only 10 losses. He had a 27-game win streak in which his opponents scored a total of 15 points. Roy was high school coach of the year in 1961, his last year at Madison. Roy then moved on to become the head coach of his alma mater, Eastern Kentucky University, for the next 33 years. His teams have been in the playoffs 16 years, far more than any other NCAA Division I-AA university in history. He won the national championship twice and was national runner-up twice. Roy will clearly be in the College Football Hall of Fame.

Every fall, a new chapter of the Roy Kidd story is written. The page turns. The characters change. What doesn't change is what the coach expects of himself, his staff and his team, and the way he deals with the world around himself. Since 1956, Kidd-coached players have been winning on football fields, then successfully moving on to life's field of play. His former players are teachers, principals in high schools, physicians, successful businessmen, NFL all-pro football stars, and high school and college coaches.

As an acronym, ROY reveals himself:

R—Respectful. Roy has always treated his coaches, players and everyone with whom he works exactly the way he wants to be treated. Roy believes you should "do unto others as you would have them do unto you."

O—Overachiever. Before Roy was a coach he was a player. Just as in his coaching career, as a player he stood out way above the crowd. In high school he was all-state in football, basketball and baseball. Kidd turned down other football scholarship offers, including one from coach Bear Bryant, because he also wanted to play his favorite sport—baseball. Eastern Kentucky welcomed the two-sport star, and in his senior year Roy was an all-American quarterback.

Y—Yearning to positively touch and successfully mold the lives of others. Along the way, Roy has had opportunities to finish his coaching career at bigger schools and make much more money, but he wasn't interested in uprooting his family. To Roy, his family matters most. He and his wife, Sue, have coached some superstars of their own: their Kidds, Marc, Keith and Kathy; and their grandKidds Seth, Samantha, Evan, Nicholas, Kirsten and Kody.

What is Coach Roy's specific formula for becoming a good Kidd?

1. Always be straightforward and honest so others know exactly where they stand.
2. Focus on things that no one can take away: education, self-esteem, heart, desire to win, work ethic, and respect for authority. Winning games will take care of itself.
3. Always deal with everyone fairly and squarely. You don't necessarily treat everyone the same, but you always treat them with exact equality, fairness, respect, dignity, and values-based principle-centered consistency.

4. Do the right thing simply because it's the right thing to do. Doing right begins with taking pride in your good name, then moves to pride in your school and community. Doing right is about honor—being a champion when authority is not around.

5. Unequivocally trust. And make sure others always trust you. Trust is the single most important ingredient in every personal and professional relationship. The bond of trust is the hardest thing to reestablish if you violate it and lose it.

6. Believe. Believe in life, in love, in God, in yourself, in your job, in your people. What goes around comes around, and they will also believe in you.

Whenever the words integrity, competition, class, character, intensity, love of the game and winning come into a conversation, if it's about college football, I guarantee Roy Kidd's name will be a part of it. I have had the rare privilege of being in a locker room to hear a Roy Kidd halftime talk. Let me tell you, the many years of coaching have not dimmed the competitive fire that drives him. He's not a good loser, and he admits it. He still looks forward to the daily work winning requires. Though he owns an amazing win-loss record measured on scoreboards, what really matters most to this motivated Kidd is winning in life, which is measured in effort. The world would be so much better if we could all become good Kidds again!

Self-Fulfilling Prophecy

Every person's modus operandi is based on a subconscious philosophy of life. Whether it ever surfaces and formally materializes into a written personal mission statement, each of us acts in accordance with a specific value-based definition of our human experience. One of the noblest individual mottoes I've ever been exposed to is synonymous with one superman's name: Mr. Normand Gibbons. Normand's every personal and professional move has always been a snapshot of his basic belief: "Every human being is worthy of a good, fun and fulfilling life."

Norm was born June 9, 1931, in Glendale, California. He grew up in St. George, Utah, and earned his bachelor's and master's degrees from Brigham Young University. Beginning with his two years of service in the U.S. Armed Forces in the Korean War, Norm has dedicated his entire existence to the service and development of others. For 38 years, he has been an educator extraordinaire: parole officer, teacher and placement counselor in a juvenile detention "industrial school"; high school counselor; junior high and high school assistant principal and principal. In 1967, Norm moved to the University of Utah. At Utah, he served the next 26 years as director of admissions, associate dean of student affairs, dean of students, and, during the last seven years before his retirement, vice president.

Normand's commitment to every human being also extended outside the classroom. He headed up the Intermountain Junior Science and Humanities Symposium. He was a specially appointed delegate to the White House Conference on Children and Youth. He has also served on the board of directors of Valley West Pioneer Hospital, United Way's Big Brothers, Utah Boy's Ranch and the Utah Youth Village for Troubled Teens.

You must be wondering why I would highlight this man when there are thousands of people from which to choose. The answer is simple: Normand Gibbons literally saved my life. When my football career ended in a paralyzing injury, my broken dreams and depressing mindset drove me to consider suicide. I had it planned and was committed to carrying it out, unbeknownst to Normand Gibbons. That day, Norm told me he believed in me and that even though I couldn't play ball any more, I still was "worthy of a good, fun and fulfilling life." He then gave me a tape-recorded speech to help me stay fired up. It was by a motivational teacher named Zig Ziglar. Think about it. I am here today and writing this tribute only because of a man and his mission. He helped me set new personal sights and understand the power of a self-fulfilling prophecy.

In February 1990, in an interesting twist of fate, Norm Gibbons' life took another turn in the direction of educational service. This time, however, he had to direct his mission at himself. While delivering a speech at a university faculty luncheon, he felt dizzy, reached for a chair and collapsed to the floor. A blood clot in the center of his brain caused a stroke, leaving his entire right side numb and dysfunctional. The ambulance rushed him to the hospital with the doctors giving him only a 20 percent chance to live. If he survived, they predicted no memory, no work and no activity beyond a wheelchair. After five days in intensive care, Normand started a miraculous recovery. Bedridden and unable to function by himself, he surrounded himself with people who believed in him and his mission. For three hours every day, Norm worked through the paralysis in his leg, side and arm. He worked with his drooping eye, slurred speech and inability to walk. After his physical therapy sessions ended, he worked hours on relearning to eat, read and write. In Norm's words, "It was always a nice day when I graduated in my mind from one problem to the next, from not making progress to making progress."

Doctors expected Norm to be in the hospital for four months. He was out in 38 days. Doctors expected Norm to never go back to work. He embraced the beast of disability and fought his way back to a 100 percent recovery. By September of the same year, he was working full-time with greater fitness and more energy than ever before.

How did he recover? How did he sustain his comeback?

In a feature article published in the popular medical journal *Pulse Magazine,* Norm answered this very question. With no surprise to anyone who knows him, he simply replied, "It was a self-fulfilling prophecy. I firmly believe that every human being, including myself, is worthy of a good, fun and fulfilling life. And I wasn't willing to die before I was dead!"

5

TEACHING IS THE PROFESSION THAT MAKES ALL OTHER PROFESSIONS POSSIBLE

Nobody in our world would even have a job if it weren't
for our teachers.
They are the smartest people in the world.
They could work for any organization or major corporation,
and yet they decide to teach us what we need to know so
we can walk out of the school buildings each day educated,
equipped and fired up to make our dreams come true.
To all educators everywhere, thanks for being teachers.
We love you. We need you!

True Nobility

A king sent word into the village that he was in search of a new court counselor and confidant. The first subject was escorted in and the king inquired what he had done. The man knelt and rattled off his résumé as an architect and mathematician who had designed the castle and the bridge with complicated statistics, plans and logic. He claimed he could counsel the king on how and why we do what we do.

The second subject was announced and the king inquired of his qualifications. The man knelt and explained that he was the one who had built the castle and the bridge. He could counsel the king and his people on the necessity of having a firm foundation and strong pillars to support them in everything they do.

The third subject was brought into the king and asked what he had done to qualify for the king's court. He knelt and bragged about his legal and medical degrees. He said he could obviously counsel the king on what was broken and how to fix it.

Distraught and disgusted with the egos and self-centered attitudes of each of them, the king reluctantly invited in the final subject. When he saw an old, white-haired woman enter the room, he lost his patience and sarcastically inquired what she could have possibly done. Quietly she answered, "I was their teacher." In response to this the king rose, stepped down from his throne and humbly knelt at her feet to pay tribute to the noblest profession of all!

Milking the Message Out of Every Moment

Mr. Millward was a junior high school music teacher. He not only helped me to play the trumpet, he also explained it in terms of success principles that I could apply to everyday life. Mr. Millward taught me that there are only 12 notes in music. They were discovered long before Beethoven or B. B. King came along. All they did was take the 12 basic notes and, with creativity and emotion, arrange them into magnificent musical masterpieces. Mr. Millward taught me the importance of mastering the fundamentals of music, art, sports, math, English and everything else in life.

Mr. Richards, our high school principal, couldn't believe his eyes. One night as he chaperoned a dance, he pulled me aside and asked, "When did they start doing this dance thing with the girl cuddled up against the guy, doing all that pelvic gyration junk?" I smiled and answered, "It's been around for awhile. They call it the 'lambada.'" Mr. Richards replied, "We used to neuter dogs for doing that to our legs!" His statement not only made us laugh, it helped us see the value in raising our own expectations of dancing from the movements of an animal in uncontrollable heat to ones of a respectful, classy, disciplined human being.

That same year we had an interschool boxing tournament to raise money for charity. I volunteered to fight a guy and needed a trainer/manager for my corner. I asked a favorite teacher, Coach Ted Weight, to assist me. After round one was finally over, I staggered back to my corner all beaten up and dejected. I sat down on the stool, looked up at Coach Weight for some encouragement, and asked, "Did I hit him at all? Am I doing any damage?" Coach solemnly replied, "No, but keep swinging. Maybe the draft will give him a cold." Coach Weight taught me to always do my best, but to keep things in perspective and always have fun while doing it. It was only a boxing match!

The other day I was at my friend's home and his 10th grade son came into the kitchen. With his speech impediment he told his dad, "I-I-I w-w-wa-want t-t-t-to try out f-f-fo-for the debate team." His dad always supported him and believed in him; his dad told him he thought he could do it. Later that day the son came home from school dejected and down. His dad asked him if he made the debate team. His son replied, "N-n-n-no. Th-th-th-they s-s-sa-said I w-w-wa-wasn't tall enough." Obviously this wonderful, empathetic debate teacher knew that if there is a reason to be negative, we should focus on things we cannot change, which always keeps the hope alive to improve the things we can change.

The Hand

Thanksgiving was just around the corner and the teacher had given the children in her class instructions to draw something for which they were very thankful. She was especially grateful for her own children who had all grown up and moved away. She missed holding them so much.

As she looked at the students she thought to herself: *This inner city neighborhood is so poverty-stricken; these poor little children have so very little to be thankful for—on welfare, very poor, half-fed, half-clothed—what would they draw?*

Boyd was a thin, seemingly neglected, extremely shy boy who participated neither in class nor in the games that the other boys played during recess. When the teacher was on playground duty, Boyd would follow her about like a shadow and often press very close to her as though for protection. She wondered what a child like Boyd could possibly be especially thankful for and what he would draw.

The drawings were completed and she held them up for the class to see.

One picture was of a doll, one of a box of Wheaties, one of a new baby brother, one of a bicycle that had been passed down by an older brother. Another interesting picture was of a dad. The little girl who had drawn it said she was thankful that he still lived with them when most of her friends had no father in their lives.

Boyd had drawn a hand and when she held it up she got many responses from the students. One child said, "That is the hand of God, for he gives us everything." Another said, "That represents all of the hands that help us." Yet Boyd had drawn only one. His picture caused more comment than any of the others, but Boyd offered no explanation.

When school let out, the teacher leaned close to Boyd, put her hand on his shoulder as she usually did when she talked with him, and inquired, "Whose hand are you especially grateful for?"

Looking up into her face, he smiled and simply said, "Yours."

At this the teacher's eyes filled with tears as she remembered the numerous occasions when he had seemed incomplete and insecure without her and how she had instinctively reached down and taken his hand and held it tightly in hers, which somehow immediately comforted him. Boyd didn't have a mother living at home and he deeply missed that special, reassuring touch that only a mother can give. Unbeknownst to the teacher, she had given something of her heart and soul to this little boy that was most precious to him simply by reaching out her tender, loving, kind, caring and keeping hand. That day she learned the difference between being a life-teacher and a "life-toucher" and so she developed a new and deeper understanding of a powerful, popular poem. Boyd's drawing was about "The Touch of the Mother's Hand."

An Educational System

In my sophomore year of high school I met the anthropology teacher, Mr. Croft. I was a tall, gangly, insecure kid who only went to class to stay eligible for athletic competition. I didn't know anything about anthropology except that "we came from the goo, went through the zoo, and now we're you, whoop-dee-doo," so I never signed up for Mr. Croft's class. The intriguing thing about this is that it didn't stop him from positively impacting my life.

Mr. Croft was a teacher 24 hours a day: in the grocery store on Saturday, in the park on Sunday afternoon, after school, before school, and in and out of his classroom. Mr. Croft inspired and taught every student at East High, especially me. He deeply touched and encouraged me to become all I could possibly be.

How could I possibly repay Mr. Croft?

A few years after I graduated from high school, I had an opportunity to coach Pop Warner football for 13-year-olds who had never played before. To get a feel for the boys' abilities, I lined them up into two rows and had each of them run out for a pass. I wanted to see who could run, catch and throw so I could formulate a team in my mind.

Two days into practice, a tall, gangly, insecure kid wearing a new shirt, new jeans and new loafers showed up on the field. I asked him if he didn't want to go home and change his clothes and he boldly replied, "I've already missed two days of practice and I don't want to miss anymore. I came to play ball!"

He got in line and when he ran out for a pass, I threw the ball. It hit him square in the head. He picked up the ball and ran it back to me. He slapped it into my chest and ran to the other line. It came time for his second pass and I hit him in the head again. With his nose bleeding and his lip swelling, he picked up the ball, raced it back to me and got back in line.

On his third attempt, I lofted a soft, easy pass but it was over his head. He dove for the ball but came up nowhere near it. Covered with grass stains from head to toe, his body messy, mucky and soaking wet, he got up, took the muddy ball, raced back to me and slapped it to my chest.

Figuring I'd better have a chat with him before he killed himself, I pulled him out of line and asked, "Why are you here? Does your dad want you to be a football star? Did your friends talk you into it?"

He looked up with his big brown eyes and said, "Coach, I'm here because I want to play football. And I promise if you'll help me I know I can do it!"

"What's your name?" I asked.

He shyly answered, "Tommy Croft."

Shocked, I asked if his dad taught anthropology at East High School? Surprised, he replied, "I think so."

"Get back in line," I told him. Here, at last, was my chance to be a Mr. Croft to a Croft! Here was my chance to give something back and the first chance in my life to understand what's meant by the term "an educational system." What goes around really does come around!

Positive Discipline

I was recently visiting with Mr. Croft, my former high school teacher. We were discussing mutual respect and support in the context of positive discipline. I was looking for a first-hand experience from the world of education that would apply to parenting, coaching and to the corporate world of management, sales and customer service. The conversation centered on how to motivate, inspire and empower others—not only to increase performance and productivity, but to keep the rules and show respect.

Mr. Croft asked for my definitions.

With regard to mutual respect and support, I said, "The only place from which a person can grow is where he or she is."

As for positive discipline, I said, "You cannot increase a person's performance by making him or her feel worse; humiliation immobilizes behavior."

Mr. Croft's eyes lit up with excitement as he shared the following experience to illustrate his point.

"I had a student who disrupted everything," he said.

"Did you send him to the office?" I asked.

With an offended look on his face, he said, "I've taught school for over twenty-five years and I've never sent a student to the principal." Mr. Croft laughed. "Most of my colleagues think the principal has all the Band-Aids. No way. Teachers are responsible for their classrooms and the development and education of each kid. You don't just throw them out when they do something wrong. We have to invite them to grow. We must catch them doing something right."

"Mr. Croft," I interrupted, "I've been to schools where a long line of students trails out the principal's office, down the hall, out the door and past the 9A bus stop. They're suntanned! And they just stand there with that look of 'yep, I screwed a goldfish into the pencil sharpener four months ago and I'm still waiting to see the principal.' If this is education, we're fooling ourselves! So what did you do with your terrorist?" I asked.

"Interesting you should ask," he replied. "I didn't give up

on him and my research uncovered that this James character played in a rock-and-roll band and that he was playing that Friday night in a smoke-filled, honky-tonk, redneck, biker bar out in the bushes somewhere. I talked five teachers into going with me so I wouldn't be stabbed all by myself."

"Then what happened?" I asked breathlessly.

"Now picture this," Mr. Croft continued. Six of us in argyle sweaters with matching socks stood at the back of the dance floor surrounded by teenagers who looked like they'd been mugged with a staple gun. The lead singer had a carburetor stuck in his nose. When James spotted us he leaned into the microphone and asked, 'What are you proctologist-looking teachers doing here?' We told him we heard his band was awesome and wanted to check them out."

Mr. Croft and his colleagues only stayed 15 minutes. That's all the noise they could take. That was Friday night. On Monday morning was James a discipline problem in Mr. Croft's class? No way. Was he a problem in Mr. Croft's class for the rest of the school year? No way! Was James a discipline problem in other teachers' classrooms for the rest of the school year? Yes! Was it because they couldn't teach? No. It was simply because they didn't care! Positive discipline means caring about a person physically and emotionally—and catching that person doing something right!

Classroom Management

A teacher asked Johnny, "How many presidents have we had?" Johnny countered, "What do you think?" The teacher replied, "I don't think—I know." To which Johnny responded, "I don't think I know either."

Being successful is not based on what happens to us, but rather on how we *react* to and *deal* with what happens to us. The effective management of our situations requires nothing more than creativity, flexibility, a sense of humor and concentration on the benefit of the end result.

Effective classroom management comes from the same mind-set. For example, let's say that you are a teacher. You have been intimidated by the pressure and stress that accompanies an official visit to your classroom to evaluate your teaching abilities—an evaluation conducted by the principal, the superintendent and/or a special evaluation committee. You feel your anxiety continue to mount as you recall similar experiences in the past. However, not to worry! With flexibility, a sense of humor and concentration on results, you can eliminate the uncertainty by creatively managing the situation before it even occurs. Whenever an evaluation team entered my teaching buddy's classroom, his students knew that if he asked a question and they *did* know the answer, they were to raise their right hands. If they *did not* know the answer, they were to raise their left hands. In this way, every student in the class raised their hands in response to every question, so the evaluators thought that every student knew the answer to every question. My friend, the teacher, only called on one of the few students with their right hands raised. This enabled him to always call on a student who knew the correct answer to every question and, therefore, he in turn always received the highest marks that the evaluation team could give! Amusing, eh?

This mind-set also applies to managing the classroom learning environment. With all the discussion about *left-brain* and *right-brain* learners, (and some of my athlete buddies, the "no-brainers"), it is important that teachers set up a classroom success system. This classroom success system must take into consideration the fact that some of us are cognitive, quantitative and auditory learners, while others of us are creative, kinesthetic and visual learners. Teachers must continually change the way in which they are connecting with their students in order to accommodate and honor every student's unique learning style. The simple formula for implementing this change surprisingly comes from network television. The high-powered marketing minds of New York's Madison Avenue advertising agencies have studied and discovered that the average attention span of most people between the ages of 5 and 65 is seven minutes. They tested this and concluded that every seven minutes we need a change—a break in the action—a different point of focus in order to maximize concentration and learning. That is why networks break their programming into seven-minute segments and sell advertising accordingly. In a 30-minute television show there are usually three or four commercials. And notice that the current trend is not the old 30-to-60-second spots, but rather the new, quicker 15-second splashes repeated a few times. Because we need a break every seven minutes, and so our recall is at its highest level of performance during that incremental cycle, we remember the commercials much more clearly and for a much longer period of time than we remember the content of the program that we are watching.

In a classroom teachers don't have to change their personalities, teaching styles or lesson plans to accommodate different learning styles. All they need to do is reorganize the lesson plan into seven-minute segments. This allows them to move from lecture, to video, to writing on the board, to participatory discussion, back to lecture, to quizzes, to film strips, to tests, to reports, and so forth. In this way every student is drawn into the information at least a couple times during every class period. The result is that as they see, hear and feel the relevance of the material, the subject becomes interesting and grades improve, even for the mentally irregular athletes who are 19 years old and refer to the seventh grade as their senior year!

Something More

In a high school of over 3,000 students, all the kids receive birthday cards in their lockers on their birthdays signed by the faculty. When a student's father died, flowers and a contingent of students showed up at the funeral in support. When the Red Cross needed blood donations, the school set up a blood drive. When Ronald McDonald House needed furniture, this school and two rivals came together and raised $10,000. When a student is absent from school, a fellow student phones her to say, "We missed you today. You are needed and important to our school family."

A school is set up for one thing: to teach a specific curriculum package in a spaced, repetitious way so that the students can regurgitate their memorized knowledge several times during the year in a test format to advance to the next level and eventually get the job they dream about instead of having to settle for a job that is left over. That's it. Period. So where do all the other things come from? From whence cometh "something more"?

The Student Council sponsors, initiates, supports, advertises and implements extracurricular activities. School clubs, dances, assemblies, convocations, pep rallies, career fairs, teacher appreciation days, and charitable volunteer work in the community all come out of the Student Council budget and its student and faculty leadership.

Student Council advisors not only teach a regularly scheduled curriculum course, they also teach a leadership course, that includes ethics, interpersonal communication and management. Yes, they do "something more." They coordinate all the activities for the calendar year. Then in the summer, they take students to leadership camps and attend the national Student Council Association conference. Putting in at least 40 extra hours per month during the school year, a Student Council advisor becomes an expert psychiatric counselor, heart nurse, chauffeur, fund-raiser, disc jockey, spirit broker, poster painter, banner hanger, magazine seller, candy dealer, soft-drink negotiator and confidant friend. Most important, they advocate student growth and development to the principal, the school board, the district and to the rest of the faculty. School life revolves around the student council advisor because they do "something more."

Not everyone can qualify and become a Student Council advisor. It requires a personality driven by the opportunity to make a difference, incredible vision, sensitive perception, patience, determination, high expectations, patience, perseverance, extreme creativity, patience, commitment to kids, passion for creating significant emotional experiences and empathetic listening. The greatest of these have touched my life for the best. They are: Dr. Earl Reaum from Colorado, Mr. Phil from Louisiana, Kay Baker from Texas, Dennis Lock from Missouri, Patty Ireland from Georgia, Ed Bailey from Washington, Michael Hassell and Bob Shogren from Arizona, Maris Aldrich from Montana, Nancy Moen from Oregon, Dan Wilson from Canada, and Mark Herman and Alden Esping from California.

It's been said that the greatest teacher is experience. If so, then logic dictates that the greatest teachers focus on experiential learning. The Student Council advisor creates and provides planning, problem solving, critical thinking, team building, public speaking and public service experiences that outlast the classroom and positively effect students forever.

Why do "something more" and put in extra time to maximize the talents of students, build their character traits, and physically and emotionally prepare them for additional leadership responsibilities in the future? So students will graduate from high school and want to do "something more." Student Council advisors understand:

> *A child is a person who is going to carry on what you have started. He is going to sit where you are sitting, and when you are gone, attend to those things that you think are important. You may adopt all the policies you please, but how they are carried out depends on him. He will assume control of your cities, states and nations. He is going to move in and take over your churches, schools, universities and corporations . . . the fate of humanity is in his hands.*
>
> *—Abraham Lincoln*

Building the Bridge

We don't learn to know, we learn to do. It doesn't do us any good to know how to read a book if we never pick one up and read it. With all due respect to the extremely intelligent and highly educated, all the information in the world isn't going to make us successful. It's like the man who has three Ph.D.s—one in psychology, one in philosophy, one is sociology. He doesn't have a job, but at least he can explain why!

I'm a huge advocate of getting a college degree. We must be life-long learners, but let us keep it in perspective and always teach "whole-person" learning. Students need employability skills that are transferable from job to job.

According to research by Dr. John Bishop, chairman of Cornell University's department of human resource studies, most employers are more interested in a job applicant's specialty skills than academic knowledge. When asked what skills they look for when hiring, employers almost always rank occupational skills, work ethic habits, initiative, and if and how an individual keeps his promises ahead of reading and math. Bishop's research concludes, "An education that does not encourage skills specialization, leadership training, the development of usable 'tools for tomorrow' and a practical bridge from 'school to work' is a barrier to excellence."

The data clearly states that employer expectations are increasing. In 1981, employers just expected skilled workers to "show up." Today, they expect employees to perform at higher levels. In 1981, it was "come to work." In 1997, it had grown to "come to work and be involved in problem solving, process improvement, peer reviews, peer training, peer hiring, safety ownership, leadership of teams and conducting team meetings, customer surveys, multiple skills for different departments, and community charity involvement."

Vocational education and the extracurricular opportunities afforded to any young person who seeks out one of many student leadership clubs is what 21st century workforce preparation is about! Educators who prepare their students to compete in a real world that they recognize are important to all of us.

Dr. Jim Koeninger of Oklahoma and Dallas, Texas, has spent a lifetime teaching life skills, marketing, leadership and management in the vocational education student organizations. His ideas have positively influenced Health Occupations Student Association (HOSA), Distributive Education Clubs of America (DECA) and Future Business Leaders of America (FBLA). As the author of The Innovative Educator, Koeninger has continued to enhance the educational learning experience for thousands of teachers and students throughout the world. Many have had equal influence, but no single person in America has impacted vocational education any more than Jim Koeninger! His Leadership Development Institute (LDI) was the first student leadership camp of its kind in America and has inspired hundreds of replica camps coast to coast.

Mr. Archie Romney of Sahuarita, Arizona, is a proud vo-tech teacher who spends a minimum of 10 extra hours a week outside the classroom preparing his students for state and national competitions. As the Vocational Industrial Clubs of America (VICA) advisor, Archie has taken over 30 students in the last 25 years to the prestigious national Skills U.S.A. Championships to compete with 3,500 students for huge scholarships, prizes and recognition awards. Mr. Romney's extraordinary commitment to his profession has earned him Arizona Teacher of the Year and Arizona State Vocational Teacher of the Year. Archie's students say he always puts success into their curriculum. "He taught me how to pay attention to the little things that tell you there may be trouble ahead. That's important in engine diagnostics and repair, but it's also important in life," said one national champion of his favorite teacher.

Mr. Mike Cardin of Ottumwa, Iowa, is a DECA advisor. He not only spends extra hours outside his required classroom curriculum teaching marketing and leadership skills, he also has a special understanding of winning and shares it in all that he does. Mike has coached state and national DECA competition winners, and has developed and directed the winning campaigns of both state and national officers. This is not all.

Mike takes the leadership, teamwork and winning

philosophies he teaches in his marketing classes and applies them to sports. He is one of the most successful high school golf coaches in the history of the state of Iowa. He has already won many state championship titles, with many more to come. He is also a superb basketball coach, basketball referee and all-around champion advocate for kids! In the words of his students, "No one gives more, demands more or wins more than Mike Cardin. He makes hard work fun, perfect practice permanent and school interesting, and he helps us make winning a habit! Most of all, he is a listening friend. Trust me, I know!"

Mr. Kent Boggs of Stillwater, Oklahoma, is relentless in his dedication, commitment and loving determination to turn young boys into real men and young girls into assertive women. Mr. Boggs eats, sleeps, drinks, talks and walks agriculture education. Future Farmers of America (FFA) is his vehicle to teach young people values, ethics, organization, responsibility, pride, class, sophistication and meticulous attention to detail. Mr. Kent Boggs is one of the finest gentlemen on earth and inherently uses his position to influence thousands of students and teachers each and every year to be all they were born to be.

In today's corporate world, when the organization interviews a prospective employee, they are asking themselves, "Can this person be a manager in five years? If not, why should we invest time and money to train them?"

Everyone knows that the greatest gap in human performance is between knowing and doing. True education is about building the bridge that connects the two so that children can successfully cross into the future. Vocational educators are helping to build that bridge. Are you?

Quiet Heroes

(dedicated to all our teachers)

The world is full of quiet heroes
who never seek the praise.
They're always back off in the shadows.
They let us have the lime-light days.
You're the one that I look up to
Because of you I'm free.
You set an example I could follow,
You helped me see my destiny.

So even though my thanks don't show
Unnoticed you will never go.
I need to say I love you so
You're my hero!

I've had my share of broken dreams
But you said I could win.
You gave me the chance I always needed
To start my dreams again.
You took the time to teach and tutor
You showed me rules to rise.
You changed my fears to glory tears.
You're an angel in disguise.

So even though my thanks don't show
Unnoticed you will never go.
I need to say I love you so.
You're my hero!

I wouldn't be where I am today,
I've won my share of time,
Unless you coached me through the maze
And pushed me on the hardest climbs.
It's just your style, the extra mile,
No glory must be tough,
You let me have the accolades.
A smile you said was just enough.

So even though my thanks don't show
Unnoticed you will never go.
I need to say I love you so.
You're my hero!

The Miracle of Casey

Little Casey was five years old when I met her. She was one of the most beautiful, bubbly, talkative big-eyed little girls in the entire world. She was diagnosed with leukemia and was scheduled for a bone-marrow transplant at Doernbecher Children's Hospital in Portland, Oregon. After the frightening, tedious surgery, Casey would need to stay in Portland for months of chemotherapy and radiation treatment. Her mother, Pam, wanted to stay by her side the entire time, but it was impossible financially.

Pam was a schoolteacher in Albany, Oregon, and couldn't afford time off from work. She prayed and pleaded for a miracle.

The miracle of precious little Casey started in the hospital with the capable doctors and nurses who treated and cared for her. The miracle extended when Pam was welcomed to stay at the fabulous Ronald McDonald House in Portland— at no charge.

The medical bills were insurmountably high. In Pam's greatest moment of despair, her fellow teachers at South Albany High School helped by creating a daily class schedule where each teacher coordinated his or her personal and professional schedules to cover Pam's classes. This allowed them to fulfill her obligations without paying for a substitute teacher, and while Pam moved to Portland to be by Casey's side, she didn't miss a single paycheck.

Casey brought hope and joy and love and dreams to everyone who had the privilege of being around her. She was in remission and on her way to recovering, so her sudden death has shocked and saddened all of us. She passed away on Good Friday 1994, at 10 years of age.

We pray for miracles, but God answers our prayers and fulfills our needs through other people. Sometimes we don't get the answers we choose and we often don't understand the answers we get. But one thing is for sure. If God had come to Casey's mother and said, "Pam, you can either have Casey for 10 years or not at all, which do you choose?" I guarantee Pam would have said, "Give me sweet Casey for 10 years."

In her short life, Casey Welzier brought a hospital staff together, a high school faculty together and my own mind, heart, spirit and soul together in priority focus. Thanks, Casey, for teaching us about unselfish service, unbridled hope and optimism, endurance to the end with a smile, and a clear understanding of what really matters most.

Wild Man

Most teachers are loving, considerate, supportive, positive individuals. But, as in any profession, there are always negative people who spread negative energy and gossip about others.

Years ago, when I arrived to speak at a high school convocation in Louisiana, I entered the faculty lounge to relax and get my thoughts together. Two teachers stormed through the door and immediately started griping about a student I'll call the Wild Man.

"That long-haired, dope-smoking, frisbee-throwing, skateboard-jumping, flag-burning hippie will never amount to a hill of beans," said one. The other joined in with ridiculous gossip about as accurate as "my wife's sister's dog's mother-in-law told me through the grapevine that he did this and that."

When I couldn't take the negative comments any longer, I found the auditorium and checked out the sound system. There I met the very positive, professional principal who explained the plan for the day.

There was a student in the school who had been a friend to everyone. Zachary was an energetic kid who supported all the games and dances. He had multiple sclerosis—a disease that affects the nerves and muscles. For years Zach had been in a manual wheelchair, moving from class to class and function to function.

A month before I arrived, Zach's condition worsened and he needed a motorized wheelchair to stay at this school. Without it, he would have to attend a school with special equipment.

It turned out that Zach couldn't afford the new electric chair, so his only choice was to check out. Today was the day Zach was leaving; he was in the counselor's office with his parents filling out the final paperwork.

The school assembly was announced and Zach and his parents were casually invited into the auditorium. The students and faculty filled the giant room and Zach took his usual spot out in the aisle on the fifteenth row. Zach assumed it was his last day and last event at this school. Before they introduced me as the speaker, the real drama unfolded.

The student body president was introduced and he came on stage for the Pledge of Allegiance. He then shocked everyone when he introduced Wild Man—the kid the teachers were degrading in the faculty lounge. With green hair, numerous rings in his ear and two fly-fishing hooks in his eyebrow, Wild Man caused a stir among the teachers.

Without saying a word, Wild Man gave a signal and four football players approached Zach, lifted him out of the wheelchair and brought him to the center of the stage. Wild Man gave another signal and two students from the band presented Zach's parents with flowers and escorted them to the stage.

Wild Man then excused himself and disappeared backstage. Seconds later he reappeared driving a brand-new, shiny, chrome-plated electric wheelchair with a giant bow in the school colors taped on the side.

Wild Man spun around and stepped out to allow the football players to place Zach in the chair. They showed him how to operate it and moved aside as Zach took two victory laps around the stage. With tears streaming, two thousand students *and* faculty members simultaneously leaped to their feet to give a five-minute standing ovation.

Were they just cheering for Zach and the fact that he could now remain in their school? No, they were also cheering for Wild Man who had used his own initiative to rally for Zach's new chair. His mohawked, tattooed, punk-rocker friends had banded together and collected enough money on their own to buy the chair.

So, it's true: we shouldn't judge a book by its cover. When given a chance to feel wanted, important, capable and needed, even the most deceiving "books" can deliver a great moral to the story. Remember, "A broken clock is right twice a day." Never give up on anyone!

Whole Person Learning

Educators teach us:

Art—that we might put ourselves in another's situation and feel what he feels.

Music—that we might not just hear, but listen.

Language—that we might not just speak, but communicate.

History—that we might learn from the successes and failures of others.

Government—that we might question authority and get involved.

Science—that we might come to know both the seen and unseen worlds.

Math—that we might always begin logically with the end in mind.

Vocational Education—that we might understand practical relevance to take what we know and apply it to what we want to accomplish.

Physical Education—that we might run and not be weary, walk and not faint.

Nature—that we might respect all living creatures, plants, and beings, and realize how we are all connected in the great circle of life.

Self-Esteem—that we might love life.

Hands-on Education

Vocational education is as important as every other subject in our educational curriculum. Vocational education is "hands-on," practical-application learning of not only school skills but life skills. Because it is an elective course it breeds a special kind of teacher. Can you imagine how teacher attitudes and behaviors would change if they made every subject an elective course and paychecks were determined by attendance?

Agriculture education is an important vocational education course, and the Future Farmers of America (FFA) is one of the greatest student leadership organizations in the world. They put so much emphasis on personal development and public speaking training that it's easy to pick these exceptional young people out in a crowd. I was in a hotel lobby and stopped a young man to ask where the men's room was. He gave me precise directions and ended with a meaningful poem. I said, "You must be an FFA officer." He said, "Yes, sir. How did you know?" It's obvious. They are all so wonderful. Let me share one of the thousands and thousands of reasons why.

Jeff was a 13-year-old boy entering the eighth grade in a small school in Oklahoma. His father was a drunk, spending more time in jail than out. His mother worked for minimum wage at a local shop. His older brother was doing prison time for arson.

Jeff was a special education student who was influenced by negative family and friends. He desperately needed some positive encouragement and direction. Sensing Jeff was lost and lonely, the "agriculture teacher" invited him to join the FFA. In the first week of class, Dale exposed the students to the many opportunities for personal growth and development available in the FFA. He assigned them to pick one and write it down as a goal for the year. Jeff came to school the next day with one word on his paper: pig. As they say, he wanted to "show a pig." Jeff did not own a pig and he had no money to buy one, but he thought it sounded interesting and exciting.

Dale, the "ag teacher," explained to Jeff that in their annual sausage-selling fund-raiser, the person who sold the most packages would win $70—the exact amount to purchase a small show pig. His mother had never seen him so excited. That night Jeff implemented his sales strategy. He opened up the three pages of his little town's phone book and started with the first name. That night he phoned every name from A through F and sold 417 sticks of sausage. The next night he finished the phone book and sold 363 more. Jeff sold more sausage than anyone ever had in the multi-year history of the fund-raiser and won the $70 first prize. With the help of his ag teacher, Mr. Dale, Jeff bought the pig.

Dale immediately set high expectations. First, Jeff could not participate in any of the twelve shows that year if his grades ever dropped below a C. Since the second grade, Jeff had earned mostly D grades. Jeff started working harder in school and received nothing but As and Bs in all of his classes for the entire school year.

Second, Jeff had to pay to feed and keep the pig ($25 per month), and earn enough spending money to pay for hotels, meals and gas while traveling from show to show. Jeff found odd jobs at farms and at school that paid his bills.

One day after school, Dale told Jeff he needed to walk and work his pig for another 15 minutes, and that Dale would come and tell him when to quit. Something sidetracked Dale and he forgot about Jeff. An hour and a half later, Dale remembered his student. Dale found Jeff still walking the pig. Six months and 12 shows later, Jeff's dedication paid off. He was paid $311 for his pig at the "premium auction," and later sold it for the market weight value for an additional $173. His $70 pig brought $484.

It's been a few years now, and Jeff has remained a constant A and B student. He has learned leadership skills, raised other prize-winning animals, participated on livestock judging teams, become a pretty darn good public speaker, and stayed out of trouble. Hands-on vocational education really works in building employability skills, self-esteem, confidence, work ethic and positive attitude. All other subjects and teachers should take note and put as much success into their curriculums.

Be Not Weary

Sally thought she saw life change for the better when a widower from her past returned with a proposal of marriage. Nicely attired, he spoke of a prosperous farm. Sally understood him to mention servants, and that meant that he must be a man of substance. She accepted his offer and crossed the river with him to view her new possessions, only to find a farm surrounded by wild blackberry vines. The house was a floorless, windowless hut. The imaginary servants were two thinly clad, barefoot children. She soon discovered that the father had borrowed the suit and boots to go a'courting. Her first thought was to go back home.

But she looked at the youngest boy, whose gaze met hers, and she decided to stay for the sake of the children who needed a mother.

Each of us has been in her position, wanting to leave the place we find ourselves in. It's always easier to let somebody else take responsibility for a seemingly hopeless situation.

But never despair. A boy is the only thing God has out of which to make a man. Sometimes all he needs is a teacher.

Sally Bush didn't know when she looked at the melancholy 10-year-old face that her new stepson's name was Abraham Lincoln.

When you are having a hard time in the place you find yourself, look into the face of just one boy or girl and try and see how great they might become with the right amount of time and patience.

You are looking into the face of the future.

Get Involved at School

Have you noticed how parents try to choose their children's friends? "You *can* associate with him, you cannot associate with *him*," they emphatically state. This forces children to have two sets of friends: those associates whom they feel they can bring home for the approval of their parents, and those with whom they really "hang out." No wonder we have parents who don't have the foggiest idea that their teenagers are in a violent street gang or wasting away getting high on drugs. Parents only see the pretend side of their children's lives. Children display this side of their lives when they are at home in order to manipulate their parents' perceptions.

So what do we do? Can we truly help our children deal with the negative influences and temptations of gangs, drug use, pregnancy, dropping out of school and suicide? Of course we can! All we have to do is get involved in their *real* lives.

Regardless of whether we want to admit it, control is only an illusion. Sure we can control our children while they are in our presence, but because they are away from us most of the time, it's what they do when we are *not* around that makes or breaks them. As parents, we need to teach them correct principles and set positive examples of what is good and right, but then give them the freedom to govern themselves.

There are two ways to check up on how they are using their freedom. First, we must open our homes in the spirit of unconditional love, so that we may engage in nonjudgmental interaction with all our children's friends. Only then can we witness the true positive and negative influences in their lives. Only then can we counsel them on their decisions and choices, for example, that the 22-earrings-on-one-side-of-the-face friends are a bit much and so is the miniature towel rack they're planning for their own earlobes!

Second, after we have opened our homes to our children's friends, we must go to our children's schools. Because of the amount of time they spend there, the very best place for us to get involved in our children's lives is school. As we volunteer our time at school, not only do we develop a friendship and rapport with our children's friends, we also empathetically grow to appreciate our beloved teachers. I guarantee that after just one day in the classroom you will leave shaking your head, wondering how anyone can be a school-teacher without massive doses of medication, psychotherapy and bodyguards! Middle school teachers could easily be prison wardens when they retire! Yet, some parents viciously complain that teachers only work 9 months a year and get paid for 12, their job is easy, and their workday ends at 2:30 P.M. Obviously, those complainers have not been in a school lately. Threats against teachers' lives, disrespect for authority, serious attempts to undermine high expectation and accomplishment, crazy concepts such as replacing English with "Ebonics" as a so-called real language, and parents referring to teachers as the bad guys all contribute to what is killing our schools and cutting deeply into the positive attitudes of our educators.

The bottom line of parenting? Good parents who really care about their children will volunteer in the schools. They will help with reading and math, chaperone dances, escort field trips, and stick up for teachers in and out of school. It's actually fun, entertaining and exciting to volunteer in schools. In the elementary schools, you'll find that the three important basics are not reading, writing and arithmetic, but rather recess, the tried and tested technique for catch-ing lizards, and show-and-tell. You'll see jewelry boxes transporting hair balls that were coughed up by a pet and hear magnificent reports on such important facts as "more Americans are killed every year by pigs than by sharks."

If you don't like your schools, don't just sit back and com-plain. Get involved and make them all that they can and should be. If you don't like what your children are doing or the direction in which they are headed, don't just complain and scream and yell and ground them. Instead, get involved in their lives. How? Where? Go where they are physically and emotionally. And where are our children most of the day? Obviously, at school. Everything in a young person's life revolves around school. Great parents get involved and stay involved in their children's lives at school!

Take It Personally

The great educator, Horace Mann, was asked to be the guest speaker at a dedication service for a beautiful new high school building. Standing on the stage of a state-of-the-art auditorium, he concluded by gesturing and saying, "All the sacrifice, hard work, time and money that went into this magnificent edifice will be worth it if we but help one child."

As Mr. Mann was exiting the building, a parent confronted him. "Didn't you overstate it a little, that all this would be worth it if we just help one child?" the parent asked. Horace Mann, in his wisdom, simply replied, "No. What if that child was yours?!"

The next time we kick against tax levies and bond issues to improve our school systems, let us take it personally and vote YES for education!

How to Pass Class

1. BRING THE TEACHER NEWSPAPER CLIPPINGS DEALING WITH THE SUBJECT. This demonstrates fiery interest and gives the teacher timely items to mention to the class. If you can't find clippings dealing with the subject, bring in any clippings at random. The teacher thinks everything deals with the subject.

2. LOOK ALERT. Take notes *eagerly*. If you do look at your watch, don't stare at it in disbelief and shake it.

3. NOD FREQUENTLY AND SAY, "HOW TRUE!" This may seem disengenuous, but the teacher will appreciate it.

4. SIT IN FRONT, NEAR THE TEACHER. (Applies only if you intend to stay awake.) If you are going to make a good impression, you might as well let the teacher know who you are, especially in a large class.

5. LAUGH AT THE TEACHER'S JOKES. You *can* tell when the teacher tells a joke. If the teacher looks up from the lecture notes and smiles expectantly, the teacher told a joke.

6. ASK FOR OUTSIDE READING. (You don't have to read it. Just ask for it.)

7. IF YOU MUST SLEEP, ARRANGE TO BE AWAKENED AT THE END OF THE CLASS. It creates an unfavorable impression if the rest of the class has left and you sit there alone, still dozing.

8. BE SURE THE BOOK YOU ARE READING DURING THE CLASS LOOKS LIKE A BOOK FROM THE CLASS. If you do math in psychology class, match the books for size and color.

9. ASK ANY QUESTION YOU THINK THAT THE TEACHER CAN ANSWER. Conversely, avoid announcing that you found the answer to the question the teacher *couldn't* answer in your younger brother's second-grade reader.

10. CALL ATTENTION TO THE TEACHER'S WRITING. This produces an exquisitely pleasant experience connected with you. If you know the teacher has written a book or an article, ask about it in class.

6

TELL THEM HOW YOU FEEL

The average person talks at a rate of between 150 and 400 words per minute, yet thinks at a rate of between 800 and 1,200 words per minute.

No one ever knows everything we feel and all that we want to say.

Thoreau was right when he wrote: "The mass of men lead lives of quiet desperation."

No one ever knows unless we tell him or her how we feel.

Pressure is not something that is naturally there.

It's created when you question your own ability.

And when you know what you can do, there's never any question!

Together We Can Make It

Bob Butler lost his legs in a 1965 land mine explosion in Vietnam. He returned home a war hero. Twenty years later, he proved once again that heroism comes from the heart.

Butler was working in his garage in a small town in Arizona on a hot summer day when he heard a woman's screams coming from a nearby house. He began rolling his wheelchair toward the house but the dense shrubbery wouldn't allow him access to the back door. So he got out of his chair and started to crawl through the dirt and bushes.

"I had to get there," he says. "It didn't matter how much it hurt."

When Butler arrived at the pool there was a three-year-old girl named Stephanie Hanes lying at the bottom. She had been born without arms and had fallen in the water and couldn't swim. Her mother stood over her baby screaming frantically. Butler dove to the bottom of the pool and brought little Stephanie up to the deck. Her face was blue, she had no pulse and was not breathing.

Butler immediately went to work performing CPR to revive her while Stephanie's mother telephoned the fire department. She was told the paramedics were already out on a call. Helplessly, she sobbed and hugged Butler's shoulder.

As Butler continued with his CPR, he calmly reassured her. "Don't worry," he said. "I was her arms to get out of the pool. It'll be okay. I am now her lungs. Together we can make it."

Seconds later the little girl coughed, regained consciousness and began to cry. As they hugged and rejoiced together the mother asked Butler how he knew it would be okay.

"When my legs were blown off in the war, I was all alone in a field," he told her. "No one was there to help except a little Vietnamese girl. As she struggled to drag me into her village, she whispered in broken English, 'It okay. You can live. I be your legs. Together we make it.'"

He told the mom that this was his chance to return the favor.

Commitment

There is a suicide epidemic in the world today. It affects everyone from 40-year-olds going through a life crisis to students in our schools. In Pano, Texas, several teenagers killed themselves in the same week. It is happening all over the country: South Shore of New Jersey; Pine Ridge, South Dakota; Orange County, California; Dade County, Florida; Toronto, Canada. In Iowa there were 100 suicide attempts in 30 days at the same high school. One girl died. The school brought Charolette Ross from California, a national consultant on suicide, and me in to talk to the kids. We split up the student body into two groups. Charolette did the left brain, cognitive therapy presentation. I did the right brain, emotional, motivational presentation. We then swapped audiences and repeated our presentations. Finally, we gathered with counselors and health-care professionals to interview each of the students who had attempted suicide and survived.

The demographic breakdown of those 99 students was enlightening:

> Seventy-three percent were on the honor roll. They said, "Thanks for the recognition, but I still have a giant hole in my heart. Something is missing in my life. Please help me!"
>
> Six students were student-body officers elected by classmates. They said, "Thanks for letting us win a popularity contest, but I'm missing something in my life."
>
> Three students were cheerleaders. They said, "Thanks for the attention, but it's shallow and fleeting."
>
> Three students were varsity football players. They said, "We were injured. Our bodies let us down. Because we can't be athletes we are nobody. There is nothing left."

In a corporate setting, they are the "employees of the month." In the community, they are the "good kids." In school, they are the stars with recognition, accolades and constant attention. So why did they want to give up, quit and take their lives?

Each one told us they lacked "commitment relationships" in their lives. That was the word they used, and it caught my attention. To help us define commitment, let us introduce another word: love. Love is a commitment, not a way of feeling. Romance is not love. Think of it this way: If I love you because you are beautiful, that's romance. But if you are beautiful because I love you, that's real love. It's a value-creating love that inspires us to be the best we can be even when the person we love is away. It makes us honestly say, "I like me best when I'm with you. I want to see you again."

Because of movies and music we say, "I love her sooo much. She makes me feel differently than I've ever felt before." Hey, so do beans. Feelings, emotions and hormones are not enough to sustain a relationship.

As important as the words "I love you" are to our mental health and emotional stability, when it comes to commitment relationships, "I need you" are the most powerful words. In the context of love, "I don't love you because I need you, I need you because I love you." Think about it. As you do, let me validate the deep yet elementary importance of "need."

My friend was getting married. He asked me to write a song and sing it at his wedding. I said no. He answered, "I need you." I couldn't say no again. I wrote the song. Two days later he phoned me back to explain that the band had just canceled, and he wanted me to prepare 40 to 50 songs to play as the dinner entertainment. I emphatically said, "No way!" He said, "I need you." I couldn't say no.

Again, let me pause and validate this discussion before I continue. If, as a stranger, I say, "I love you, come on, let's go," you will interpret it as sexual harassment and say, "Absolutely not." But if I say, "I need you to help me," you react by saying, "Where's the fire? We can put it out. Let's go."

I practiced and prepared my music. My friend's wedding finally arrived. I sang the song I wrote for the couple, and then one of the 40 to 50 I had practiced for the dinner. Before I could sing another song, the band arrived. There was a miscommunication. I didn't want to sing all night, I wanted to eat and socialize like everybody else, so I helped the band set up their equipment. When I arrived at the wedding reception, I arrived with the attitude that my friend needed me. I would have stayed until four o'clock in the morning if necessary because he needed me. I would have waited tables, mopped the floor and contributed in any way I could. But the second the band showed up, I was no longer needed. In all truth, they could do without me. We can fool others, but we can't fool ourselves. Why hang around if I was no longer needed? I didn't. I left the reception and went home.

This is the message coming through loud and clear from adults and young people across North America, especially from those we interviewed in Iowa who attempted suicide. Each one of them told us they knew they were loved, but they didn't believe they were needed.

In the corporate arena, when a sales champion or outstanding executive jumps ship to work for the competition, it is not about money. They no longer feel needed where they are, so they go where they do feel needed. The students in Iowa put on a good outward show that all was well. Most of us buy into thinking outside attention and recognition motivates us. It doesn't, and yet we emphasize it in our marriages, personal relationships, business contracts and athletic endeavors. No, no, no! We desperately need to be needed. That's what keeps us motivated and hanging around.

The tough reality is that we can't afford to wait for someone else to tell us or show us that we are needed. It might not ever happen. We could go months before we experience this crucial validation. So what do we do: give up, quit and kill ourselves? Most definitely not. Private victories must precede public victories. Whom are we fooling to think it is society's responsibility to give our lives meaning and purpose and excitement? It is our responsibility to do something on a daily basis to prove to ourselves that we are needed. The solution then is to participate more and be involved! We must reach out and make the move to establish and nurture commitment relationships based on action, participation and proactively creating symbiotic desired results.

In a relationship, "I need you" is not codependency. Rather, it means "I am okay, but I would be so much more with you. You complete me." At the beginning of the wedding, I felt as if I was not just good, I was good for something. I felt that my little weird-shaped puzzle piece really did fit, that I could make a significant contribution. When the band showed up, I lost that understanding. The way we recapture it in any phase of our lives, especially in our personal and professional relationships, is to change our attitude from "what's in it for me?" to "what's in it for others?" The best way for us to prove to ourselves that we are needed is to go out of our way to lift everybody else's performance up to a higher level when we are around. We could call it the "Michael Jordan factor." Let's face it, we work harder in relationships, in sports, in church, in school, in our communities, and in everyday life when we know we make a special difference to others. "I need you" is "telling them how you feel," expressing that without them, there wouldn't be *everybody.*

Forgive the Mistakes of Others

Paul was nervous as he sat on the train; the old man sitting next to him sensed this.

"Son, what's the matter with you?"

"I just got out of prison," replied Paul. "My mistake broke my parents' hearts and caused them a lot of shame. I don't know if they can love me after what I did. I never let them visit me in prison. I told them they didn't have to let me come home if they were too ashamed of me. I live in a small town with a large tree by the railroad tracks. I told them to tie a ribbon around that old tree if they were willing to let me get off."

Paul paused as the old man listened, then continued.

"The reason I'm so nervous is that we're almost there and I'm scared to look at that tree. I feel I don't deserve my parents because I hurt them so much."

Paul looked down in shame. Neither man spoke as the train slowed down to stop at the next station, Paul's home town.

Then the old man nudged him, "I think you can look now, son."

Paul glanced up slowly. The old tree was covered with ribbons—red, blue, yellow, orange and green—hundreds of them. Paul turned to the old man with tears in his eyes and said, "They still love me. I'm going home."

Whether you first heard a story like that in a well-known song or are hearing it for the first time, it's a great example of unconditional, non-judgmental love. If you aren't getting along with someone in your family because of something they've done, maybe it's time to let them know you still care. Tell them how you feel!

Pass It On

The scene was a national convention of a well-known Fortune 500 company. The speaker at the opening general session interrupted his presentation to interact with the audience and make a significant point. He asked everyone to stand up, team up two by two, and face each other. "With all sincerity," he said, "and with a straight face, tell that person 'I love you' and then give them a hug." Everybody laughed and proceeded with caution. Man to man laughed and turned sideways to slap each other on the back inside shoulder to inside shoulder. Woman to woman laughed and actually hugged face to face. Woman to man was different. With bodies poking way out and one shoulder leaning way in, they awkwardly stood at arm's length and quickly patted each other on the back as if they were burping a wee baby. "And rightfully so," you emphatically agree.

The speaker's point was to get people to think and step outside their comfort zones. Through this simple exercise it became obvious to everyone that we change only when it's safe, only when it's required and, most likely, only for that moment.

When the speaker finished, the President/CEO stood up to thank him. "The speaker was great and said some magnificent things, but the most powerful thing he did was invite us to break the old-mold expectation that work relationships must be all business, cognitive, stand-offish and nonemotional. When he invited us to say "I love you" to a business associate it hit me hard that this is one of the major ingredients missing in our organization. From this day forward our corporate culture will stress emotional human connection. I trust each of you will continue to use good judgment and remain first class in your treatment one to another, but please, I repeat, please, freely express your appreciation to each other. And when given permission, don't be afraid to 'appropriately hug.' You never know, this thanking, needing stuff could be contagious. Pass it on!"

The CEO left the meeting, got in his chauffeur-driven Town Car and headed home. As he thanked his driver for opening his door, he leaned over and briefly hugged him. "Thanks," the CEO said. "For four years you have been my company driver and I don't think I have ever told you how wonderful you are. You are the best driver on the road. You are a first-class gentleman and an asset to our organization. I need you and deeply appreciate your friendship and loyalty."

The chauffeur walked through the front door of his home, whistling and smiling like never before. He picked his wife up off the floor and hugged her close. "I changed my mind. I'm not going to quit my job after all." "Why?" she asked. "Did you get a raise or something?" "Yes I did. You know my boss pays me way more than other drivers, and I make a great living. I wasn't looking for a money raise. Today Mr. Allen gave me an emotional raise—the raise I've been seeking and needing for over a year! Get ready. I'm taking you to dinner."

They went to a restaurant they had never been to before. Their son worked there. His father had kicked him out of the house a year ago. When the son saw them walk in, he tried to hide, but couldn't. His purple Mohawk hair stood up and the ring and chain in his nose dinged off his dog-collar necklace. The son didn't know what to say or do, but his father did. He walked straight over to his son and hugged him. With tears in his eyes he said, "I love you, son. I appreciate you for you. Please come home. I miss you and need a relationship with you."

The startled boy nervously hugged him back and excused himself to go into the kitchen. "I've decided not to quit this job and move to San Francisco," he told the manager. "I've just decided to move back in with my parents. I'm going back to school to get my GED." "Why?" the manager asked. "I just discovered my parents actually care about me and I'm sick of letting them down trying to prove my independence. It's time to make them proud!"

Great story, but let's take it further. This son's eventual children will now benefit from his education, higher expectations, inner peace and stability, and most likely be the recipient of his unconditional love, hugs and appreciation. As he and his wife pass it on, their children's children will be the recipient of their hugs and appreciation. As they pass it on, their children's children will be . . .

Nothing Wrong with Wealth

There is nothing wrong with being wealthy. Growth and financial increase are a part of mankind's inalienable rights. We all desire more, and capitalism provides us the opportunity to get more than we have. It's perfectly natural to want to be financially comfortable.

When I was asked if I thought money would change me, I said gleefully, "I sure hope so!"

What's pathetic are the people who believe they can only get ahead at somebody else's expense. They are afraid to share, fearing there's not enough to go around. What they lack is an abundance mentality.

The people who really get rich enrich others. One of the best formulas for becoming wealthy is to give more than you take. That way you build credit for yourself with those around you. Someday you will be able to use that credit.

The people who are really successful—whether they are in business, the arts or sports—take out less than they put in. They leave the world a better place than they found it.

When you start making an effort to live this way, things begin to happen. People appear with opportunities. You'll find yourself in the right place at the right time. People will seek you out because they know you won't take advantage of them.

Dreams for Sale

When you see him running a basketball court and soaring through the air in a graceful slam dunk, or walking down the street signing autographs whenever he's asked, or donating time and money to charity, you realize he is a special man with dreams for sale.

He's called a lot of things, but the people who know him best call him "The Mailman" because he delivers. Karl Malone has stopped every NBA basketball franchise for the past 12 years. At six-foot-nine, 260 pounds, Malone delivers almost 30 points a game for the Utah Jazz. He was named the league's Most Valuable Player for the 1996-97 season and critics call him the greatest power forward ever to play the game.

He's not the kind of guy you would call an angel by any means—at least not in basketball. But Malone delivers in other ways.

He has become a guiding spirit to one 13-year-old boy living in Salt Lake City. The two met in 1995 when the Utah Jazz made their annual visit to the Primary Children's Medical Center. As Malone puts it, "The kids were all great, but when I met Danny, it was just different. It did something to me personally."

Danny has terminal leukemia so Malone decided to make the dying boy's last few weeks extra special.

"The second I met him I knew he was a Jazz fan, a Karl Malone fan. Those eyes lit up and he high-fived me. As sick as he was he never had any complaints. Danny's best day is being tired, being sore, taking chemo and being sick. His story is so courageous that more people should know about it."

"Karl's my angel," says little Danny to his mother, when Malone visits him in the hospital. "He's been a good friend. He's helped brighten my days."

After game six of the 1996 NBA Western Finals, Karl Malone gave little Danny the famous number-32 jersey he had worn during the game. Danny Ewing knew immediately what he wanted to do with the jersey. He asked his mother to bury him in it. She did, and Karl Malone was a pallbearer at the funeral.

In 1996 Karl was honored by the Make-A-Wish Foundation as their National Celebrity of the Year. In Utah, year after year, he is everybody's Man of the Year. Thanks for every delivery. For young and old, male and female, sports fan and not, you truly have dreams for sale. We love you and need you Mr. Malone! God bless you, Kay, and your beautiful family!

Cancer Can't Beat His Old Friends

Jim Wilhemly could only watch as his 200 acres of soybeans and corn grew ripe and heavy. He was deeply in debt and knew the time had come for harvesting. He feared all would be lost.

At 52, Wilhemly could no longer work the fertile fields he and his wife, Eileen, had nurtured for 20 years. As harvest time approached, word of Wilhemly's plight spread through the countryside southwest of Chicago. Amazingly, an army of neighbors arrived at the Wilhemly farm in a caravan of tractors, combines, huskers and wagons—50 farmers and 25 of their sons. The women brought fresh pies, covered hot dishes and jugs of steaming coffee. Their men already were harvesting the corn crop.

Old Charlie Jackson said, "I picked six thousand bushels of corn myself for Oscar Walling the time he caught his hand in a picker and tore it off. Don't know why you do these things. Hard to explain. You just do it. This is the natural thing farm folks do for each other."

Touched by the display of humanity as old and dependable as the land itself, Mrs. Wilhemly's eyes filled with tears. Her husband, once a vigorous farmer and township clerk, stopped by and shook hands, grateful he had such friends.

For two Saturdays the army in overalls rolled across the farmland bringing in the soybeans. Too ill to stop by, Wilhemly stayed home wondering how to thank the kind folk who came to help. But before he could come up with an answer, Jim Wilhemly died from the lung cancer he'd been fighting for two years. His wife paid off the bank and was able to keep her home.

All she could say was "I'm grateful."

It was a simple heartfelt sentiment that needed no embellishment. What's true is true.

Feel

Sometimes the most important factor in a situation is not IQ but EQ.

Being a high-performance person comes not from our Intelligence Quotient but rather from our Emotional Quotient—our feelings. IQ gets you the job, but EQ gets you the promotion.

Wouldn't it be a tragedy if we let technology completely overrun our human connections? Wouldn't it be a shame if technology replaces the human touch in a doctor's office and you only get voice-mail?

"If your pain is below the waist, press one."

Will they put the Catholic Church confessions on voice-mail? "Call 1-800-FESS UP. If you're into bigamy, press two, if you're worshipping the devil, press 666."

Let's hope not!

One of the most magnificent flying machines ever engineered and built is the United States Armed Forces F-18 fighter jet. This state-of-the-art weapon has every conceivable computer chip crammed somewhere in its cockpit. It flies faster than the speed of sound and costs $20 million to produce.

To fly the jet with pure precision at supersonic speeds, a highly trained pilot climbs into the cockpit, surrounded by wall-to-wall gadgets, dials and gauges, and straddles a control stick. To steer the airplane, the pilot need only move the control stick one inch in any one of the forward, backward, right or left positions, and it changes the entire direction of the aircraft by 45 degrees. When asked what the secret was to flying these high-tech planes, pilots simply answered, "By feel. Once you're airborne, it's all about feel."

Feeling is important, not just flying.

7

LOOK BEYOND IT

When you are describing
A shape, a sound or tint;
Don't state the matter plainly
But put it in a hint;
And then learn to look beyond it
With a sort of mental squint.

—LEWIS CARROLL

Don't fear obstacles!

It's no fun to run
across an empty field.

The excitement and
growth come
when there

are eleven
—guys out there
trying to knock you out!

Full Contact

I attended a full-contact karate meet in which a friend of mine competed. I was asked to hold two 1-inch-thick boards out in front of me as my friend, Todd Peterson, attempted to break through them to demonstrate his punching power. I braced myself firmly for his effort and held the boards at arms' length. Todd hit the boards as hard as he could. WHAP! His hand landed with a thud.

The boards didn't break, but his knuckle did. I had practiced this routine with Todd before and I had seen him break one board of this thickness, but never two. I thought he might give up, but giving up was not in Todd's nature. Quickly, he punched again. THUD!

It was the only sound I heard as I clenched my eyes shut. There was no sound of breaking boards and another knuckle on Todd's hand began to bleed and swell. The crowd giggled at his lack of mastery. Todd quickly recoiled and punched again, this time breaking the boards on the third effort.

As I walked off the stage I asked Todd what had gone wrong. He quickly replied, "I made a great mistake, Dan. Instead of looking through the boards at your chest, I looked at the boards. To do it right you have to imagine a point past the point of impact."

The lesson is a good one for all of us.

If all we ever see are the hurdles in our way, we will never reach our destination. Look past the obstacles in your life, not at them. You only get stopped when you take your sights off the goal! As Todd found out, getting to the finish may involve pain, even broken bones and broken dreams. So see the goal clearly, make full contact with life, break through every barrier and don't give up until you make the dream come true.

Say Something Nice

A young couple had a baby who was physically perfect except for one thing. She was born with no ears. The parents of this young child were extremely worried about how difficult life would be for their offspring. They feared the ridicule that would surely occur when she was old enough to attend school.

They wanted to introduce their daughter to other children before that dreaded day in order to see what the reaction would be. They asked a neighbor to bring her little girls to the house and let them look at the baby.

Instead of showing up with her daughters, the neighbor showed up with her eight-year-old son who was known for his mean mouth. If someone had bad breath he wouldn't simply say it, he would fall to the floor and faint!

With many reservations they introduced their daughter to the little boy and waited for a reply. He looked at her lying in the crib. Finally he asked, "Are her eyes good?"

"Yes, why?" asked the concerned parents.

"Because she's going to have a hard time wearing glasses."

Even the brattiest, most obnoxious person doesn't have to say something mean. Why notice everything that is wrong with people? Instead, try to see the positive side. If you look a little closer than first appearances you'll find it.

Chances are they already know what's wrong. They have heard the ridicule and scorn already. Surprise them by saying something nice.

Mall Memoirs

#1

When I looked beyond the obvious experience of going to the local shopping mall, I learned three significant lessons on successful living.

I had borrowed my neighbor's truck to pick up a large package. On the way to the mall the truck stalled twice. When I arrived at the mall parking lot, it stopped again; this time I could not restart it. Concerned that I had broken my friend's truck, I walked to a repair shop and brought the mechanic back to take a look. He lifted the hood, fiddled around for a few minutes, poured a few drops of fuel into the carburetor, hooked up the jumper cables and immediately started the engine.

"What's the problem?" I asked.

His reply knocked me over. "You are out of gas."

I paid him $50 for the road call and laughed. I learned that attitude is everything. We can own a brand-new car or truck, but unless we motivate it by putting gas in the tank, it can't take us anywhere.

#2

The second lesson I learned at the mall came from inside.

A mother with three small children was approaching the down escalator. Her eight-year-old son inadvertently stepped on the moving step before the rest of the family. Halfway down he turned around. At the same moment his mother realized he had slipped away.

"Come back up here right now!" she yelled.

With wide eyes and a determined look on his face, the little lad began sprinting up the moving escalator. A group of us started cheering, "C'mon Johnny, you can do it!"

The little guy climbed and puffed and climbed some more. But he was going against the tide. One step from the top he ran out of gas, just like the truck. Too exhausted to continue, he stopped and let the escalator whisk him back to the bottom.

Life is the same way.

It's a fast-moving escalator that never stops. If we want to stay competitive and eventually reach the goals we set in our professional and personal lives, we must keep climbing just like Johnny. But unlike that little lad, we can't stop—or we'll end up back at the bottom!

#3

The third lesson I learned at the mall summarized and combined the other two.

We need motivation—fuel in our tanks—but it must be high-octane product motivation, if we expect to get the desired results.

What do you fill up with?

It was a Saturday morning at the mall. An expensive sedan stopped near the doorway and a teenager got out. His mother yelled from inside the car, "I'll pick you up at 7:30 tonight. Stay out of trouble."

For eight hours the mall was designated as this teen's baby-sitter. His pals arrived and they formed small groups, wandering through the mall, amusing themselves by getting in the way of shoppers, making fun of senior citizens and knocking over trash cans.

For too many teenagers, cruising the mall is the leisure-time activity of choice. When these kids do get in trouble, they make excuses and tell the police that no harm has been done. Sadly, the parents of these youngsters usually don't care. Such parents think their own interests are more important than the mall merchants. Do they understand that we reap only what we sow—input equals output—garbage in/garbage out?

Troublesome youngsters wandering through shopping malls are the product of irresponsible parents. Do you leave your most valuable possession wandering for hours unsupervised?

Is that the kind of quality time you want your offspring to put in their tank? What is the input? What is the end result? I guarantee that they will run out of gas and quit before they make it to the top.

If you look beyond the obvious, isn't it interesting what one can learn at a mall?

Overcoming

Michael Dowling was president of one of the largest banks in Minnesota, a father of five, and U.S. Chamber of Commerce Man of the Year. Because of his success, he was often asked to speak to soldiers during World War II. On one occasion he went to Europe to visit wounded soldiers in London.

He spoke to a large group of bedridden men who had lost eyes, legs, arms. He began to minimize the seriousness of their wounds, telling them to stop feeling sorry for themselves—that they should get up, fire up and again be productive. The enraged soldiers started yelling, booing and throwing whatever they could.

In response, Michael began to walk toward them while commanding them to set high goals and to get on with their lives. The soldiers continued to shout obscenities until he finally sat down on a chair and took off his right leg. The soldiers calmed down a bit, but they still resented him. He then took off his left leg. The booing stopped but Michael didn't. He took off his right arm, flipped off his left hand, and there he sat, a stump of humanity.

Now that he had their attention, Dowling finished his speech on taking personal responsibility for success through setting goals and perseverance. He was a man who could deliver his remarks with authority. Because he had been a bit indignant pointing out their pathetic attitudes and physical predicaments, Michael told them it was only fair that he share his story with them.

At age 14, Michael Dowling fell from the back of a wagon in a blizzard. Before his parents realized it, he had been severely frostbitten. Both of his legs had to be amputated, one at the hip, the other at the knee. His right arm and left hand were amputated as well. Not much future for a young lad like that was there?

In his disabled condition, he went to the local board of county commissioners and said that if they would educate him and equip him with artificial limbs, he would pay them back in full and make them proud.

So what's your excuse? What's holding you back? This physically challenged man became a giant of achievement, not with his body but by setting a target in his mind and his heart. What is possible if you believe? Everything.

Goals and Why They Exist

Winning is only an excuse to play the game, so we must learn to appreciate the daily practice that prepares us—even when it's a grueling workout. Remember, happiness is not in the destination, it's the journey. Having said this, let me say a few words about motivation

I was asked to speak to a group of fathers and sons about setting goals. We were in an auditorium with no basketball standards around, so it was a perfect place to show the guys how important goals are.

One of the boys in the audience had a basketball with him so I had him come forward with it. I told him to dribble a few times and to shoot a basket. The boy followed my instructions, shaking his head. He shot.

"Did you make it?" I asked.

"No," he said grumpily. "There aren't any baskets. There isn't anything to shoot for!"

With that simple answer I had made the point I wanted to make. Nobody would want to play basketball without any hoops to shoot for. There would be no point to it, no way to keep score. And everybody wants to know if they have won or lost.

Life is the same way. You need goals if you want to score and feel good about life. Targets show us where we've been and where we still have to go. It's always comforting to see the finish line so we know how far we have to run.

Remember, if you go through life without ambitions, you'll never make the grade. There is only one way to really play the game—whether it's basketball or the game of life.

Aim for something and shoot to score!

Never Say Never

Richard Nelson, a 16-year-old junior at Manti High School in Utah, was an outstanding athlete. He was the number two singles player on the state championship tennis team and had just made the basketball team that would go on that year to win the state championship. He was looking forward to much success as a senior during the following season. But on October 23, 1996, most of his athletic future was suddenly taken away from him, dashing all his goals and dreams.

Richard was riding his bicycle at night from Manti to Gunnison to visit his girlfriend. The road was very steep in some places, which allowed Richard to reach the speed of about 40 miles per hour on the downhill slopes. Because it was dark and difficult to see, Richard was following the white line on the shoulder of the road to ensure his safety. As he came around a blind curve and was looking down at the ground, Richard failed to see a parked car on his side of the road, jacked up to fix a flat tire. With no warning he hit the parked car and ended up in the hospital, where he didn't regain consciousness for another two days. Besides bad cuts on his head and knee, he broke his collarbone and right arm, necessitating that he wear an L-shaped cast on his arm for two months. The cast came off on December 19 and Richard's doctor gave him a series of tests to determine the success of his healing. He failed all the tests. His triceps muscle had lost all its strength—he could not push out with his arm. The doctor diagnosed that he had suffered a pinched nerve and that he might never regain the use of his right arm. Richard's once strong but now puny right arm just hung at his side and the doctor gave him no real hope of recovery.

Because of his injury Richard wasn't able to play on the basketball team during the rest of that year, but the coach did make him equipment and statistics manager so that he could come to practice and be around the guys on the team.

His junior year ended, the summer came and Richard was determined to do whatever he had to do to make the basketball team the next year. He realized that he couldn't make it right-handed, so he started working on his left-handed skills. All summer long, each and every night, he practiced making left-handed baskets at the outdoor tennis courts in the center of town. Every night he shot 200 left-handed baskets and practiced left-handed dribbling and left-handed passing of the ball against the park retaining wall. Instead of going to the summer dances sponsored by the high school, Richard practiced basketball.

When the next season arrived, Richard was ready to try out for the team—and he made it! He never became a starter but he was always the first substitute to go in the game.

The season boiled down to the final game of the year against Richfield High. This game would determine which team would win the league championship and advance to the state tournament play-offs. It was a "must win" for both teams.

The Friday night of the final game arrived and the gym was packed. The starting guard for Manti had sprained his ankle earlier in the week, so Richard finally got his big break—he started the game! However, before the first quarter was over Richard was replaced. It was hard to compete when he could only use one arm. The game continued until the last 30 seconds when Manti's other guard was injured, forcing Richard back into the game. Richfield was ahead by three points and Manti had the ball. The Richfield team's coach tried to take advantage of the situation by having one of his players immediately foul Richard. Undaunted, Richard stepped up to the free throw line with a "one and one" situation (if he made the first foul shot, he would get a chance to shoot and make a second basket). Confidently, Richard picked up the ball, braced it in his left hand and shot. *Swish!* He made it and the crowd went wild! He then made the next shot, bringing Manti High to within one point of Richfield. The crowd stood and went crazy again!

Richfield then took the ball out of bounds and threw a long pass down court to the player Richard was guarding, trying to make a quick, easy basket. But Richard, with his undying determination, leaped through the air to intercept the pass. When he landed he was fouled again, giving him another "one and one" opportunity at the free throw lane. With 10 seconds left on the clock, Richard balanced the ball in his left hand, took a deep breath and shot. The crowd was deathly quiet until—*swish*! He tied the game! His next shot went up, down and through! *Swish* again! He made it— he made all four shots—left-handed! Richard Nelson won the game and became the hero of the school! And how and why was he able to do it?

According to Richard Nelson, he was not a hero. "Anybody could have done what I did," he said. "I was supposed to make those shots. Everybody was counting on me to win the game when I was put in that situation. All I did was believe in myself, work hard when others didn't and persevere. Anybody could have done what I did if they had shot as many foul shots as I had that summer before. As Earl Nightingale said, 'The only difference between me and some-body else—between a successful person and an unsuccess-ful person—is that the successful person will do what the unsuccessful person will not do. The key is the successful person does not want to do it either, but then does it any-way.' Hang tough, work hard and never say 'never'!"

Discipline

Responsibility brings freedom and freedom provides opportunity. That's the principle of self-induced discipline.

Self-discipline sounds like some kind of punishment you administer to yourself. It really means you are in control of your actions and the outcome—at least to some degree.

Self-discipline means avoiding outside discipline by doing the right thing. Arabian horses are a perfect example of the kind of self-control each of us is capable of achieving.

These magnificent horses with intelligent eyes, well-formed heads, and flowing manes and tails win many championships because of their stamina and courage.

While they are all hearty specimens, some stand above the others for endurance and intelligence. To determine which they are, trainers teach them to drink only when they hear a whistle. Once they have learned to obey, they are placed in a corral under the hot sun until they are parched. Then water is brought and placed outside the corral out of their reach, forcing them to wait even longer. Finally, a gate is opened and most of them stampede for the trough to drink with reckless abandon. Only a few stand poised with pride, holding their heads erect, and don't give in to the terrible craving. Only when they hear the whistle do they allow themselves to drink.

The ones who obey and resist the urge to drink are reserved for special training. The other steeds are led away.

So it is with humans. The mark of a champion is not on the outside but somewhere deep inside, where self-control resides. To gain control of yourself and become self-disciplined is the second step to becoming successful. First, see yourself as a conqueror. Then discipline yourself to become one.

Unfortunately, many folks who see themselves as champions are not willing to put in the extra effort and self-imposed discipline to become winners. Consequently, they lose out to those with restraint.

The Wisdom of Youth

Rebecca sat down and wrote God a personal letter. It read, "Dear God, I've been a good girl, so please send me $100 so I can buy a bicycle. Love, Rebecca."

When the postman saw the letter addressed to God, he didn't know what to do. So he added an address and sent it on to Washington, D.C. When one of the secretaries at the government agency opened the letter, she was touched by the little girl's request. In response, she immediately put a $10 bill in an envelope, addressed it, and mailed it back to Rebecca.

Rebecca was excited when she received the letter, but she was puzzled as to why it said "Washington, D.C., Confidential." She quickly opened the envelope and found the $10 bill.

She sat down and wrote a thank-you letter.

"Dear God, You are wonderful! Thank you for the money. But next time, don't send it through Washington. They kept $90 of it!"

In any discussion of government taxation, this story is an amusing anecdote. It illustrates that the methods our government uses to generate revenues don't always seem fair to the working people who pay the bulk of the taxes.

Nevertheless, there are situations in life that are best endured by maintaining a good sense of humor. Everybody wonders where those tax dollars go and this story seems to illustrate our feelings about the politics of government.

Sometimes it takes the wisdom and observations of a child to help us get a grip on our gripes.

Work for the Company

It's been prophetically written: "Where there is no vision, the people perish." It is blatantly obvious in the National Football League.

Certain teams are perennial champions and others are perennial losers. Why? The answer came when the players on the last- and first-place teams were interviewed, and asked "Why are you here?" The last-place players' eyes were downcast. They mumbled excuses for their poor playing as if their cholesterol count was higher than their SAT scores. They each answered the question, "I'm here to play football." Observe the operative word *I'm.*

Contrast these losers with the champions. When the powerhouse players were questioned, they stood taller, with confidence and enthusiasm oozing from every pore. They knew their purpose and they expected positive results. When asked, "Why are you here?" they boldly proclaimed, "We're here to win the Super Bowl!"

Can you see the difference?

In one instance the losers had no vision. They were content to be in a mediocre, short-term survival mode, just hanging on to finish the season and pay the bills. In the other instance the winners had vision. They focused on purposes instead of just setting goals. They want it all, and are willing to work hard toward achieving that long-term, peak-performance result.

What is your vision—personally and careerwise? Where will *you* be in 5, 10 or 20 years? Are you working for a pay-check or working for the company? Do you only look forward to Friday instead of to every day of the week? Do you think you are paid by the hour or do you realize that you are paid for the value you bring to that hour?

Young people give up opportunities to get good grades and participate in extracurricular activities at school just to work for minimum wage so they can have a fancy car or nice clothes. The sad truth is they will struggle the rest of their lives. An education allows them to have options—so they can get the job of their dreams, instead of settling for the leftovers. All of us need a long-term vision! What is yours?

No Free Lunch

With freedom comes responsibility to take control of our lives. It has been said, "The only thing we are not in charge of is whether or not we are in charge." See if you agree.

How many of you are waiting for your ship to come in? Then let me ask, have you done anything about it?

When you were in your mother's womb, things were comfy—if you didn't mind close living quarters and poor lighting. The meals were free, you got to sleep a lot and all your needs were met.

On nights when things haven't been going my way, I pull up my shirt and stare down at my belly button to remind myself of the good old days, when life was easy.

But many people don't realize that you can't go back to that comfortable place. You can no longer get something for nothing. And, ultimately, we should never be tempted to crawl back into the womb. The umbilical cord was cut for our own good.

So why is it then that so many folks spend their whole lives trying to plug it back in? The quicker and earlier we accept the fact that there's no going back—that there's no such thing as a free lunch (unless someone else is picking up the tab)—the faster we can start preparing ourselves to fend for ourselves and get what we want out of life.

If you are sitting around and hoping your ship will come in and doing nothing to guarantee that it will arrive at the dock, you will be disappointed at the end of your time on Earth. "Successful people are just lucky," you say? "I wish I had some luck," you say? Well, my friend, the harder you work, the luckier you will get. It isn't going to happen by chance. And that goes for all of us, me included.

Halftime Score

In our highly competitive world, we must understand that there is nothing more insignificant than the halftime score.

When I was in college at the University of Utah, we played football against UCLA. Prior to the game our coach pepped us up, "UCLA doesn't have to win this game. 'You can if you think you can.' Just believe in yourselves. We can win!"

The game started. We got the ball first. They quickly took it away from us. It was our turn to stop them. The guy in front of me was so big I had to look through his legs to see what was going on. He could have kick-started a 747 jet! When they hiked the ball, he hit me so hard that he knocked my helmet around my head so that I was looking out my ear hole! As I stood there crying I realized my coach was lying. *UCLA does have to win and I quit,* I thought to myself as I started to walk off the field. The coach wouldn't let me quit and he pushed me back into the huddle. The next play we sacked the quarterback. I did! I have to admit that I ran into him by accident, but I still tackled him for a loss. He fumbled the ball. We recovered. We scored. We stopped them and scored twice more. Halftime score was 19-0 in favor of the University of Utah. During the first half UCLA's quarterback thought he was caught in one of those revolving doors at the mall! We lost the game, 23-19.

On another occasion we played the University of Oklahoma. We were ahead, 7-0. Yes, we were whooping 'em. It was those last 59 minutes that killed us! We lost, 63-7.

In another game, against the University of Arizona, we were behind at halftime, 21-0. By the end of the third quarter we were losing, 27-0. However, this time we won, during the last seconds of the game, by 28-27!

We also beat Jim McMahon's BYU team. We were losing at halftime, but came from behind to win on a last-second pass, by 23-22. What is the point?

Teams that are ahead at halftime are faced with a decision. Either they keep fighting and playing to win; or they stop taking risks, try to live off their past successes and start playing "not-to-lose." Playing "not-to-lose" is when we stop our aggressive offense and replace it with defensive carefulness. It's when we lose that "eye-of-the-tiger" intensity that gave us the competitive advantage in the first place. On the other hand, there is playing to *Focus* and *Finish*. *Focus* to *W-I-N* represents *What's Important Now*. Then we *finish* each play from "hello" to "good-bye," one play at a time, until we finish the game. Successful sales managers teach that anybody can make a presentation. It's closing the deal that wins the business. Successful parents teach that, "If it's worth doing, it's worth doing right" and "If it's worth starting, it's worth finishing."

Whether it's "halftime" in your business year or "halftime" in your life, whatever you do and wherever you are in life, don't let up now. Look beyond the "halftime score." The only way you can win is to endure to the end!

Who'll Jump In?

We can't always choose the situations we are in, but we can decide how to manage them. It's not always what happens to us that matters, but what we do when it happens.

A wealthy businessman had his employees over to his mansion to celebrate their year-end success. For this party he had filled the pool with crocodiles in an effort to see who was the most loyal and daring of all. After dinner the man put forth the ultimate challenge to his employees, as they stood at the edge of the pool watching the crocs swim back and forth in the water a few feet below them.

"Who here is loyal?" he asked. "Who will dive into the water and swim from one end of the pool to the other?"

The man offered a $10,000 bonus to the person who took up the challenge. But there were no takers. Nobody raised a hand.

He upped the ante to $20,000.

Suddenly there was a loud splash. One of his office staff had jumped in and was swimming for his life, with the crocodiles hot on his heels. The loyal follower grabbed the ladder and leaped to safety in a single bound.

"Good heavens," said the businessman, "you're the bravest, most loyal, risk-taking employee I've ever had. Nobody has ever taken me up on that challenge. Why did you do it?"

The man stood there dripping in his wet dinner jacket and simply replied, "Do it? All I want to know is who pushed me in?"

Whether we are pushed in on purpose or choose to do something of our own free will, it's not what happens but how we deal with it that matters.

Remember, the only thing we are not in charge of is whether or not we are in charge!

End in Mind

I remember a summer vacation with my family: my parents and the four kids—my sister, my two brothers and me. At the time we ranged in age from 5 to 14. We traveled 12 hours across the hot Arizona/Nevada deserts, stuffed in a car with no air-conditioning—destination: California. Needless to say, this was a death wish for most families, with endless arguments, teasing and restlessness.

What kept our family sane? We kept the end in mind.

Every time the hot car filled with gripes and hollering, my mom and dad would simply remind us about Disneyland, our cousins and their swimming pool, and the beach on the other end of the journey.

There is a lesson here in terms of excitement and enthusiasm. Excitement comes from the anticipation of financial rewards or personal pleasure. It is in the now: a first date, making the team, getting the job.

Enthusiasm begins in the present tense and extends into the future. It lasts throughout the endeavor until the task is completed. The excitement of a first date turns into a steady relationship; once you make the team you play every day to the best of your ability; once you get the job you give your best effort every day.

As we contrast excitement with enthusiasm, obviously it is important to be excited. But its effect quickly dies off. Then we must be ready for the long haul, with enthusiasm, if we are to become successful—or in the case of our summer vacation—to arrive in one piece at Disneyland.

Enthusiasm stems from self-motivation—from an understanding of why we do what we do. To test your enthusiasm, ask these three questions: Why should I? What's in it for me? Will it make me feel wanted and important? Enthusiasm comes when we keep our sights on the passion of our purpose, instead of just setting goals.

8

BEST SHOT

I firmly believe that any man's finest hour,
his greatest fulfillment of all he holds dear, is
that moment when he has worked his heart
out in a good cause and lies exhausted on the
field of battle...victorious.

—VINCE LOMBARDI

It's better to
shoot for the stars
and miss,

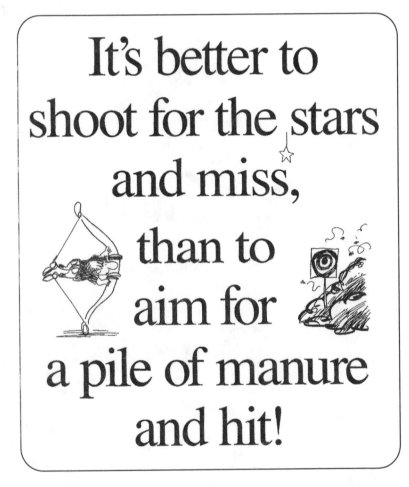

than to
aim for
a pile of manure
and hit!

Fear

In the movie *Rocky III,* Rocky had already lost his title to the vicious character, Clubber Lane. Rocky was scheduled to fight the man again and was truly afraid. But his wife, Adrienne, talked him through his fear.

"You've never quit anything before, why quit now?" she asked.

"Because in all the other fights my trainer made me feel I was better than I was," he answered. "It doesn't matter that I have the title. I don't believe in myself anymore. And when you don't believe in yourself, you're through—finished. For the first time in my life I want to quit."

"I'm afraid, too, but there's nothing wrong with being afraid," she said. "The important thing is to overcome your fear or it will bother you the rest of your life. No matter how hard it might be you've got to fight. I think you can do it, but you have to do it for yourself—for you, alone."

"And if I lose?"

"Then you lose! But at least you lose with no excuses, with no fear. You lose with your head high, knowing you gave it your best shot and no one ever needs to be ashamed of that. Never."

We all have to do things in life that are frightening. But if we give our best effort, there is never any reason to be ashamed. Once Rocky knew that, he pushed himself harder than ever before. He came back to beat the fear inside of him—and Clubber Lane as well. So can you.

We are born with two fears—the fear of loud noises and the fear of falling. We learn the other fears we have: our fear of the dark, of the bogeyman and of the unknown; our fear of what others may think of us; our fear of taking tests; our fear of speaking in public. Fear is real and we must deal with it or continually run and hide from it for the rest of our lives. What will you do?

Zig Ziglar defines *fear* as False Evidence Appearing Real. Statistics validate this: 40 percent of our worries never happen, 30 percent are in the past and cannot be changed, 12 percent are needless, leaving a mere 8 percent that are real. For this reason, don't let fear make you an emotional hostage. Face that 8 percent immediately and continually.

Instead of fearing the worst, expect the best. President Franklin D. Roosevelt did. Whether it was because he was undertaking the presidency during the depth of the Great Depression or because of his experiences as a wheelchair-bound person, he emphatically reminded us: "We have nothing to fear but fear itself."

Who Has *It*?

There are doctors who have *it*, salesmen who have *it*, mothers who have *it* and farmers who have *it*. Clara Bow, a doe-eyed actress from the 1920s, had *it*. In fact, they called her the "*It* Girl."

So what did they have that you don't?

The *it* is a little bit more—that extra something they put into everything that makes them special, above average. *It* is the fighting heart and burning desire to be the best they can be.

Usually what *it* people do matches their natural talents. They took the time to discover what they did well, then they pursued *it* and perfected *it*—until they had *it*.

So *it* all boils down to developing confidence. Clara Bow won a contest that promised the winner a trip to Hollywood. That was all the incentive she needed to do whatever *it* took to come out on top. The rest is history, as they say.

Make a Difference

On a cold, snowy day in Washington D.C., amid the debris of a tragic plane crash in the Potomac River, a real-life hero emerged from obscurity.

Flying too low, Air Florida's Flight 90 had crashed into the 14th Street Bridge, catapulting plane, baggage and terrified passengers into the freezing water. A flight attendant was floating in the icy current doing everything she could to stay alive. Someone on shore threw her a rope, but she could not grab it. She went under and popped back up, waving her hands and screaming for help. For a second time she went under—this time for much longer. Wide-eyed, scrambling and gasping for breath, she finally came up for one more attempt to save her life.

A shy, unassuming man named Vinnie Skutnick was standing on the bridge watching the tragedy. Believing that he could make a difference, he quickly removed his heavy overcoat, kicked off his boots and dove into the sub-freezing river. Swimming like an Olympian, Skutnick found the flight attendant, lifted her head and shoulders out of the water, and whispered, "You will live." As he pulled her from the river, Skutnick was asked why he risked his life to save the stranger.

He replied, "I couldn't save everybody, but I knew I could make a difference to one person."

Random acts of kindness *do* make a significant difference.

Learn from Others

In 1965, a championship game was being played between two of America's finest high school basketball teams. DeMatha Prep of Hyattsville, Maryland, was playing against undefeated Power Memorial from New York City. Power had a 71-game winning streak coming into the game. The only chance DeMatha had of defeating Power Memorial was if it stopped Power's seven-foot-one center, Lew Alcindor.

DeMatha put its two biggest men on Alcindor and the strategy worked. They won 46-43.

The loss was Alcindor's first since he was a high school freshman. It popped a dream and ended a nationally recognized winning streak. He was heartbroken about the loss, but not for long. When interviewed, Lew Alcindor taught us something invaluable.

"Anybody can lose," he explained. "The idea is to make losing a novelty, not a bad habit."

Even today, Lew practices what he preaches. He's become the greatest center ever to play college or professional basketball. Even though he's now known worldwide as Kareem Abdul Jabbar, he understands that the world is not interested in the storms—only if you can bring the ship safely to harbor.

Henry Aaron

Henry Aaron broke Babe Ruth's career record of 714 home runs to became the greatest long-ball hitter in baseball history. He now holds the record for the most career homers.

Hank Aaron didn't start at the top. In fact, he didn't even play baseball in high school because his school didn't have a team. Instead, he considered himself a bookworm. It wasn't until he was in his early twenties that Aaron finally caught baseball fever and decided to pursue a professional career in sports.

At the time, there were few Blacks playing in major-league baseball. So he joined a semipro team called the Indianapolis Clowns of the Negro American League.

Henry played for $200 a month, waiting and praying for his first big break. Then a Milwaukee Braves scout spotted him and signed him to the "big time." When Henry stepped to the batter's box for the first time in his major league career, he was understandably nervous. There were two outs. The pressure was on. Thousands of eyes waited for him to perform. To cap it off, the opposing team catcher sneered at Henry as he came to the plate. As Henry held the bat with a cross-handed grip, the catcher sneered, "Hey, kid, you're holding the bat wrong. You're supposed to see the label."

Henry turned and looked straight into the catcher's eyes. "I didn't come here to read," he said, "I came here to hit." With that, he drilled the next pitch into the outfield for a single and laughed his way to first base.

Henry Aaron became one of baseball's all-time greats. And from firsthand experience, he understands the saying, "Believe in yourself. At times you're the only one who will."

Billy Casper:
Back to Basics

Billy Casper is one of the greatest golfers of all time. He's also a dear friend of mine and one of my idols. Why is he my idol? His story sets an example of excellence for the world to follow.

As soon as Billy was big enough to swing a club, his dad started giving him golf lessons. By the time he was 15 years old he was captain of his high school team. He won the San Diego County California Amateurs and Open Championships and turned pro at age 19. Once Billy became a professional in 1955, financial success came quickly. He was the second golfer in history to win $200,000 in one year and the first golfer ever to win $1 million. He was named Golfer of the Year on several occasions, and for many years he had the lowest average score, the fewest bogeys and the fewest putts per hole. In the 1960s Casper was golf's greatest and most consistent performer—among the top-five money winners every year for over a decade.

The story that typifies Billy's unbelievable ability to concentrate and perform under pressure took place during the 1966 U.S. Open at the Olympic Club in San Francisco. Billy had won that match in 1959 at the tender age of 29. Now he had an opportunity to win it again, even though nobody thought he could, since he'd been in a slump for several months.

Going into the last nine holes of the final round, Casper trailed Arnold Palmer by seven strokes.

"Impossible," they all said.

But Casper shot an amazing 32 on the last nine and Palmer shot 39. They tied for the championship in regulation play.

So they went head-to-head in a sudden-death playoff. Casper fell behind by two strokes after the front nine holes. But he hung in there—believing in himself and in his ability—and overtook Palmer again, shooting a 69 and winning by four shots. Billy Casper understands that when things start going wrong, and you feel like the wheels are falling off of your wagon, you should go back to the basics. Master the fundamentals and you'll find victory is in your grasp.

Sports heroes are like heroes in all walks of life. They all share a common denominator and fully comprehend the words of William Jennings Bryan: "Destiny is not a matter of chance, it is a matter of choice; it is not a thing to be waited for, it is a thing to be achieved."

Bryan didn't expect to find life worth living. He made it that way, like Billy Casper and thousands of others.

We should, too!

Determination

Glen Tenove is a man who has more determination and production power than most. He was supposed to be too small to play defensive end in NCAA Division One college football. But he did it and became a star!

In his first semester at California State University at Long Beach, he was an outstanding student athlete. Tenove enrolled in a conditioning class, where the instructor asked each student to perform nine different physical skills. Tenove finished in the top four in each one. The following day Tenove asked for the names of the people who had finished first in each category. Then he watched them in class to see what they were doing. Tenove stayed late in the weight room, working out and strengthening his muscles.

At the end-of-the-semester test, Tenove ended up first in seven categories and came in second in the other two.

"I don't just want to be good," says Tenove. "I want to be the best!"

Tenove has a notebook that spells out this deep belief. The inscription on it reads, "God, make it as tough as you like, but make it possible."

"I don't care how tough it is," he adds. "If it's possible, I'll make it happen!"

To most people, some of what Tenove did borders on the impossible. For example, he played the last three football games of his senior year with a separated shoulder. For the rest of the weekend following the injury, he worked at moving his arm until he could do it without reacting to the pain.

"After a while, you get used to the pain," he says. "It's like it isn't even there."

A few days after his injury, he cheated on the examination to determine whether his shoulder was separated. The doctor asked Tenove to hold weights in each hand. If his shoulder was separated, the weight would pull that arm down.

But because Tenove had practiced moving his shoulder all weekend, he was able to withstand the pain and to hold his arm in place using the muscles around the shoulder. He passed the test even though his shoulder was separated.

"I knew if I couldn't lift that arm, I couldn't play any more," says Tenove. "And there was no way I was going to have them tell me I couldn't play."

And when his coach told him to skip practice and rest his shoulder, Tenove ran up and down the steps alongside the student union building for more than an hour. He says, "I like to practice hard and go into a game a little bruised and beat up. I love to have the feeling that I've outworked everyone else."

Tenove's intensity isn't limited to the football field. He had a 3.75 grade point average and he was a candidate for All-American academic honors.

Glen Tenove is now through playing football and is spending the majority of his time and effort playing a more crucial game—the game of life. But he is as intense and competitive now as he was in school—constantly striving for perfection.

Life is a game in which production, not potential, is rewarded. That's Tenove's kind of game.

P.S. Tenove is currently coaching football at a California college and still bench-presses 500 pounds. He even recently started a professional boxing career. Someday I guarantee he'll be the world champ—if he wants to be. For Glen Tenove demonstrates in a boxing ring what he demonstrates in life: he's not in there to prove his strength—he's in there to win the fight!

Fighting Back

Why is it that no matter how many times you tell some people they can't do something, they just try harder? Brian Piccolo was one of those people. And he should serve as an inspiration to us all.

Brian played pro football for the Chicago Bears and died at the age of 26, after a courageous battle with cancer. Off the field, on the field, and in the hospital, his motto was profound and simple: "You can't quit—it's a league rule!"

Another player is Rocky Bleier.

In the late 1960s and 1970s, this country was engaged in the Vietnam War. One of the victims of that terrible time was Rocky Bleier. While in action one night, Rocky's platoon was ambushed in a rice field. At the end of the fighting one of the men dragged Rocky Bleier out of a rice paddy more dead than alive—with shrapnel embedded into the muscles of his legs.

Nobody gave Rocky Bleier even a slight chance to ever play football again—nobody except Rocky. Some people believe in fighting back and Rocky fought back all the way from that rice paddy in Vietnam into the starting lineup of the Pittsburgh Steelers. He rehabilitated that injured leg through months of hard physical therapy. First he learned to walk again, then to run, then to play ball.

There's a movie about Rocky Bleier, appropriately called *Fighting Back.*

In each of our lives comes a "Mission Impossible"—something we'd like to avoid, if possible. If we knew what was coming, we'd run and hide. But we don't know and we can't hide.

I've been through my Mission Impossible. I fought back. And the best advice I can give you is that the body will endure almost anything. It's the mind that needs convincing. The simple truth is that if we think we can, we can!

Just a Little Extra Effort

Jim McMahon, the great quarterback for the 1985 Super Bowl Champion Chicago Bears, is the epitome of effort. From his days of Pop Warner football, through his high school, college and professional days—every time he walked on the field he knew he could win. Not by accident, fate or fluke, but by extra effort.

It was December 19, 1980, Holiday Bowl III. Jim McMahon's nationally ranked BYU Cougars were playing against SMU. There were four minutes and seven seconds left to play in the game. SMU was winning, 45-25. BYU called time-out and Coach Lavell Edwards motioned McMahon to the sideline. Edwards said, "Let's see if we can save a little face and score before the game ends."

McMahon got upset. "Coach, what do you mean? We're not quitting! It's not over until it's over!" McMahon went back onto the field, called the team together and said, "We're gonna win!" The very next play he threw a long pass—touchdown! BYU recovered the ensuing onside kick and scored again on a one-yard scamper by a running back. BYU kicked off, held SMU for 3 downs and then blocked the punt and recovered the ball with 13 seconds left on the clock. McMahon's first 2 passes were incomplete, but on the very next play, with 3 seconds left in the game, McMahon completed a 46-yard bomb to Clay Brown in the end zone. Brown leaped high in the air to catch it and the game was tied! Gunther came onto the field and kicked the extra point. BYU won, 46-45.

In 1981 McMahon was runner-up to Marcus Allen for the Heisman Trophy, was a first-round pick by the Chicago Bears and was named Rookie of the Year.

In 1984 Doug Flutie proved the same thing and, along with his Boston College teammates, won an important game in exactly the same miracle catch manner. Flutie also won the Heisman! These two athletes not only have superior talent—they have the superior determination and drive that enables them to make the extra effort that always makes the difference. Not just in games, but most important, in practice.

The difference between *good* and *great*, between *winning* and *losing*—between receiving enormous rewards and no rewards at all—is just a little bit of extra effort.

- In 1974 the winning jockey of the Kentucky Derby received $27,000. Less than two seconds later the jockey who crossed the finish line in fourth place received only $30.
- In 1982 Gordon Johncock won the Indianapolis 500 by 16 hundredths of a second—the length of his car. His paycheck was well over 10 times that of the second-place finisher, whom we don't even remember.
- In the 1984 Summer Olympic Games the competitors in the women's long-distance cycling race engaged in a back-and-forth, hard-fought sprint to the finish line. The winner won the race, and thereby the gold medal, by the length of a bicycle wheel.
- In baseball the difference between a .300 hitter who is a millionaire star and a .200 hitter who earns a minimal salary (and finds himself traded from team to team as often as a team manager changes his dirty socks) is 1 hit in every 10 times up to bat. And in those 10 times at bat, if both these batters let their batting count go to "full-count" (three balls and two strikes), then the difference between them is only 1 hit in every 60 pitches!

Sure it's important to have good practice facilities and great coaching—and also some talent to go with it. Sure it's important to believe you are somebody special, equal to the guts and deserving of the glory of McMahon and Flutie. But without that little bit of extra effort, becoming a champion remains only a dream.

9

LIFE IS A STORY

If we are strong, our character will speak for itself.
If we are weak, words will be of no help.

—JOHN F. KENNEDY

From Slums to Judge

Joseph Serrentino, a juvenile court judge from Los Angeles, proves that life is a story.

He was born and raised in Brooklyn. He was the second eldest in a family of seven children and he grew up in an atmosphere of street gangs and hoodlums. By the time he was 20 years old, Joe had served time in reform school, jail, the brig and even a padded cell for incorrigibles. He flunked out of school four times, went through nearly 30 jobs and was literally kicked out of the Marine Corps.

As a high school drop-out with no skills and no money, he tried his hand at professional boxing. He soon quit that as well.

One day, as he was passing Brooklyn's Erasmus Hall High School, Joe saw a sign that invited passersby to enroll in night school. Suddenly, he realized that his only chance for a better life was through education and his inadequacies hit him like a ton of bricks.

Joe enrolled, found that he loved to learn and graduated with the highest grade point average in the history of Erasmus Hall's night school. He then decided to attend the University of California at Santa Barbara, where he became president of the student body and graduated magna cum laude. After graduation, he began reviewing his life with all its defeats and decided there was one more thing he should do before he tackled the real world. He reenlisted in the marines to remove that embarrassing blemish from his record. After an honorable discharge, he entered Harvard Law School and graduated as class valedictorian in 1967.

His valedictory address touched everyone present, as he recounted his life story and concluded with these words: "Do not look for tragedy or trauma to explain the change in me; it came mainly from inner resolution. Life is a story and as the author of my own never before written story, I had the right and the charge to write it and rewrite it so that it would play out in whatever way I desired."

Attitude Leads to Ability

Playing college football taught me some valuable lessons.

We had just been trounced by a much inferior team and we were watching a video of the game the next day. Play after play passed on the screen as the coach ranted and raved. On one play he stopped the video to run the play again. It wasn't a spectacular play but he made us watch it seven times. It had a message the coach wanted to teach.

We were on defense and one of our linebackers came up to make a tackle on a running back. Our linebacker hit him with great force but he just bounced off. The running back kept running—he covered 25 yards before he was finally tackled from behind.

"See that," exclaimed our coach. "That guy missed the first tackle but he didn't give up. He went downfield and tackled his man 25 yards later. That's my kind of player! You see, when your attitude is right, your ability will always catch up."

Although the coach didn't plan to have that linebacker play much that year, he decided right then and there to start the player in every game.

Gifted people fail due to their negative attitude while less talented people succeed because of their positive attitude. Which way do you want to play the game of life?

Attitude Determines Altitude

We hear a lot of stories about being in the right place at the right time. But success doesn't just happen. Your job is to discover and develop the man or woman you ought to be. This experience helped me realize how true that statement is.

My friend's wife had just given birth to their first child— healthy and certainly destined to succeed. I left the hospital and went downtown to mail some letters. As I drove past one building I saw four drunken bums leaning against a wall, each hugging a wine bottle as if it were his only friend. Across the street were some law offices with well-dressed professionals walking in and out.

Then it hit me. The three different scenes—the baby, the bums and the attorneys—explained the importance of attitude. We all are born to succeed, but we don't all end up that way. Mothers only give birth to boys and girls, never to attorneys, doctors, educators, mechanics or bums. Who and what we become is a direct result of what we think we can become. It is the attitudes we acquire during our childhood that make the big difference.

Attitude determines the altitude we achieve when we soar into life. Luck doesn't have a great deal to do with it. Almost always, the luckiest people worked the hardest to stack the odds in their favor. When a break comes their way, they have spent years getting ready to take advantage of it.

"The only difference between a successful person and an unsuccessful person is the successful person will do what the unsuccessful person will not do," said Earl Nightingale. "The successful person doesn't want to do it either, but they do it anyway."

The Magic in Us All

The Los Angeles Lakers and the Philadelphia 76ers were battling it out in a seven-game NBA championship series. In the sixth game the great and overpowering center for the Lakers, Kareem Abdul Jabbar, was hurt—he had a migraine headache and a torn ankle. He wasn't able to make the trip to Philadelphia for the final championship game.

It was a devastating blow to the Lakers. The players lost hope of winning the championship. But instead of making excuses, the Lakers' head coach decided to make some adjustments. He knew they were winners—that they'd come too far to lose.

The coach, Pat Riley, took a 20-year-old rookie and moved him from his guard position to center. That adjustment was tough enough for the six-foot-eight guard, but when he went up against Darryl Dawkins—a mass of muscle and intimidation who shattered backboards and opposing centers just for kicks, and who stood three inches taller—the rookie was terrified.

That young player's name was Earvin "Magic" Johnson and he showed his genius that night. He scored 42 points, grabbed 15 rebounds and earned the Most Valuable Player trophy for leading the Lakers to victory.

Earvin Johnson is another example of the magic we all have within. We can all rise to the occasion when the need arises.

Positive Anxiety

In a world full of emotional disorders, at first glance or mention you might think positive anxiety is a bad thing. Earvin "Magic" Johnson is a living example of the necessity of positive anxiety. In the many years he was in the National Basketball Association, Magic couldn't sleep during the playoffs.

"Imagine living on adrenaline for weeks," Johnson says.

Normally congenial, he would snap at people. Still, it was his favorite time of year. For a few special weeks, the man who loved crowds and noise would enter into a tunnel of silence and solitude. Now, after numerous awards and championships to his credit, Magic is using positive anxiety to fight another opponent—death from the human immuno-deficiency virus (HIV).

As Johnson battles for his life, his ability to get excited about upcoming games and his family creates adrenaline rushes and positive thoughts that overcome the anxiety of dying.

"My whole life has been a challenge, and this is just another one," he says. "I love to beat the odds."

Although he made a costly mistake and tarnished his image as an ideal role model, the world prays for Magic Johnson as he attacks a terrible disease with all the psychological tools he has already applied to win games. Magic reminds us that we are all human. When we make mistakes, we must get up, dust ourselves off and make the best of a bad situation.

The Weight Came Off

If a young woman is five-foot-nine and weighs 168 pounds, is she too fat to model?

Everyone told Cheryl Tiegs that she was too heavy and would never be able to get in shape. But it didn't matter. She knew her face was pretty enough and her body could be toned and trimmed. She never let the naysayers get her down.

With a regimen of diet and exercise, Cheryl began slimming her body and firming her muscles. She was single-minded in her commitment, discipline and effort. The weight dropped away and, sure enough, underneath the chubby cheeks was a stunning face—bubbly and vivacious—smiling for the world to see. That famous face has graced almost every magazine cover in the world. It was the face of the 1980s.

Cheryl has graced many covers of *Sports Illustrated* magazine's swimsuit edition—not an easy task with the fierce competition in the world of high-fashion models. She's the tubby little girl who became a legend because she wouldn't let go of her dream. The last time I checked, she had gotten her body in shape!

A Special Trip

Have you ever wanted to get away for a while? Take a nice long vacation?

Michael King wanted to cross America. Like many of us, he thought it would be great to roll across the Midwest plains, up and down the mighty Rockies, and through the big cities.

So Michael saved his money, planned his trip and set out. But Michael King's cross-country trip was quite different from a regular vacation. During his five-month ordeal he wore out four sets of wheels and went through 14 pairs of gloves in order to make the 5,000-mile journey—in a wheelchair!

He also took the trip for a unique reason.

"I wanted to show people they can fulfill their dreams, and they can do anything they set their hearts on doing," he said. While Michael made his point he also raised $30,000 for handicapped centers across the country.

Through his courage and determination, he set an amazing standard of faith, grit and determination. Even being paralyzed from the waist down, Michael was undaunted. He rested his aching arms each night and set out each day to enjoy the endless beauty around him. He pushed and persevered, living a lifetime every day.

A Working Guy

Doesn't it seem that the harder we chase happiness, the more it eludes us? So let me share with you the wisdom of Michael F. Wittowski.

Michael is a wise man. He's not a college professor or a famous philosopher. He's an average working guy and, as a matter of fact, that is the secret of his wisdom. He likes his job, he does it well, and he gets a kick out of contributing something to society every day by using his hands and his brain.

Too many of us get the idea that work is a curse of the lower classes when, in reality, work is a sacred privilege. Doing a good job is one of the best sources of happiness this life offers. Mike Wittowski knows that, so when he came into some money and had the chance to quit he said he was happy to keep working. He took the money, helped his family and friends, then gave the rest of the money to charity. He figured somebody else could use it.

We're not talking small potatoes here. It was more than winning the football pool. Mike won one of the largest lotteries in history—about $40 million—enough to do nothing for the rest of his life. Instead, he did something great by leaving it to charity and going back to work.

Mike lacks nothing. By being productive, Mike feels wanted, needed and important. He's a happy man.

Player of the Year

Anemia is a condition in which your blood is deficient in red blood cells and total volume. If it is not corrected, you could die. If you live, you are weak and constantly fatigued.

That is what a doctor told a young boy in Worthing, Texas, back in 1971. The doctor also told him he would never be able to compete in sports competition. But that young boy had a dream to play football and was determined to prove the doctor wrong.

In his freshman year of high school he was told he was too small and weak to play. So he became the team manager. But after everyone else had left, he stayed and ran laps and windsprints. He struggled lifting weights. His sophomore year he told his father his goal was to make the team and get a uniform like the rest of the guys. He got a uniform but never played. He stayed after every practice and, all alone, worked out and ran.

In his junior year he told his father he wanted to get into at least one game. The last game of the season his team was way ahead and he was sent in to play the whole fourth quarter. After that game he told his father he wanted to play in every game his senior year and earn a scholarship to college. He got a chance to go to Baylor University. After injuries to three other linebackers in his first year, he was moved to starting linebacker. In his junior and senior years he was a unanimous choice for All-American. He signed a pro contract as a second-round draft pick of the Super Bowl Champion Chicago Bears.

Mike Singletary wound up the best middle-linebacker in the National Football League, anchoring one of the best defenses in NFL history, and was honored as NFL Defensive Player of the Year. If he had listened to all the limitations other people had placed on him, Mike would have never reached the goals he had set for himself. Do what is inside of you, regardless of what others tell you you can't do.

Champions See the Goal

In 1980, Eric Heiden won five Olympic gold medals and set five world records as a speed skater. For four years prior to the Olympics he practiced four hours a day, six days a week. Because of the brutal winters, much of his training was on an indoor stationary skating machine.

An ABC television crew went to Wisconsin to film these special training sessions. The camera focused on the incredible intensity, rhythm and determination. Heiden's strength and finesse were unbelievable. One might have expected Heiden's face to be strained and grimacing. But there was no anguish, no complaining—just a smile.

Staged for the camera?

No. What we did not see on the screen, but what was in full view of Heiden, was a giant picture of five Olympic gold medals. Heiden could see the gold medals the entire time he practiced. When fatigue set in, he visualized and imagined what he would feel like when he won them.

Any champion, like Eric Heiden, willingly pays the price to win. They know the benefits of winning are worth the effort. This is the third step to becoming a champion. First, see yourself as a winner. Second, discipline yourself to become one. Third, be willing to pay the price in hard work.

10

WILL THE FUTURE
EVER ARRIVE?

Hope is a prodigal heir, and Experience is his banker.

—CHARLES C. COLTON

No matter what your past has been,

you have a spotless future!

Give Yourself a Second Chance

Have you ever heard the old saying "A lot of people die with their best music still in them?" Let me tell you about a fellow who almost made that saying come true for himself.

The rocky road to musical fame has left many striving artists by the wayside. Starting out has never been easy. Every artist who ever sold out a concert started out an unknown entity—even such greats as Barbra Streisand, who began her career in bars in Greenwich Village, New York.

Lonely nights, smoky dives and unappreciative customers are the norm. They were for this singer. As a matter of fact, there were too many nights like that. At a certain point, he was convinced no one would ever want to hear the songs he wrote and, for a moment, considered taking his own life.

Before he could put his plan into action, he wrote a song about those terrible nights. He called it "The Piano Man" and his career took off.

Years later he wrote "Second Wind," which urges us not to hate ourselves for the mistakes we've made—a song which pleads with people not to take their own lives, like he almost did.

Billy Joel almost died with his best songs in him. Now he persuades us to give ourselves a second chance when we get down. The only difference between the ones who succeed and the ones who don't is a dream. Don't let your dream die without playing it out.

Painful Preparation

The incredible courage shown by tiny, tenacious, inspirational Kari Strug in the 1996 Olympic Games in Atlanta, Georgia, reminds us all about the powerful cliche "Proper Prior Planning Prevents Poor Performance." It also reminds us that both physical *and* mental toughness are required to be a champion.

A few years ago I went to a workout session of the University of Utah women's gymnastic team. I learned why they win consistently.

Her name was Missy Marlowe and she eventually competed on the U.S. Olympic gymnastics team in 1988. She was also named one of the prestigious top six—one of the six best male and female athletes in the United States—and received the Broderick Award as the NCAA Outstanding Female Athlete of the Year.

When I first saw her, Missy was a young freshman on the uneven parallel bars, trying to execute a difficult maneuver. I watched her crash 10 times in a row. After the tenth fall she sobbed and limped away, but it didn't stop her. She came back and I watched her fall four more times, each time smashing hard into the mat. Finally, on the fifteenth try, Missy spun off the bar, reached out and completed the maneuver.

Coach Marsden told me afterward that every new girl goes through the same thing to learn each one of the many difficult moves required to win meets and please judges. Nobody clapped that day. There were no cameras to record her victory. But her face showed personal satisfaction. And when she eventually won the national championship that year in the All-Around Competition, the hard work, sacrifice and painful endurance were all worth it.

Would you have quit on the first crash? The tenth? The fourteenth?

How many of us would have realized that just one more attempt would make the difference between failure and success?

Any great achievement in life requires hours of lonely,

deliberate preparation and work. Don't make the mistake of thinking that champion athletes, successful artists, doctors, attorneys, writers or actors didn't spend years learning how to perform in their areas of expertise. You can be sure they paid their dues in time, effort and lonely solitude. They were convinced, however, that there's no gain without pain.

"It's Gonna Hurt!"

Did you ever look down the road and see something that means trouble in the distance? It may be a police roadblock ahead and you forgot to bring your license, or a final exam ahead and you forgot to study, or you have to give a speech and you're afraid you won't even remember your own name. Most of us know what it's like to sit in the waiting room of a dentist's office waiting to have canal work done. We know that eventually that sore tooth is going to feel better, but in the meantime the noise of the drill coming from the other room sounds like someone is hanging shelves and we cringe at the anticipated pain.

Life is full of these horrible expectations. Unfortunately, we sometimes blow them all out of proportion. We can turn a scary little fantasy into a full-fledged Frankenstein if we let our imaginations run wild. On the other hand, if we just grit our teeth and say, "Hey, I'm gonna get through it," we usually do. Shun Fujimoto did!

Shun was one of the greatest gymnasts in the world. He was a member of the Japanese Olympic gymnastics team that was within grasping distance of a gold medal. Shun knew that he had trained for the better part of his young life for this moment and he knew that his teammates needed him. He mounted the rings, performed his breathtaking routine and dismounted. When he landed he broke his right leg and collapsed on the mat in excruciating pain. That night his teammates visited him in the hospital and offered their support. The next day when Shun's name was routinely called over the arena's public address system during the competition, to everyone's surprise, a limping Shun emerged from the athlete's entrance tunnel and mounted the rings.

With the audience riveted in gasping disbelief, there he was poised on the rings wearing a cast on his right leg. Could he carry that extra unbalancing weight through his routine of flying, soaring and twisting? It would be a superhuman physical feat if he could. He knew that the accomplishment of such a feat would meet with not only cheers, applause and perhaps a gold medal, but also with razor-sharp, stabbing, mind-numbing pain throughout his whole body, because the cast on his leg surely would collapse on the landing.

Shun not only had to perform with his leg in a cast, but that night in the hospital he had meticulously figured out that he also had to achieve a score of 9.5 out of 10.0 in order to do his part towards winning the gold medal for the team.

Suddenly, Fujimoto began his routine and faultlessly performed the aerial ballet on the rings. The crowd and the judges were amazed and enthralled. As he finished his routine, he sailed off the rings, did a double twist followed by a triple somersault, and landed like an arrow embedded in its target. With tears streaming down his cheeks, he stood ramrod straight, the sign that he had finished his routine. He then collapsed and his teammates carried him off the floor, his broken leg in a now shattered cast. The scoreboard flashed 9.5—his team won the gold medal! Later Shun said, "The pain shot through me like a knife. It brought tears to my eyes. But now I have a gold medal and the pain is gone."

The next time you're faced with something difficult, even though "it's gonna hurt," grit your teeth and get through it. There is always something good at the end.

The Wrong Foot

Some people seem to start life out on the wrong foot. Let me tell you about one girl who was lucky to even get out of the starting block at all.

She was born prematurely at four pounds. By the age of four, doctors discovered a double attack of pneumonia and scarlet fever had crippled her left leg. At age eight, she finally began to regain the use of her leg. After two years of therapy, three times a week, she was finally able to limp. With a special brace she could walk by age 12.

But she didn't want to just walk, she wanted to run, and run faster than any woman ever. By the time she was 15 she was running well enough to become the star of her high school track and basketball teams. She won a track scholarship to Tennessee State University.

In 1960 she made the U.S. Olympic team and won three gold medals in Rome. She won the 100-meter and the 200-meter dash in world-record time. Then she anchored the four-by-100-meter relay team to a world-record win. All this from a sickly girl who was never supposed to run at all.

Wilma Rudolph was named America's Female Athlete of the Year. The woman who got out of the starting blocks faster than any woman at that time almost didn't get out of the blocks at all.

But there's more than a history lesson to this story. Remember, it doesn't matter where you begin, only where you end up. The people who believe that and act according to what they believe live dreams they could only imagine. Every successful champion in every field of endeavor started somewhere. And even if they started on the wrong foot, they finished a winner.

One Step at a Time

How do you do something great and noble with your life? One step at a time is a good way to start, according to Mrs. Charles Philipia.

She wanted to raise money for charity and didn't have the means to do it herself. She was poor, retired and lived on a very meager income from the investments she had made during her working years. When she heard of a walk-a-thon to raise money for handicapped children, she approached local businesses with the proposal that they donate a certain amount for each mile she walked. Most people walked their standard 10 miles, but Mrs. Philipia went the extra mile—and then some.

This 63-year-old woman didn't just walk through the streets of her hometown. She walked from Miami, Florida, to New York City—a distance of over 1,500 miles! She didn't ride a bus or hitch any rides.

Reporters gathered in New York for interviews about her amazing accomplishment. When they asked how she did it, Mrs. Philipia had her answer ready.

"It doesn't take courage to take one step at a time. And that's all I did. I just took one step, then another and another. Step-by-step is the only way to accomplish anything, no matter how great or small the task might be."

Mrs. Philipia was right! The most noble things ever accomplished were accomplished a little at a time. Inch-by-inch, life's is a cinch—yard-by-yard is when it's hard.

Obstacles and Barriers

How much time do you spend thinking about reasons you can't do things? Do you complain about obstacles being in your way? Consider what car maker Henry Ford said about obstacles.

"One of the great discoveries people make—and one of the greatest surprises they will ever enjoy—is when they find out they can do what they were afraid they couldn't do. Most of the barriers we beat our heads against and worry about were put there by us, and only we can take them down."

Of all the barriers, there are three that plague everyone. First, we get distracted. We have great plans and goals but we don't set aside time to work for them. Instead, we do something meaningless.

The second barrier is that we tell ourselves tomorrow will be better. We put off starting something by thinking there will be more time tomorrow or next week. There never is.

The third barrier is the worst. We lose faith in ourselves. We begin to feel we aren't competent. We listen to every criticism and dwell on our every mistake. We lower our expectations.

We usually bring these blockades on ourselves. Therefore, it is up to us to overcome them.

Who gets it right the first time? I don't know anybody. Do you?

If you haven't failed a few times, it means you're not pushing yourself hard enough. Failure is a necessary step on the road to success.

All around us people are failing miserably. We feel sorry for them. Don't. The only way to succeed is to fail. It's better to try something and fail than never to try. The only people to feel sorry for are those who haven't tried for fear of failure. The people who try the impossible are getting closer to success every time they fail. The guy watching other people fail while he tries nothing is missing out on one of life's most important lessons.

Thomas Edison failed by discovering the light bulb.

If you fail, consider it a blessing. If you knew what good company you were in, you'd be proud. Henry Ford is!

The Lousy Lawyer

Did you ever fall flat on your face as a total failure? One lousy lawyer did.

He came from a wealthy family and was the pride of his parents. He had every advantage: the best schools, a law degree and an introduction to important people.

But he had to prove himself a capable lawyer—without the help and influence of his father and his social standing. In the courtroom he presented a terrible image. He was too frightened to stand up to the opposition and was easily overwhelmed.

As he reached his lowest, most wretched level of suffering, he realized there were people worse off than himself. He began to consider how he could help.

He never did become a prominent lawyer. Instead, he developed his own philosophy which led his native country of India to independence from British rule. His name was Mahatma Gandhi.

In the moments of suffering during our worst failures, if we look around we might gain a new perspective on life. When you are at your lowest point, it might be the time to plant the seeds for the future.

Gandhi looked around him and turned his life into an astonishing success. The world is a better place because when Mahatma Gandhi looked at himself, he didn't like what he saw and did something about it.

Miss America

One five-year-old wanted to be Miss America. She started to pursue her dream by enrolling in piano lessons. She also took voice lessons. But her dream and pursuit of musical excellence almost came to a screeching halt when she was 11 years old. A serious car accident left her physically challenged. She would never walk again.

For 10 months she wore a total body cast. When the cast came off, she could walk but only with a severe limp. She had 100 stitches on her face as a result of the accident.

But she had a dream so she continued on. At the age of 17, through hard work and undying faith, her leg miraculously got better and she tried out for her first county beauty pageant. She lost, not even finishing in the top ten. The next year she entered again and didn't make the five finalists. On the third try she won the county pageant, but lost in the state pageant. The fourth year she again won her county contest, but again lost by a landslide at the state level. The fifth year, at age 22, she not only won locally but finally won the state contest and became Miss Mississippi.

Over 75 million television viewers watched teary-eyed Cheryl Pruitt gracefully walk down the runway to be crowned Miss America. In all the glitz and glamour of that special night, in front of the lights, the American public didn't realize that the elegant, talented, articulate young woman almost didn't make it to Atlantic City at all.

It wasn't just a pretty face, a particular evening dress or a smile that got her there. It was heart and soul and a relentless pursuit of personal excellence.

Opportunity at Your Feet

Let me tell you the story of a man who saw golden opportunity walk right across his foot. Come back with me to a garage in the Midwest, half a century ago.

Inside, a struggling and half-starved illustrator was trying to make a living with his pictures. As he sat there exerting his brain for an inspirational idea, a mouse ran right across his foot.

Generally speaking, mice are not particularly welcome. They smell up the place and make a nuisance of themselves. The young illustrator watched the mouse scurry into the hole in the wall and thought about how miserable his chances were of succeeding as an artist. Then he began to imagine things in that pesky, yet perky, mouse and he began to draw.

America and the world have never been the same since that unknown mouse ran across that man's foot. The mouse was named Mickey and the illustrator was Walt Disney.

The next time you see a sign of failure crossing your path like a repulsive rodent, look again. It might be an opportunity trying to get your attention. Walt Disney built an empire on that silly mouse. He and his hard-working employees have entertained millions. He looked down, then soared as high as a man can fly.

Where Do Words Come From?

What we've been in the past does not make us who we are today. What we hope to become in the future does.

A few millennia ago, when written language was invented, a critic said, "The discovery of the alphabet will create forgetfulness in learners' souls, because they will not use their memories. They will trust to the external written characters and not remember of themselves."

The critic's name was Socrates. Thanks to writing, we still remember much of what he said so long ago.

Centuries later, Gutenberg invented printing. Critics said the same thing about print technology. A priest named John Trithemius said printing would weaken the gift of memory so people would forget the vital words they memorized in church. Instead, printing has expanded our memories. Gutenberg's first printed book, the Bible, has been read and remembered more than any other in history.

When television arrived, critics said we would stop reading. In fact, television stimulated reading. We publish more books, sell more books, and read more books than ever before. And we know more about what's happening throughout the world than ever before.

Now "the information superhighway" has arrived. It can provide instant access to all knowledge, everywhere. Critics say the human mind can't handle it—the Worldwide Web is too much. We'll lose our ability to remember and think.

Will the critics be wrong once again?

As in the past, new information technologies will expand the human mind, improve learning skills and make life better than it was yesterday.

11

FOR A MOST UNUSUAL PERSON

THAT'S RIGHT, I'M TALKING ABOUT YOU

I have known many things in my lifetime.
I've known the loneliness of the long sad nights
that drift on memory.
I have known the glorious abandon of
unencumbered space,
And soared to unimaginable heights of ecstasy
Holding the hand of nature as I ran.
I have known the great sadness of separation
And the unparalleled joy of being reunited.
In my lifetime I have known the many joys of solitude . . .
And Happiness . . .
And Beauty . . .
And then I met you . . .
And you're the darndest thing I ever did run across!

—M. A. BARNES

If you're not failing
a few times, it means
you're not pushing
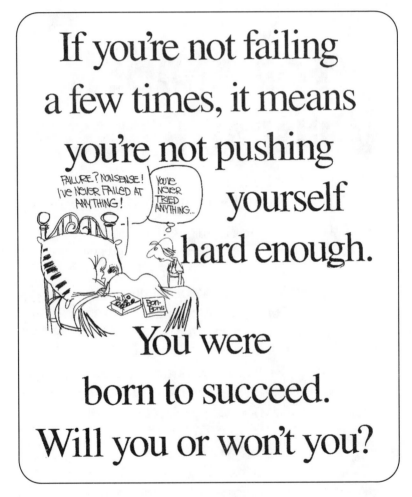
yourself
hard enough.

You were
born to succeed.
Will you or won't you?

To "Mine" Own Self
Be True

Everyone was in awe of Seth Goldberg's principles, values, inner strength and total peace of mind. As a devout Jew, he was faithful to his beliefs and true to himself. Even though he was mellow, Goldberg was definitely not a passive soldier. When it came to fighting the enemy, he was always the first to volunteer for the terrifying missions. In fact, Goldberg saved the life of every single man in his platoon at least once. He was a highly decorated soldier at the end of World War II and his story will help each of us put the war in its proper perspective.

Because Goldberg was a true hero in every sense of the word, you would think that he would have received many promotions and become a high-ranking officer during the war. Quite the contrary. The officers were afraid to promote Goldberg because he had the reputation of being a German-lover. Even though he was Jewish, he didn't hate the Germans like everyone else. He said they were about the same as us, perhaps a little bit more hardheaded, but basically the same. He said they had wives and girlfriends and families who loved them and prayed for their well-being just as we had. Goldberg was not only empathetic, but he also spoke excellent German. Just before the war broke out, Goldberg had attended college for three years in Germany where his German roommate became his best friend.

If Goldberg liked the Germans so much, how was he able to fight them so well? He simply replied, "The only way to stop the evil, corrupt Hitler and his Nazis is to defeat the German people who have let themselves be deceived by Hitler." He said it was wrong to kill the Germans, but it was more wrong for Hitler and his Nazis to annihilate innocent people and deceive the entire world. Goldberg said that sometimes we are forced to choose between two evils, and Hitler had to be stopped at all costs!

Once, Goldberg stayed up all night trying to help save the life of a young German soldier who had a bullet in his chest.

The boy died early the next morning and his fellow ∪oidiers knew they saw a tear in Goldberg's eye as he began digging the grave.

Seth Goldberg's final story unfolded a few months after that incident took place. In it lies the true nature of war.

The platoon next to his caught a German trying to steal supplies. One of their men was injured while arresting the German. The captors brought the German to their camp on the way to the brig. The captain sentenced him to be shot at dawn. As the night wore on the men sat around the fire talking about the homes they wondered if they would ever see again. The German prisoner was walking toward the brig, and suddenly as the light of the fire illuminated his face, Goldberg sprang to his feet. The muscles in his neck and arms were bulging and tense. He shook his head and blinked his eyes to confirm what he thought he saw. Then he leapt toward the German. The guard's first reaction should have been to protect the German, for it wasn't uncommon for a soldier to try to kill a prisoner when he remembered that the prisoner had killed one of his buddies. But in this instance, that was not the case. Before anyone had a chance to do anything, Goldberg and the prisoner were hugging each other and kissing each other on the cheek as they exchanged a few words in German. Everyone watched in stunned amazement. That is, everyone except the guard, who shouted, "Weiterlaufen schwein." The German broke Goldberg's grip and resumed walking toward the brig. The guard looked at Goldberg and said, "You ought to be shot, you pig-lover."

The only thing that kept Goldberg from smashing the guard in the mouth was his deeply instilled respect for authority. He turned around. Every muscle in his body quivered and he clenched his fists so tightly that he forced the blood out of them. He sat back down and just stared at the ground.

The captain received word of this little episode and immediately ordered Goldberg to report to his tent. Tents are not soundproof and everyone within the immediate vicinity clearly heard the captain order Goldberg to be the fifth man on the sunrise firing squad.

When Goldberg came out of the tent, the men asked him what he was going to do. They reminded him that his refusal to obey a direct order would result in his being shot himself. Goldberg replied, "I understand the consequences, but how can I shoot my best friend, the man who was my college roommate? How can I shoot a man my family loves— a man who has a wife and kids—a man who actually has changed my life for the better?"

So what did Seth Goldberg do? Before I tell you the rest of the story, what do you think you would have done? It would be hard to shoot your best friend, but the German was going to die regardless of whether you personally pulled the trigger. Refusing to shoot would mean that two men would die instead of one. What good would you be to your country if you were dead? Right? On the other hand, what kind of life would you have if you knew that you knowingly had served on the firing squad that executed your best friend?

If you understand the rules of war, you will argue that Goldberg's role in the firing squad wouldn't make him guilty of the German's death. The German would die as a victim of martial law and Goldberg, as a participant in martial law, would be acting as a soldier not a murderer.

The end of the story? Early the next morning, the firing squad executed both Seth Goldberg and the German soldier who had been his best friend.

Let us all seriously contemplate Seth Goldberg's legacy— the blatant reminder of the brutal ramifications of war—so that we no longer think of it in terms of country against country or one political system and its leaders against another. War is common person against common person; man, woman and family against man, woman and family. We, as brothers and sisters in the family of man need to love, tolerate and mutually respect one another—only then can we "give peace a chance."

In honor of Seth Goldberg, let each of us first identify what principle we would be willing to die for and then passionately live for that principle every single day of our lives. Only then can each of us claim, as did Seth Goldberg claim, "to *mine* own self I have been true."

The Price of a Soul

On a Friday in April of 1949, a three-year-old child was laughing and playing with her friends in a vacant lot next to her home. Suddenly she disappeared. And so began the nightmare of Baby Kathy.

The unlucky little girl had fallen into an abandoned well. Within minutes firemen were pumping oxygen into the small opening.

"Are you all right?" they called down, as rescue crews frantically tried to figure out a way of retrieving Kathy.

"I am," came the tiny, muffled voice from below.

Men and machines raced the clock in a frantic effort to move the earth and free the child. The acts of heroism were unbelievable, but it was in vain. Fifty-three hours after her fall, little Kathy was pulled up from her death chamber. Was it worth it? You bet.

The same thing happened in 1987 when Baby Jessica McClure fell into an abandoned well in Midland, Texas. Again, efforts of fearless heroism drew men, women and machinery to that small unknown town to rescue a child nobody had ever heard of until that fateful afternoon.

This time there was a happy ending. Baby Jessica was brought out in one piece, alive and kicking—even after nearly three days alone underground.

When things get tough, the tough get going. And every soul is worth saving. Remember that the next time things get tough.

What Are You Worth?

At one time in his remarkable career, Fred Astaire's legs were insured for $650,000. Betty Grable's were worth a cool million. During the making of the movie *Dick Tracy*, Madonna's body was insured for the same sum. Michael Jackson's voice is insured for millions, so are some athletes' knees.

How much are you worth?

I'm not talking nickels and dimes—or even millions for that matter. I mean how much are you worth in terms of making a contribution to the world while you are here on Earth?

It's up to each of us to make our lives worth something— like directing a movie. The show must go on. But will it be a box-office smash or just another flop?

You are the only one who can answer that. If you're proud of the way things are going, then keep the cameras rolling. If you don't, rewrite the script. Create a role you really want to play.

It's your life. You are the star, the producer and director. Make it a role that will be cherished for posterity—a classic— like the musicals made by the late, great Fred Astaire.

Be Above Average

Think for a moment about the effort it takes just to be average, then consider how much energy Elaine Dart must put forth to be average.

Elaine appears to be a typical girl with typical hobbies and interests, born to a middle-class family. She paints a little, embroiders a little, knits sweaters, types on a computer—the basic run-of-the-mill things most average girls do.

But Elaine has to work much harder. As a victim of cerebral palsy, she cannot use her arms. All the things you and I do with our hands, Elaine has to do with her feet. It took her two years to paint a picture, six months to embroider a pillow, two years to knit a sweater. She can type a page in minutes, thread a needle in seconds, even write with a pen—all with her toes.

Consider the amount of effort Elaine must put forth just to be average and compare it with the individual effort you are making in your life. How do you stack up? Have you ever put that much effort into anything in your entire life? Imagine what you could you do if you did?

Elaine Dart is a winner! She made the most of what she was given. For an average person it doesn't take much effort to remain average. But the goal of every person should be to become something better. A winner is an average person who gives an above-average effort to make things happen.

Desire

Desire is an extraordinary, intense determination. It is a fighting heart, with a burning commitment to a cause. This desire burns through in the field of athletic competition—where struggle is fierce and perseverance is profound. Sports competition is life personified.

To be successful in life, you must think like sports champions think: they believe they can run faster, jump higher and throw farther than anyone else. That's why they continue to break world records. They understand desire and they are willing to fight for it, regardless of the situation.

In 1975 during the U.S. Open Tennis Championships, a young tennis star from Spain named Manuel Orantes was struggling. No matter how hard he tried, the ball just didn't bounce well in his court. Nothing seemed to be going his way.

Being a great competitor, Manuel never gave up. He persevered one shot at a time through this long streak of bad luck. His toughness paid off. In the qualifying matches Orantes was matched with the South American tennis star Guillermos Vilas.

As the match began, Manuel's confidence was once again restored. Certainly he could win. But contrary to his desire and belief, his string of misfortune continued. And before Orantes could even get focused, he found himself on the brink of being excluded from the tournament. It was the last point of the match. Vilas needed only one point to advance to the finals.

According to the best odds makers in the world, there was no believable way that Orantes could win. He was just too far behind. But did he believe this? No. Manuel Orantes is a champion; he is a winner and winners never give up.

Orantes started by winning the critical point and came back to win the semifinal match against Vilas. It was a grueling match lasting over five hours and ending at 1:30 in the morning. Worn out physically, mentally and emotionally, it was theoretically impossible for Orantes to win. But he did!

In the finals, luck should have been on his side of the

court. But it wasn't. He was scheduled to play the top-ranked Jimmy Connors for the championship early the next day.

Because Orantes hadn't had much sleep, and because almost every ounce of energy had been drained from his body in winning against Vilas, the odds again were against him. Somehow, however, Orantes found the strength to walk out onto the court and once again gave it his very best effort. As the underdog and with everything going against him, including a low energy level, lack of sleep, blisters on the bottoms of his feet, aching muscles—drained emotionally and physically—how could he possibly rise to the occasion?

His opponent, Jimmy Connors, was well rested and ready to go. It just didn't seem fair.

But Manuel Orantes beat Jimmy Connors in straight sets, 6-4, 6-3, 6-3. He fell to his knees after winning the last point and said a short prayer of thanks.

In an interview after the match, Orantes was asked how he did it. He replied, "When I walked out onto the court, I knew exactly what had to be done, and I knew that I didn't have the time or energy to dink around with Connors. If I was going to win, I was going to have to put him away as quickly as possible and beat him three sets to nothing. If I was going to win, it would be because of my desire."

What a great champion! He never gave up. He won because he believed that he could do it. It would have been easy for Orantes to concede defeat when he was so far behind against Vilas, but he didn't. He wanted to win; therefore, he did win.

Remember, champions are average people like you and me. But they always give an above-average effort. That is their secret. Winners don't just dream and talk about winning—they do it!

P.S.—After this loss and the lesson it taught him, the great, proud competitor Jimmy Connors developed his own never-say-never attitude. Since that turning point, he has racked up more come-from-behind victories than any other tennis star in history. The name Jimmy Connors is synonymous with *desire, heart* and *willingness to win.*

Absorb the Bumps

Bill Latimer was one of the greatest athletes in America, an intense competitor. As a student at the University of Utah, he was a star on the tennis team and one of the best competitive skiers. All was going well for Bill. Things couldn't have been better, until Bill had a skiing accident and they had to amputate his left leg just below the knee.

Needless to say, Bill was totally devastated. However, he realized if he continued to compete and compare himself to others, he would feel handicapped and not capable. But if he looked at what he now had to work with, he could turn the negative label of "handicapped" into a positive opportunity to overcome a physical challenge.

And Bill was a guy who had sought out physical challenges his entire life.

With this newfound understanding of self-competition, Bill promised himself that he would never let anyone see him walk with a limp. He vowed that he would not let this accident stop him from competing.

So Bill had two kinds of artificial legs made for him. One has a foot with a convex bottom and a rocking-chair effect, so when he walks he does not limp. No one knows he has an artificial leg unless he wears shorts. With this leg, Bill still plays tournament tennis and wins. He's an amazing racquetball player. He swims long-distance marathon races.

The other artificial leg he had made is constructed so that he can wear a ski boot. Bill is still a fantastic powder skier, but sometimes it's hard for him to negotiate the bumps. One day when he was flying down the side of a mountain, he hit a bump and his leg flipped off. A ski with a boot and a leg hooked on it was speeding down the hill without Bill!

Standing below was a lady making her very first ski run. When she looked up she screamed, "Ski! Ski! No, leg! Leg!" Then her jaw dropped open when she saw Bill skiing down the mountain on one leg, chasing his other.

The runaway ski and leg stuck in the snow right in front of the lady. But Bill, nonplussed, brushed the snow from it, strapped it back on, and said, "It's okay, ma'am—happens all the time."

Bill Latimer is a great man. He didn't stay down when he got knocked down. He didn't let obstacles and disappointments stop him. He overcame great emotional and physical barriers and succeeded.

Bill knows that you're never beat till you quit. One single event—even one as traumatic as an amputation— is merely a bump on the long ski run of life. With a sense of humor, and a belief in self-competition, we can get up and do whatever it takes to succeed.

You've Got to Want It

I was once asked to be the guest speaker at the Helena High School commencement exercises in Montana. After I had delivered my remarks, I noticed a very young-looking girl walking up to receive her diploma. She appeared to be about 12 years old, and I figured she must be a genius who had finished high school early. When her diploma was presented to her, the crowd arose and gave her a standing ovation. This deeply moved me, so I asked the principal sitting next to me about her.

This beautiful girl was Laurie Mitchell. She was 18 years of age. And although Laurie was not a genius, she was close to it. She graduated as an honor student, third in her class of 347. So what makes her story so extraordinary?

Laurie was born with numerous physical handicaps. Her right hand, the one she took and held her diploma with, has only a thumb. Her left arm extends only to the elbow. Laurie's right leg has no femur bone and she has no left leg at all. She walks on one artificial leg, with a brace on the other. Laurie stands only four feet, two inches tall.

Laurie's condition is serious but she doesn't let it bother her. Instead she concentrates on how she can overcome the obstacles that she encounters on a daily basis. Laurie Mitchell truly wants to become the best she can be. She has courage, determination and an exceptional ability to accept a challenge. She will never be labeled a quitter or a loser since she has the ability to turn the impossible into reality.

At the age of six she was determined to learn how to swim. Three months later—after long hours of practice—Laurie achieved her goal. Today she is an excellent swimmer.

Living on a ranch exposed her to yet another goal: riding a horse. After several months of practice, and with a specially designed saddle, she could sit on the horse and ride it. However, she found that she had difficulty using her legs to command the horse to move forward, so instead she bites the horse's ear.

There is an interesting lesson here. Laurie can't kick the horse or use both reins to turn it, so she taught it to respond to what it *feels*. By Laurie's simply leaning to the left or right, the horse knows where she wants to go.

Oh how wonderful it would be if each of us were in tune with ourselves to the same high degree that Laurie is and could teach others to model our behavior by simply following our example.

The Olympics

In 1896, the United States sent its first Olympic team to Athens, Greece. Thirteen competitors set out by boat—a far cry from the 700 athletes who competed in Atlanta in 1996. The men in the boat were due to arrive the day before the Games began. Their stories are inspirational.

James Connolly, 27, quit Harvard, hoping to return after the games. But the dean told James he couldn't guarantee readmission. James took that chance. He had a dream to follow.

After a 12-day journey across the Atlantic, the team took a train across Italy. In Athens, they were met by a procession speaking only Greek—naturally, they didn't understand a word. On the day the games opened, Connolly won the triple jump—making him an instant celebrity.

Robert Garrett, 20, a student at Princeton, had never held a real discus. But he'd seen pictures of an athlete throwing one, and he thought he could be quite good at it. Being unable to locate a discus with which to practice, he paid a blacksmith to make one. The handmade discus weighed over 20 pounds and Garrett could barely lift it. Nevertheless, he practiced faithfully.

When he arrived in Athens, he was pleasantly amazed to find that a discus weighed slightly more than five pounds. As the event started, Garrett went up against the reigning Greek champion. He easily beat the favored contender and won first place. The following day he entered the shot put—with over 100,000 Greeks cheering their national champion. To their dismay, Garrett won again.

American tennis player John Boland traveled to the Olympics intending to be a spectator. On a whim he entered the tennis tournament and won gold medals in singles and doubles.

In those days, athletes competed against one another to win, not for the fame or the money. Competing for the right reasons always lifts our expectations and performance to the highest level possible. Strive to be an Olympian every day, no matter what the reward.

12

COMMUNICATION CONCERNS

You cannot speak of *ocean* to a well-frog—
the creature of a narrower sphere.
You cannot speak of *ice* to a summer insect—
the creature of a season.

—CHUANG TZU

You can if you
think you can!

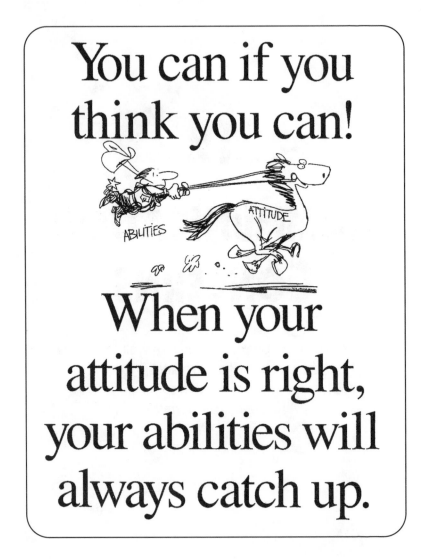

When your
attitude is right,
your abilities will
always catch up.

The Art of Communication

Things aren't always what they seem to be. Perception isn't always reality. It should be, but it isn't. Too many people are outdoing by overdoing and in the process, eventually redoing reality.

When Emanuel Leutze painted *Washington Crossing the Delaware*, he depicted the Stars and Stripes being carried in the boat, even though it was not adopted as the American flag until June 14, 1777—six months after Washington crossed the Delaware!

In his renowned oil painting, *Israelites Gather Manna in the Wilderness*, Tintoretto armed Moses' men with shotguns. The earliest known appearance of a gun was approximately 1326 A.D.—somewhat after the Exodus!

In the biography *Abraham Lincoln: The Prairie Years*, Carl Sandburg wrote about Lincoln's mother singing "Greenland's Icy Mountain" as she stood at the family's log cabin door. Quite a feat considering the song was not written until 22 years after Lincoln's death!

No wonder life seems so complicated. We bring it upon ourselves. Analyze a bank for instance. It's an institution where you can borrow money only if you present sufficient evidence that you don't need it.

What about the American voter who yells at the government to balance the budget and then borrows $50 "just until payday"? What about the father who cheats on his income tax, yet can't understand why his son cheated on his math test? What about the mother who, while in the midst of lecturing her daughter about always being honest, hears the telephone ring and says, "Tell them I'm not here"?

It's true. Things aren't always what they should be. A *fire-fly* is actually a beetle—and if we have a bug called a *fly* why not a *walk* or a *jog*? A *Douglas fir* tree is actually a pine. A *panda bear* is actually a relative of the raccoon. An *English horn* is actually an alto oboe from France. A piece of *catgut* is actually made from the intestines of sheep. A *Turkish bath* is actually Roman.

The other day even a reputable radio program threw me

for a loop when the disc jockey said, "Now for a partial score—Chicago 7." Those whom we expect will know what they are doing often don't. The United States Naval Academy of Design held an art competition and awarded second place to a work by Edward Dickenson. The judges later learned that the award-winning piece had been hanging upside down! At the signing of the Treaty of Versailles in 1919, David Lloyd-George of Great Britain advised the leader of Italy that his country could make up its commercial losses by increasing the production of its banana crop. This pronouncement neither heartened nor excited the man since Italy does not produce bananas!

Today's world is even stranger: a woman pays $50 for a beautiful lace slip and gets annoyed if it shows beneath her dress; a man puts up screens to keep insects out of his home, air conditions his home, car and office, then attends an outdoor picnic!

Let us stop the absurd madness of trying to be so sophisticated, complicated and grandiose. Simple, straightforward connection should be the required standard for all human interactions. It's the only way we will ever align our perception with reality. When we "tell it like it is" not only do we enjoy honest communication, but we also may often find that our conversations are entertaining and unobtrusively funny!

When my son was five years old his mother woke him up for the second day of kindergarten. He snapped, "What again?"

When asked what hitting advice he gives to gives player Ken Griffey Jr., the batting instructor for the Seattle Mariners major league baseball replied, "I tell him, attaway, Junior!"

I heard two golden nuggets of straightforward, unadulterated truth the other day while I was at an airport. An elderly southern woman was at the counter yelling at the top of her lungs, "Don't you lie to me. Don't you dare lie to me. If the pilot of this plane can fly in the dark and can find Springfield, Illinois in a snowstorm, I know you can find my bag!" A man stood beside me with his suitcase on the floor next to him. The suitcase bore stickers from Hawaii, Toronto, Jamaica, Oklahoma, Utah and Florida. Upon seeing the suitcase, the same woman blurted out, "My oh my, have you been to all those places?" The man replied, "No, but my luggage has!"

Art Form

Communication is not just two people taking turns talking. It's an art form where an open line of complete understanding exists. Tragedy lurks amidst poor communication.

A mother's young three-year-old daughter had opened the front door and walked down the busy street. From her window she could see her little girl standing on the curb as trucks, buses and cars whizzed by. She raced out toward her daughter, grabbed her and scolded, "How many times have I told you 'Don't go near the curb'?" Her daughter looked at her innocently and asked, "Mommy, what's a curb?"

Good, comprehensible, effective communication breeds understanding on an intuitive, spiritual plane that words cannot explain.

My car broke down in the rain late at night on an obscure country road. No one knew I was out there. Within 15 minutes my dad pulled up and said, "Hop in. We'll tow it in the morning." He never told me how he knew I was in trouble. Parents mysteriously communicate with their children heart to heart, spirit to spirit, sometimes without speaking a single word. Dads give goodnight kisses and tuck us in bed to officially eliminate fright. Mothers kiss an "ouchie" and somehow magically make it all better.

Communication can always be good, clean, pure, powerful and positive. It should always be this way. It will always be this way if you want it to be, choose for it to be and allow it to be!

Uniquely Smart

Parents have taken communication to another level. How many times have we heard our dear mothers say things like, "Don't climb up that tree. If you fall down and break both your legs, don't come running to me!" Or, when we've been in an accident, how many times have we heard our mothers' classic question, "Do you have on clean underwear?"

I have observed parents spanking their sons and yelling, "Don't you hit your sister!" And other parents reprimanding their daughters, "Why are you talking with your mouth full? Answer me!"

I remember a conversation between my parents and my teenage sister. "Remember your 12:00 A.M. curfew," my mom reminded. "The sex monster comes out at midnight." And my dad's reaction to the boy's vehicle: "You can't go out with him. He's driving a van." My mother asked, "Why can't she, dear? You used to drive a van." Remembering that van vividly, my dad responded, "That's what I mean. You cannot go out with a guy who drives a van!"

One night I phoned my dad and he taught me about urgency. He said, "I was just watching a pro basketball game on TV. They should just give each team 100 points and let them play the last two minutes of the game. More happens during the last two minutes than during the rest of the contest."

Parents are the ultimate teachers. They help us laugh, feel, think and learn the lessons of living. I love my parents and wouldn't trade them for any other parents in the world!

The Competitive Advantage

If plants grow from sunlight, people grow from praise. So give it freely, it costs nothing and it's so nourishing. Giving compliments always comes back to you—in one form or another. If you give it, you'll receive it, and everybody likes to hear they've done a job well.

Put this theory to the test. Start fertilizing your social circle with some recognition and accolades. You'll see the difference soon enough.

The need for praise is basic to everyone. When we receive it, we grow; without it, we shrink and fade. Look for an occasion to give an encouraging word or a compliment. Constantly strive to make people feel wanted and important and capable. Let them know they can succeed. By doing this, it forces us to concentrate on the positive side of people, instead of the negative. This makes us all more productive and pleasant to be around.

In sales we call it psychological reciprocity, which simply means this: In the course of our conversation, if I make you feel intelligent, significant, special and important, it automatically creates a subconscious moral obligation for you to make me feel equally intelligent, significant, special and important before the conversation ends.

It's true. What goes around comes around.

Straight Talk

"Do unto others as you would have others do unto you" is a pretty general statement.

A note on my mother's refrigerator door served up a deeper explanation. She called it "The Golden Goodies":

- If you open it, close it.
- If you turn it on, turn it off.
- If you unlock it, lock it up.
- If you break it, admit it.
- If you can't fix it, call someone who can.
- If you borrow it, return it.
- If you value it, take care of it.
- If you make a mess, clean it up.
- If you move it, put it back.
- If it belongs to someone else, get permission to use it.
- If you don't know how to operate it, leave it alone.
- If it's none of your business, don't ask questions.
- If it will brighten someone's day, SAY IT!
- If what you have to say will hurt somebody, DON'T SAY IT!
- If something isn't broken, don't try and fix it.
- If you think you know it all, look around and see how little you really know.

Don't Be a Wrecker

It's unbelievable the number of hit shows being patterned after an old formula called a soap opera. In the early days of television they were called soap operas because the shows were sponsored by soap companies.

These programs seem to have recurrent themes and one of them is the character who is always out to ruin the lives of others. He or she creates slander and gossip. These people are insecure and miserable and want those around them to feel the same way.

WRECKERS

I watched them tearing a building down,
A gang of men in a busy town,
With a ho-heave-ho and a lusty yell,
They swung a beam and the side wall fell.

I asked the foreman, "Are these men skilled,
And the men you'd hire if you had to build?"
He gave a laugh and said, "No indeed!
Just common labor is all I need.
I can easily wreck in a day or two
What builders have taken a year to do."
I thought to myself as I went my way,
Which of these roles have I tried to play?
Am I a builder who works with care,
Measuring life by the rule and square?
Am I shaping my deeds to a well-made plan,
Patiently doing the best I can?

Or am I a wrecker, who walks the town,
Content with the business of tearing down?

Free Speech Is Out of Control

When we support good, clean, pure, powerful and positive elements in life, we become fully charged. We should genuinely care about our neighborhoods and the people who live there. And we should make a stand against those things in our society that are indecent, immoral and promote violence.

In Philadelphia, a woman disguised as a man shot 21 bullets into a parked car where a second woman, who was eight months pregnant, waited for her husband. Miraculously, neither the woman nor the baby died.

Police identified the shooter and arrested her. When they searched her apartment, they found a library of do-it-yourself crime books, including *The Anarchist Cookbook, How to Disappear Completely and Never Be Found, The Homemade Mortar Construction Manual,* and *Kill Without Joy: The Complete How-to-Kill Book.* One book told how to wear oversized shoes and ankle weights to disguise footprints.

Perhaps we should not be surprised that such how-to-do-it books are on the market. Our cherished principle of free speech makes it impossible to censor them. But it takes a sick mind to write, print, buy and read such books. Every book is a collaborative effort. The author must find a publisher. Retailers must stock the book.

Along the way to the book shelves, dozens of individuals have the opportunity to say "I won't have anything to do with a book like this." Instead, they supplement the madness of the author with a little madness of their own.

The Philadelphia shooting was tragic, but the abuse of freedom that contributed to that shooting was more tragic still.

Hypnotism and Lifestyle Changes

The average human brain has unlimited potential. To help us understand the importance of positive thinking, let's look at hypnotism.

Any of you who have seen a hypnotist at work will surely agree they are amazing and magical. But hypnotism is nothing more than blind trust. Through concentration, the hypnotist suggests to the mind of the person being hypnotized, and those hypnotized do whatever they are asked to do.

Here are three examples of how powerful the mind can be.

1: The hypnotist tells a shy, timid introvert that she is an exceptional orator, a great entertainer and comedienne. Incredibly, this quiet, intimidated soul is suddenly transformed into an extroverted speaker who cannot shut up. She says more in five minutes than she has all year.

   The hypnotist helped the girl overcome her negative feelings about herself by suggesting a positive thought, which the girl accepted as truth. The positive thought replaced the negative, and she responded accordingly.

2: A friend of mine has trouble with math. Yet under hypnosis he becomes a math whiz in a matter of seconds. How? Does the hypnotist give him a crash course in mathematics? No. The hypnotist simply told him he could do it. He broke down my friend's self-constructed barrier—the one that's been holding him back from his innate, and previously suppressed, potential.

3: Two strong football buddies are made into weaklings. Normally they can lift hundreds of pounds, but because of a negative mindset they cannot even lift a rubber ball or a three-ounce shoe off the table.

   The mind controls our muscles. When the brain says it can't do something, it really can't.

   Yet the reverse is also true. When the brain says it can, it really can.

So these hypnotic demonstrations simply show that we can do anything we make up our minds to do. We have the potential to do the impossible if we firmly believe that we can.

Remember, the hypnotist didn't change the strength, knowledge or experience of the participants. All he did was make suggestions.

Each of us is also hypnotized in a very real sense. As though we are under a hypnotic spell, we do only what we tell ourselves we can do. Therefore, if you're negative, introverted, uncoordinated, weak, stupid or slow, it's because you tell yourself you are. And because it's up to you, you can change!

Self-Talk

Robert Redford is a man who believes in taking risks. Someone asked Redford about the trappings of fame that go along with being a movie star.

Redford replied, "I don't have any illusions of how fleeting fame might be. I constantly remind myself that I only have a few years on earth to say some things. The important thing is to take risks in getting those things said. If you quit taking risks you're liable to lose everything you've worked for."

Again and again, people at the top of their professions are forced to take risks in order to stay there. A researcher named Charles Garfield noticed that many peak performers follow a formula for success.

They ask themselves, "Can I survive if the risk I am about to take doesn't work out? Will I be able to go on if I fail?

If the answer is yes—that they could survive the worst possible consequences—then they take the risk. Do they fail? Of course they do sometimes, but they know they will be okay, even if they falter.

Self-talk is about creating the right questions. Only when we ask the correct questions can we get the correct answers and solutions, which are the decision-making tools necessary for taking calculated risks.

To become successful at whatever we do, we have to take chances. Sure, they scare us. They take us out of our comfort zones. But with positive self-talk we can *go for it!* The people who rise to the top—the cream of the crop—talk the talk, then take the risks and walk the walk to success and achievement. You can, too.

Hold On

Carol Burnett was once asked to describe labor pain. She said, "If you want to know what it feels like to have a baby, grab your bottom lip and pull it up over your head."

Pain before joy is a formula that occurs often in the world. After the trials and tribulations of labor comes the wonder of a new life.

Most of us have heard the expression "no pain, no gain." Sure, we can push our bodies way beyond their limits, but it's the mind we must convince. Mental toughness is every bit as important as physical toughness. To ultimately succeed, we need both. But how do we develop them? Most people don't—the reason being that we grow up thinking life will always be one-dimensional and when it changes, instead of hanging tough and weathering the storm of negativity surrounding us, we give up and quit. Consequently, we never develop either kind of toughness and never cultivate endurance.

If you grew up thinking life was a linear plane, you're not alone. But nothing stays the same. Just because things are going well doesn't mean they will always go well. If they did we'd become complacent and lose our competitive edge.

Heavyweight boxing champs often lose their titles to an inferior opponent because they think of themselves as *the* competition. It turns their offensive strategy to a defensive one and they lose their advantage. They must realize that once the fight begins they no longer own the title. It's up for grabs—winner take all.

Likewise, when things go wrong, we can't allow ourselves to believe that the trend will continue. For instance, I was driving down a highway for about an hour. Through my windshield I saw a sunny, clear blue sky turn dark and dismal. It rained so hard I could barely see. Then it cleared up and a brilliant rainbow stretched across the horizon. See what I mean? Life changes.

There are high times and low times. The goal is not to eliminate the low, negative times, for we learn more from our losses than from our victories. The goal is simply to reduce the duration and intensity of the negative cycles and increase the duration and intensity of the positive cycles.

When we hit one of those lows, we must remember to hang tough and learn the lesson being taught. Then when the negative cycle comes around again, it won't last as long. Remember, "no pain, no gain;" boundless joy and love for the newborn child always follows the pain of giving birth; there's always a storm before every rainbow—hold on!

Locked Doors

Everybody has heard of Harry Houdini, the master magician escape artist. He often boasted he could escape from any jail in the world in less than an hour—if he was allowed to wear street clothes.

A small town in the British Isles took Houdini up on his challenge. When Houdini arrived at the town's new jail, excitement was at a fever pitch as he was taken to the cell. Confidence oozed from every pore as the door was closed.

Hidden in his belt was a 10-inch piece of steel which he used to work on the lock. At the end of 30 minutes his confident look had disappeared. At the end of an hour he was drenched in perspiration. After two hours he literally collapsed against the door. And, amazingly, the door opened.

It had never been locked—except in Harry Houdini's head. One little push would have opened it. But since he thought it was locked, he didn't try.

The doors of opportunity are the same. If we think they are locked, we won't try to open them. But sometimes all it takes for them to swing wide open is one extra push.

Are you trying everything you can to open the doors of opportunity in your own personal world? Maybe some of the doors you didn't think you could open are waiting for you to use them. Try believing the door is open before you give up.

13

AMERICA THE BEAUTIFUL

America—love it or leave it?
No! Change it or lose it.

You can't "try" to do anything.

Either you do it or you don't.

The world is not interested in the storms you encountered, but did you bring in the ship!

An Important Song

In 1893 a teacher from Wellesley College journeyed west. Travel was difficult in those days and relatively slow. She had to stop often along the way, so she had plenty of time to look around and see the beauties of this great land.

Katherine Lee Bates visited the Columbian Exposition in Chicago. Then she was on her way again, travelling across the plains of middle America with mile after mile of ripened grain blowing like ocean waves. She came to the Rocky Mountains, purple in the late summer sun. And she climbed Pike's Peak to reach the Continental Divide, where she could see America stretching from horizon to horizon.

Katherine Lee Bates was so moved by the experience that she jotted a few words to capture her feelings.

> *Oh, beautiful for spacious skies,*
> *For amber waves of grain,*
> *For purple mountains majesty*
> *Above the fruited plain.*
> *America. America.*
> *God shed His grace on thee.*
> *And crown thy good with brotherhood*
> *From sea to shining sea!*

She wrote about pilgrim feet beating a thoroughfare for freedom, about heroes who loved their country more than self, about a patriot dream that sees beyond the years and about alabaster cities undimmed by human tears.

One hundred years after Katherine Lee Bates penned those words, they still describe this remarkable land of freedom. Is it any wonder we love to sing "America the Beautiful" so often?

The Teamwork of Sergeant Irwin

America is not beautiful merely because of her "purple mountains majesty and amber waves of grain" but because of her people. The backbone of America's freedom and productivity is, and has always been, volunteerism.

Volunteering is at the core of building a team, and true teamwork comes only when we understand commitment to service above self.

The first great American B-29 airplane strike against Japan in World War II was flown from a land base. It was led by an airplane dubbed *City of Los Angeles*. Aboard this aircraft were 12 men—11 regular crewmen and a colonel, flying as commanding officer. They were to rendezvous with other planes at a place 65 miles off the enemy's mainland, then assume regular fighting formation and fly in on the target.

They reached the appointed place on time, and Colonel Sprouse ordered the dropping of the phosphorous bomb, which was supposed to let off its yellow fumes as a marker for the dropping of regular bombs. Sergeant "Red" Irwin skidded this dangerous bomb down the airplane chute as ordered, but the flap at the end of the bomb chute had somehow become stuck. When the bomb struck it, it exploded ahead of time and burst back into the interior of the airplane, right into the face and chest of Sergeant Irwin.

Dropping to the floor, it began to swiftly burn its way through the thin metal floor separating it from the incendiary bombs stored in the bomb bay below. The *City of Los Angeles* and its crew were in danger of being blown to bits far out over the ocean in enemy territory.

Terribly wounded, Sergeant Irwin got to his knees, picked up the bomb in his bare hands, cradled it in his arms and staggered up the passageway. Crashing into the navigator's table, he had to stop and unlatch it with fingers that left burn marks on the hardwood. By now the airplane was filled with eye-stinging smoke, blinding the pilot. They hovered less than 300 feet above the water. Irwin staggered into the pilot's compartment, shouting, "Window! Window!" He could not see that it was already open. He threw the bomb out of the window and collapsed on the deck.

Colonel Sprouse ordered the *City of Los Angeles* back to base in the slim hope that Irwin's life might be saved. Two hours later they reached Iwo Jima, a small island in the Pacific. Irwin's flesh was still smoking with embedded phosphorous when he was removed from the plane by comrades who had to shield their faces from his awful wounds.

Sergeant Irwin lived to receive the Medal of Honor, his country's highest honor for extreme bravery, and survived nearly 50 plastic surgeries that helped restore him to an almost normal life. He married and became a father. Because of him, 11 other men lived to tell about the experience.

In the military the idea of teamwork means life and death, not just winning the game. Sergeant Irwin's courageous act is a prime example of selflessness and teamwork. As the Three Musketeers said, "All for one, and one for all!"

Why Should I?

Have you ever volunteered for something? Why did you do it? How did you feel when you finished?

Volunteers arrive early, stay late, go without breaks, work hard and always smile. Why? They are not paid, yet they give their all. Can you imagine what would happen to the work ethic of our workforce if everybody approached his or her job in the volunteer spirit of "I want to" rather than in the contractual agreement spirit of "I have to"? Contracts bind performance and breed minimum required involvement. Volunteerism also binds performance, while simultaneously breeding maximum productivity.

Imagine what America would be like without volunteers. Consider the organizations that depend on volunteers: churches, youth groups, health care agencies, hospitals, schools, civic organizations, sports leagues, arts and humanitarian associations, environmental groups—in every community throughout this country. Our quality of life would be infinitely less rewarding if it were not for the volunteers who selflessly offer their time while receiving no pay—and often little or no recognition.

What is the force behind these remarkable efforts and desire to help others? Volunteers find the work extremely satisfying and fulfilling. Volunteering builds self-esteem and develops personal skills. It teaches us how to use our time more productively. More important, it teaches us that it isn't always what you have, but more often what you give away that matters most in life. It teaches us to place a greater value on what we contribute to society than on what we accumulate.

Our sense of community is the strongest tradition in the history of American values and it's the volunteers who provide this strength. Through volunteering we make more than just a living with our lives—we make a difference and create "ordinary" miracles. May each of us volunteer to make and keep America the greatest, freest, bravest, friendliest, cleanest, kindest, most peaceful, most loving, most helpful and most courteous country in the world!

Duty, Honor, Country

These three hallowed words reverently dictate what we ought to be, what we can be and what we will be.

They are rallying points:

- to build courage when courage seems to fail
- to regain faith when there seems little motive for faith
- to create hope when hope becomes forlorn

These three words build character—they let us know when we are weak; they make us brave enough to face ourselves when we are afraid.

They teach us to be proud and unbending in honest failure, but humble and gentle in success. They help us face the stress of difficulty and learn to stand up in the storm. They help us have compassion for those who fall and to master ourselves before we seek to master others. They remind us about the past as we reach into the future. They say be serious, but never take ourselves too seriously. They tell us to be modest and to keep an open mind.

They temper the will and give vigor to the emotions. They create a sense of wonder and joy and inspiration in life.

These three simple words, made famous by General Douglas MacArthur, may have meant something entirely different to him than they do to each of us. Nevertheless, it's wonderful that he shared them with the world.

Veterans Day

On the eleventh hour of the eleventh day of the eleventh month in 1918, combatants signed the armistice ending World War I.

Later, Congress selected the symbolic date of November 11 as Veterans Day to honor the men and women who have served in the nation's military.

Since the Revolutionary War, over a million men and women have given their lives in military service. Another million and a half have been wounded.

Significant sacrifices were also offered by Americans who became prisoners of war during major military engagements. Some were held by the enemy for years under the most brutal and demeaning conditions. They suffered mental, physical and moral indignities beyond belief.

The largest numbers came during the bloody Civil War, when more than 400,000 were taken prisoner by Union and Confederate forces. Fifty-six thousand died in captivity.

During World War II, 120,000 Americans were taken captive. Twelve thousand died in prison camps—many of them in the Pacific.

While the Korean Police Action saw fewer prisoners, four out of every ten died in the barbarous North Korean camps.

On Veterans Day, let us remember the millions of men and women who served their nation in order to protect the freedom American citizens enjoy daily. Let us also prove our appreciation by honoring them with an equal commitment to country. We must take full advantage of our freedoms by doing the right thing: treat others as we want to be treated, be honest, trustworthy, helpful, courteous, kind and reverent. In this way, Veterans Day becomes an annual commitment by the living to those who have gone before.

Women Fought, Too

Women don't get enough credit for the part they played in the American Revolution. We've all heard of Betsy Ross and how she made the first American flag, but women have been in the thick of things since the beginning. One of them was only 16 when she took a midnight ride as dangerous and exciting—but far less publicized—as Paul Revere's.

On the night of April 25, 1777, two thousand British soldiers began destroying rebel storehouses. They found rum among the supplies, got drunk and started burning the town. A wounded messenger rode to a farm 20 miles from the town. The man who lived on the farm was the captain of the local militia. If he left to warn the surrounding cities, he would not be able to lead his 400 volunteers into battle.

His daughter, Sybil, offered to go in his place. Mounted sidesaddle, she rode 40 miles—twice as far as Paul Revere—through a perilous region filled with hostile Indians. As she traveled, she shouted warnings and banged on doors with a stout branch to alert the townspeople along the way.

It took Sybil all night to make her ride.

Women have always been brave, heroic and patriotic. Sadly, we don't hear as much about their acts as we should. It's time we realized that heroes aren't just men.

The Price of Freedom

People often confuse peace with freedom. They speak the words as though they were the same. They're not. Convicts locked up in prison may have peace, but they have no freedom. People living in communist countries may have peace, but they have no freedom. Freedom is the most cherished gift on Earth. Freedom is having the free will and choice to do what you want.

Everybody desires freedom, but most never count its cost. To put it in perspective, let's relate it to a billion.

In each day there are 1,444 minutes. In one year there are 525,600 minutes. In 1,000 years, there are just over half a billion minutes.

Now let's relate that to money. If you spend one dollar a minute, it would take you 1,903 years to spend $1 billion.

With that figure in mind consider this: every year we spend over $200 billion to protect this country and the freedom it brings. At that price do you think there must be something worth defending in America? But, ultimately, no price can be put on freedom.

That's your math lesson for today. A billion dollars is more than just a word. This country spends many billions of dollars to make sure that the lifestyle we have created here in America will never be taken away from us. Throughout history men and women have fought—even given their lives—for the right to be free.

Freedom to become whatever you want exists here in America. So use that liberty to be all that you can be.

To Vote or Not to Vote

One of the greatest privileges of living in America is the right to vote. In the last presidential election, only half the registered voters bothered to come to the polls. That means tens of millions never exercised their privilege to determine who makes decisions for their city, state and country.

Surely too many people figure one vote, their vote, isn't going to make a difference. But they are wrong.

In 1776 one vote gave America the English language instead of German.

In 1845 one vote brought Texas into the Union.

In 1868 one vote saved President Andrew Jackson from impeachment.

In 1876 one vote gave Rutherford B. Hayes the presidency of the United States.

In 1923 one vote gave Adolf Hitler leadership of the Nazi party.

In America we have the right to vote. It's a right men and women in other countries wish they had. They are willing to die for it.

One vote has made a difference in many elections. Millions of men and women have fought and died for the right to vote freely during the elections that shape their lives. So use it, don't abuse it. Register and vote. Your vote counts.

America's Number One Gang

Gangs are formed for the right reasons: friendship, acceptance, loyalty, support and a sense of stability. The police department is a gang, the National Teachers' Association (NEA) is a gang, of sorts. So are high school student leadership organizations and the athletes who proudly display their school colors on their lettermen jackets. Gangs are all around us; they're not necessarily a bad thing.

What gangs do is what makes them good or bad, productive or destructive.

One powerful, positive, productive gang is the Boy Scouts. In the area where I live, around Salt Lake City, Utah, there are over 100 registered, highly active Boy Scout troops for every known teenage street gang. The Scouts provide everything a street gang offers in terms of support and stability. The exception is that the Scouts act in positive ways with community cleanups, food and clothing drives, and assistance for the homeless. Think in terms of time management as the Scouts go hiking, camping, white-water rafting and fishing. They conserve natural resources and engage in projects that stimulate personal growth.

If our boys do something positive instead of worrying about saying no to drugs, alcohol and violence, they won't have time to be involved in negative activities. The Boy Scout's Promise, Law and Motto says it all:

> On my honor, I will do my best to do my duty to God and to my country, and to obey the scout law.
> A Scout is honest, trustworthy, loyal, helpful, friendly courteous, kind, thrifty, brave, clean and reverent.
> Be prepared.

May we wholeheartedly support our local Boy Scouts, emotionally and financially—even to the degree that each parent sign up his or her son as soon as possible. The Boy Scouts is the one gang of which any young man can be proud to be a member.

Cookies for All

Juliette Gordon Low, the founder of the Girl Scouts, had a purpose when she started the organization. She said, "The work of today is the history of tomorrow, and we are its makers."

Taking that thought one step further, she created the Girl Scout Promise, which goes like this:

> On my honor, I will try to serve God and my country, to help people at all times and to live by the Girl Scout Law.
> I will do my best:
> To be honest and fair
> To help where I am needed
> To be cheerful, friendly and considerate
> To be a sister to every Girl Scout
> To respect authority and cautiously use resources
> To protect and improve the world around us
> To show respect for myself and others
> In all I say and do.

The Girl Scouts' mission is to inspire girls with the highest ideals of character, patriotism and service so they may become happy and resourceful citizens.

The next time a girl in uniform knocks on your door with cookies for sale, you won't see the people they have served, the funds they have raised, or the activities they have offered to so many people around the world. What you will see is a smile and a sense of accomplishment. Behind that face is a high level of self-confidence, for Girl Scouts are taught about commitment to shared goals. Girl Scouting builds self-esteem and self-worth—the keys to positive behavior. They also sell some of the finest cookies you'll ever taste.

Let's support the Girl Scouts of America.

Free Enterprise

Because every person possesses the ability to get what he or she wants and to rise to the level of his or her own expectations, we need to become acquainted with an incentive system principle of success: free enterprise. This system proves that there is no such thing as a financial crisis; it's only an idea crisis. Ideas create income. All we have to do is select what we want, find out how much it costs and put together a step-by-step plan to make the necessary money. A few years ago I had some dramatic opportunities to put this philosophy to the test.

Porsche (Project #1)

I had my eye on a charcoal gray 911 Porsche for some time. Because of the high purchase price, I had to carefully budget my money so I could buy the sports car on the date that I chose—September 11.

For more than six months I had been putting money aside so I could accomplish my goal. On September 1, 10 days before the preset purchase date, I realized I was $2,000 short. How could I come up with that much money in a week and a half? Well, well, well. Here was my chance to prove the *financial crisis theory* versus the *idea crisis theory*. Supposedly, all I needed was an idea—the right idea—and my financial crisis would be resolved.

I went to the local hardware store and explained my idea to the manager. He loved it and sold me 325 specially designed brass apparatuses at cost—$2.85 each. I purchased a drill bit that perfectly fit the diameter of the apparatuses, grabbed my electric drill and headed into a neighborhood to try out my brilliant idea.

After an hour of practicing with my tools on an old piece of wood, I knocked on the first door. It opened and a lady and her husband stood in the doorway. I said, "Ma'am, how do you know that I'm not a rapist?" Her husband immediately started to flex his neck and walked toward me with his fists clenched. I continued, "I'm not a rapist, so don't worry, but don't you think it would be a great idea if you could see who was on the other side of your door before you opened it?" The woman and her husband both agreed that it would be. Holding up some packages containing my invention, I said, "Good, because I'm selling these little peepholes and I'd like to put one in your door!"

The man gave his okay and asked, "Could you put one in our back door, too?" On that Thursday, Friday and Saturday I installed more than 300 peepholes, made a little more than $2,100.00 and immediately went to buy my Porsche. Not bad, eh? The philosophy works!

Paint (Project #2)

The next weekend I had to prove to myself that my success hadn't been a fluke. I invested about $10 in some stencils, purchased some large cans of spray paint and went into another neighborhood to test my next idea. I don't know if your neighborhood has the tradition of painting your house numbers on the curb in front of your house, but this was my new service for sale. And if someone didn't have a curb, I sold him or her a big rock and painted the numbers on it! If they didn't want a rock, I painted the numbers on the mailbox! There was always a place to paint numbers; all I had to do was use my imagination. Several people I knew drove past in their cars and saw me sitting in the gutter painting. I could almost hear their conversations just by looking at their surprised faces. They seemed to be saying, "Oh look, Ethel, Dan Clark is in the gutter. Will he ever get a real job?"

I laughed to myself—all the way to the bank. Exactly one week from the day I bought my new car, I was completing a second Thursday, Friday and Saturday sweep. I earned $1,942.00 painting numbers on curbs and rocks. It worked again and I purchased some exotic accessories for my Porsche.

Entrepreneur (Project #3)

Two weekends later I was in San Antonio, Texas. I phoned one of my fun-loving friends to see how he was doing. It just so happened that he and his wife were planning to go to their local fair, so I tagged along for the company. Ted's wife attended some demonstration classes, so we decided we would do something to pass the time while we waited for her. I told Ted about my experiences with peepholes and painting and he thought they were amusing. We started to brainstorm and laughed so hard thinking about the idea we had just had that we decided to go and pay the required $50 to open up a booth at this fair. We found some supplies, made a sign, stapled it across the top of the booth and started to package our product. I filled small plastic Baggies and Ted drew labels. We sealed the Baggies by folding the cardboard labels over the opening of the bag and stapling the sides of the folded labels together. What a professional job—they looked almost store-bought! And I'm sure our satisfied customers appreciated our first-class touch.

What did we successfully market? What was the gimmick that made people giggle and buy our product to show their friends? We put a few Cheerios in a Baggie and cleverly sold them for $1.50 as "Doughnut Seeds!" By the end of the day, we had developed such a large clientele that we were forced to develop other product lines to accommodate the tastes of clients from other regions. The same Cheerios magically sold under a new name—"Bagel Seeds." Then we introduced little thistle burrs (the small parts of weeds that stick in our socks when we walk through a field). We bagged them and sold them as "Porcupine Eggs!" That day Ted and I sold 457 Baggies, splitting the gross income of $685.50 to net $300.00 each.

Yes, the free enterprise system, with its countless opportunities for entrepreneurship, works! But it only works when we do!

Sweet Liberty

I need to share a love affair about a lady in my life,
She's always there, her beauty rare, a stalwart strength in
    strife.
A knight in shining armor, she stands so proud to see,
Defending God's great plan for man, to be all we can be.

She says: "Give me your tired, give me your poor . . ."
No matter what your race or creed,
Her flame's burning bright, lighting freedom's door.
A symbol of our destiny,
To some she's just a lady,
But to me, she's my Sweet Liberty.

I've been alone with her at night as she lights the harbor
    sky.
I've watched her pray for peace each day, her hand and
    torch held high.
She whispers words of love and hope and faith that free will
    be
Why can't the whole world listen in and live in harmony?

She welcomes in the hungry child; the homeless, helpless
    friend.
They come to her with yearning hearts, their huddled
    masses blend.
She teaches justice is for all, a brother/sister plan;
She's there to keep life's dream alive for the family of man.

She says: "Give me your tired, give me your poor . . ."
No matter what your race or creed,
Her flame's burning bright, lighting freedom's door.
A symbol of our destiny,
To some she's just a lady,
But to me, she's my Sweet Liberty.

Attention!

The occasion was the state high school conference for the Texans' War on Drugs. The setting was a high school gymnasium, crammed with over 2,000 teenagers waiting for the opening general session to begin. A young man strolled up to the stage, stood on one foot with his left elbow resting on the podium, put his right hand on his stomach and casually began to recite the Pledge of Allegiance. Suddenly a tall, dark-haired man rose from his chair on the stage. It was apparent that he was the director of the organization presiding over this event. The man walked to the podium and interrupted the young man's recitation.

"My name is General Robinson Risner. I was the highest ranking prisoner-of-war in the Vietnam War. I spent seven years locked up in solitary confinement. I was tortured beyond belief. I limp because of it. Today I still have a hole in the front of my skull from the Chinese water torture inflicted on me. I willingly and proudly gave up years of my life defending our flag and our country and all the sacred and wonderful principles that they represent. America is the greatest country on the planet, the international leader of human rights and of the free world. And you should show this country and her flag abiding respect. Hundreds of thousands of American soldiers have died for this flag. This young man's actions today were a disgrace to everything we hold dear—especially to the very freedom that allows us to gather here today. Therefore, let's do this again."

General Risner continued, "When we say the Pledge of Allegiance we stand at attention. We place our right hands over our hearts, we look directly at the flag and we say the words with conviction and pride. Please join me." A respectful silence filled the room. He then recited the Pledge in a way that I had never before heard—in a way that touched my life forever—in a way that taught everyone present the true meaning of *patriotism, duty, honor* and *country*.

It's been a few years since that significant experience, yet every time I see an American flag I vividly remember it. The flag is more than colored cloth. It symbolizes everything for which America stands—every little thing and every single person that have ever contributed to making America great. Flag-burners and disrespectful leaders who flippantly mouth the words of our Pledge should rethink their actions. You can be anti-war, anti-democrat, anti-republican, anti-guns or anti-abortion—but don't ever be anti-American. The flag is not a symbol of any special interest group, political or social faction, racial group or sexual preference. The flag is the symbol of a free republic and democratic society wherein we can all celebrate our differences, and most important, be free to do so. The flag is what binds us together.

The flag is part of you and it is part of me and it waves for all the world to see everything we have the opportunity to be. Standing at attention for our flag is key. Show some dignity!

Lucky Loser

Cecil Burns, the son of a Texas gambler, was born in a tent and grew up in the West. He never set any goals, had no material cravings, and had no ambitions other than hunting and fishing. He was content as a drifter. He was also a regular customer at the Salvation Army Harbor Light Mission in Seattle.

Then one day an unbelievable thing happened to Cecil. A once-in-a-lifetime opportunity not only stared him in the face, it actually grabbed him and filled his pockets.

At the age of fifty-six, Cecil hopped on a train and ended up in Las Vegas, Nevada. On April 3, 1982, he walked into the Circus Circus Hotel and Casino and began playing a slot machine. A few minutes later he took a walk to stretch his legs. When he returned he found that someone else was using that machine.

While he was waiting for the person to finish, he plunked a few silver dollars into the nearby Silver Strike slot machine and hit the jackpot. Cecil Burns won $400,000 in cash and became instantly wealthy. In fact, this opportunity could have set him up financially for the rest of his life. All he had to do was put the money into a no-risk money market certificate at his local bank. Since interest was a phenomenal 15 percent at that time, he could have lived nicely for the rest of his life.

The night he won the money, Circus Circus gave him the royal suite. The next day he bought a new car and hired a chauffeur. Not only had he "made it," but he was going to make it even better. Leaving his car and driver behind, he caught a plane to Reno, Nevada, played the slots there, returned to Vegas, played there, and continued back and forth from Reno to Vegas for the next several days. During this week of weakness, Burns lost over $300,000 trying to hit another $400,000 jackpot.

Returning to Skid Row no different or better off than when he left, Cecil Burns had a brand-new car, but no money to buy gas, and took up life as he knew it. It was as though the magical jackpot had never happened.

The lesson? In America we can be really lucky. Luck is the moment when opportunity, timing, proactive risk taking and hard work all coincide. But if we are not prepared when luck comes calling, it will be as though we hit a magical jackpot and never even knew it.

The American Family

General Colin Powell said it best: "We have to start thinking of America as a family. We have to stop screeching at each other, stop hurting each other, and start caring for, sacrificing for and sharing with each other. We have to stop criticizing, which is the way of the malcontent, and instead get back to the can-do attitude that made America great!"

General Powell was talking about rebuilding our sense of community when he asked us to think of our nation as a family. We may be of different races and creed—which is nothing more than being tall, short, fat, thin, blonde or brunette. Even so, we're still considered American.

One characteristic of American culture is that when problems arise we solve them—the Great Depression, the bombing of Pearl Harbor, World War II, the Korean War, the oil shortage, the Vietnam War, the Gulf War. We reject the psychology of cannot in favor of the can-do attitude.

Despite those who want you to believe otherwise, the system is not broken. It works. The system is the United States of America.

In fact, it requires only an elementary understanding of history to appreciate how robust and healthy the system is.

The United States and other democracies were challenged by fascism in World War II. We were challenged by communism during the Cold War. The system was able to shake off the antiestablishment strife during the 1960s and 1970s and master the dramatic economic shifts of the eighties. We have overcome the assassination of two presidents and the resignation of another.

Within our land the concept of racial equality was once compromised by misdirected segregation laws. The Civil Rights Movement rectified that injustice. The system is still in the process of working. It works well and it will continue as long as we pledge our allegiance with confidence and trust.

Blurring the Lines

Talk radio is the verbal salt and pepper of lunchtime conversations. It fills the editorial pages with letters to the editors. Certainly, part of this fascination with protest results from the information explosion. We think we know at least as much about issues as those in positions of authority. In this widely divergent nation, whatever any authority chooses to do, someone will find objectionable.

And it's usually the passionate critics who write or call or complain. Supporters are less motivated to express their views. Besides, complainers generate more readers and listeners than do backers.

There's nothing wrong with criticism.

It may be healthy to condemn a government policy; it is decidedly unhealthy to condemn the institution of government. It may be appropriate to bring down a president; it is not appropriate to bring down with him the office of the presidency. It may be worthwhile to denounce a senator; it is worthless to denounce the United States Senate.

There's a fine line between attacking the individual and attacking the institution. When we blur those lines, we inflict damage upon the institutional structure of the nation. Why is it we never hear from the people who are content?

Remember that America was founded on a dream and now it's our turn to keep that dream viable. Americans have always been courageous, determined, fearless and bold. Who among us ever wants to say that we no longer possess those qualities?

We look to you, the backers and supporters, the positive movers and shakers, to refute the negative complainers. You must meet the great challenge, reach beyond the commonplace and not fall short as a result of a lack of either creativity or courage. To do this all you need is the desire to do better than ever before—all you need is the faith that you will achieve your goal. All you need is to act—and the time to act is now!

That's the Way It Is

For 30 years Walter Cronkite covered the events that shaped American history. He was one of the first television journalists; he later become the anchorman for CBS News.

Cronkite would always end his evening newscast with the short phrase "And that's the way it is."

In a recent television special Cronkite was asked what he saw coming for Americans in the 21st century. He said, "Well, it's been the best of times and the worst of times. And as we run down now to the end of this 100 years, we can all recite our litany of despair: overpopulation, pollution, a faltering education system, the rich getting richer, the poor getting poorer, racial tension, drugs and too many guns. But if there's anything I've learned, it's that we Americans have a way of rising to the challenges that confront us just when it seems that we're most divided. We show our remarkable solidarity. The 20th century may be leaving us with a host of problems, but I've also noticed that it does seem darkest before the dawn. There's reason to hope for the next century. And that's the way it will be."

14

GREATER
SENSITIVITY

If a man is called to be a street sweeper, he should sweep
streets even as Michelangelo painted or Beethoven
composed music or Shakespeare wrote poetry. He should
sweep streets so well that all the hosts of heaven and earth
will pause to say, "Here lived a great street sweeper who
did his job well." We must celebrate our differences
and be sensitive to who we are.

—DR. MARTIN LUTHER KING JR.

Don't be afraid
to fail and confess.
If you fail more
than most even
try and
learn why,

you'll *fail your
way to success.*

Needed?

I was speaking to members of Our Primary Purpose (O.P.P.), a highly acclaimed program for chemically dependent teenagers in Des Moines, Iowa. At the third meeting, just for parents, a mother shared this story:

Her 20-year-old son John (who incidentally was not enrolled in the O.P.P. program) was handsome and talented, a good citizen, a good student, a good musician and a good athlete. He also had a lovely girlfriend and seemingly no problems. One day he stopped talking as much as he usually did. Thirty days passed and his conversation dwindled to nothing. He was depressed and his parents and girlfriend continually told him that they loved him. He knew that they loved him and he expressed his love for them. Everyone was concerned about his well-being and wondered what they could say or do to help him, since "I love you" obviously wasn't enough to improve the situation.

John finally made a move. He locked himself in the cellar. Although he was down in the dim dampness for three days, without food, he continued to acknowledge his parents' love for him and his love for them. His depression deepened and his loved ones were convinced suicide was imminent. Health care professionals were brought in but the counseling, kindness, caring and love were all to no avail.

On the third day of John's isolation, the local high school football coach (who incidentally didn't know what was going on in John's life) called his home to talk to him. John's mother said John was busy and took a message at the coach's request. Then she went to the cellar door and called down the stairs, "John, Coach Ivers just phoned. He said that his players voted last night on who they wanted as their assistant coach. They said you were the greatest Pop Warner football coach they had ever had and now they think they can win the state championship if you help coach them. Coach Ivers said they need you—he needs you! He said if you're interested you should be at football practice at 2:45 this afternoon."

Do you know what happened? Sure you do! John came out of the cellar and went to practice. He accepted the coaching job and by the time he came home from his first practice, he had snapped out of his depression. He once again felt needed, wanted and important, and was back to his old self.

No One Helped

In New York, Joel Shulman never felt so alone and terrified in his life.

"I could feel the chain links of her leash slipping through my fingers, but there was nothing I could do," he told me.

Shulman, a blind jazz pianist, stood on a subway platform on a Sunday night as his Seeing Eye dog fell onto the tracks. Shulman could only cry out, "Bess, Bess come on up here, girl."

Moments later the 17-year-old Labrador retriever was crushed beneath the wheels of a subway train.

"As the train got closer, I could feel the momentum of the approaching cars and I knew there was nothing I could do," said Shulman. "There was no way I could stop the train. I cried out but the people on the platform just watched, not one took 10 minutes of their time to help me, even after they'd seen my dog crushed under the weight of the train. Nobody answered my screams, they just boarded their trains. I shook all over and had to inch and feel my way up the subway platform alone."

Shulman didn't go to work that night. He stayed home and mourned the loss of the most gentle and affectionate animal he had ever known.

Has our society reached a level of paranoia so great that hundreds of people would leave a blind man stranded on a subway platform because they're afraid to help? Have we let the crime reports turn us into an entire generation of persons too afraid to get involved—too scared to help someone in need? Ask yourself: Would I help someone who couldn't get me a starting position, a better job, a fancier car or an elected office? Would I stop a fight, put out a fire or administer first aid to a stranger?

When we see people in trouble we should ask how we can help, instead of pretending we're watching a television program. We must check our level of human decency. For even if there is no immediate and tangible reward, the kind deed will surely come back to us in some other way.

Pause and Patiently Ponder

A man came out of his home to admire his new truck. To his puzzlement, his three-year-old son was happily hammering dents into the shiny paint. The man ran to his son, knocked him away, hammered the little boy's hands into a pulp as punishment.

When the father calmed down, he rushed his son to the hospital. Although the doctor tried desperately to save the crushed bones, he finally had to amputate the fingers from both of the boy's hands.

When the child woke up from surgery and saw his bandaged stubs, he innocently said, "Daddy, I'm sorry about your truck." Then he asked, "But when are my fingers going to grow back?"

The father went home and committed suicide.

Think about this story the next time you see someone spill milk at the dinner table or hear a baby crying. Think first before you lose your patience with someone you love. Trucks can be repaired. Broken bones and hurt feelings often can't.

Too often we fail to recognize the difference between the person and the performance. People make mistakes. We are allowed to make mistakes. But the actions we take while in a rage will haunt us forever.

Pause and ponder. Think before you act. Be patient. Understand and love.

Think Before You Act

An Alaskan trapper lost his wife and was left to care for his two-year-old daughter. At times he had to leave the little girl with his faithful dog so he could work in the woods.

While away one afternoon a terrible blizzard came up. The trapper was forced to take refuge in a hollow tree. At daybreak he rushed to his cabin and found the door was open. His dog was covered with blood. There was no little girl anywhere. The father was terrified that something awful had happened. Fearful that his dog had killed and eaten his child, the trapper reached for his ax. In one swift move he smashed the skull of his loyal and trusted canine companion.

Like a maniac he tore through the cabin searching for his missing girl. Suddenly a faint cry came from under the bed. There was his daughter, safe and sound. Looking further he found the bloody remains of a wolf in the corner. Then he knew—the dog had saved the child from the fangs of the wolf.

If he had only stopped to assess the situation rationally, the trapper could have held both his child and his dog in his arms. Weigh all factors before you make a move.

Those who act hastily regret their actions later. It happens all the time. Judgments made irrationally are clouded by a lack of information. The whole picture is hazy. So get the facts before you act.

A Very Bad Day

Michelle had a terrible day at school. When she got home she found her little brother and his friend playing with her lipstick. "Stay out of my stuff, you little pest," she shrieked.

Her brother's face turned beet red. He apologized but Michelle didn't let up. She ignored him during dinner and even the next morning as she got ready for school. He begged her not to be mad at him and to forgive him. But she decided to hold her grudge and make him pay, thinking she would accept his apology later that afternoon.

Sadly, when she came home from school, it was too late. She found her brother's badly twisted bike on the lawn. Her mother and father were sitting in the front room crying. There on the ground, with a sheet over his head, was her little brother. Johnny was dead.

Michelle begged him to be alive. She thought of all the reasons she loved him. She wished she could take him in her arms and say, "I love you, I forgive you. Playing with my makeup was no big deal."

Do you ever have those bad days when you want to scream at everyone—even at those you really care about? If you do, think again.

In life we can't afford to wait to tell others how we feel. Call, phone, write, tell, listen, learn, laugh and love today!

Killing Time

Dr. Robert McCarthy was a man to be admired—a successful medical doctor with a lovely wife and three beautiful daughters. He loved helping people and was greatly appreciated by his patients.

Doc McCarthy knew the secret of maximizing time. Every hour was 60 precious minutes and he didn't waste a tick of the clock. When he wasn't healing the sick he was playing with his little girls. At night while his neighbors watched TV, Bob was busy with projects and new ideas. He and his wife would lie awake in bed and talk for hours. They were afraid to lose a minute of living. And for good reason. The leukemia in his body was draining Bob's strength. He knew he was dying and he wanted to live life to the fullest, loving every blessed breath.

So the next time you're killing time, remember Dr. Bob McCarthy. Make the most of every precious moment. Our life on Earth is limited. There is always more we can do with the time we have. Make the most it.

The day will come when an accounting is due. What will you have on your ledger sheet?

A Shocking Word of Wisdom

Steve was careful about his drinking because his wife Melba worried. She said liquor made him too confident and not cautious.

Women never really understand their men, he thought. Instead, they always worry about things that never happen. Steve snapped up the shot glass, tilted his head and nodded to the bartender as he left.

Outside he thought about how happy he was. Steve owned a house and Melba was pregnant again. He hoped it would be a girl since they already had an 18-month-old son.

Steve was hurrying to pick up Melba at the doctor's office. Although the car skidded slightly on the icy roads, he wanted to hurry since he'd stopped at the bar. He speeded up a notch, then suddenly realized he couldn't make the turn at the bottom of the hill. The car was headed for the guard rail that was set around the edge of the lake. To compensate, Steve propped his door open with his briefcase so he could get out when they hit. He planned to jump out and swim to the bank.

People saw the old car coming and watched as it splashed into the water. As he planned, Steve got out safely and swam for shore. People cheered when he arrived safely. He thought, *See, I can handle my liquor.*

As he stood there smiling, waving to the crowd and watching his car submerge, Steve's heart sank. His little boy Jared was still strapped in his car seat in the back of the car.

Mixers

Maybe you were waiting for a traffic light to change from red to green when you noticed you were just a tad too far into the intersection. You backed up a little to play it safe and when the light changed you were still in reverse. Or maybe the guy in front of you was driving for the last 50 miles with his turn signal flashing and you couldn't pass him for fear that "this might be it."

When we drive we all make some dumb mistakes. But there's one fatal mistake none of us should ever make. Every year 50,000 people are killed—and even more sustain injuries that permanently affect them—as a result of drunk driving. Eighty percent of first drunk driving offense accidents end in death. That means you don't get a second chance—your first mistake is your last.

When I was in high school a drunken joyride turned a car into a deathtrap for four 17-year-olds with everything to live for and what had, the day before, seemed like their whole lives ahead of them. If you drink, don't drive. If you're driving, don't drink. In fact, if we're really honest with ourselves, we probably shouldn't drink at all. If we drink to "take the edge off and eliminate our inhibitions," we are insecure. If we drink because "it is expected in certain circles as a social grace," we are weak. Nonalcoholic beverages are equally accepted for toasts and significant celebrations.

On a financial note, anyone who drinks beer knows how long it stays with you. They shouldn't sell it, they should rent it! It's a waste of money, usually a waste of time and, when irresponsibly consumed, a waste of life. How many breadwinners stop at the local watering hole on their way home from work and drink away much of their paycheck, when the responsible thing is to spend it on their families? Think of the countless, wonderful things we could do for charities with the money we squander on "catching a buzz."

"Yeah, but . . ." they say, as they block this common sense thinking out. "Be reasonable, you fanatical prude," they scream:

It's nobody's business what I drink!
I care not what the neighbors think.
Or how many laws they choose to pass!
I'll tell the world "I'll have my glass!"
Here's one man's freedom that cannot be curbed,
My right to drink is undisturbed.

So he drank in spite of law or man,
Then got into his old tin can:
Stepped on the gas and let it go,
Down the highway to and fro.
He took the curves at 50 miles
With bleary eyes and drunken smiles.

Not long till a car he tried to pass;
There was a crash, a scream and breaking glass.
The other car was upside down,
About two miles from the nearest town.

The man was clear but his wife was caught,
And she needed the help of that drunken sot,
Who sat in a maudlin, drunken daze,
And heard the scream and saw the blaze,
But was too far gone to save a life,
By lifting the car from off his wife.

The car was burned and the mother died,
While a husband wept and baby cried,
And a drunk sat by—and still some think
It's nobody's business what they drink!

Look Hard Before You Leave

Why is the grass always greener somewhere else? Some people spend their whole lives looking for happiness when it's right under their feet. Teenagers run away looking for a better life, but they rarely find it. Divorce is rampant. The truth is happiness is where you are—you make your own.

In the mid-1800s, a man sold his ranch in northern California to look for gold nuggets. The new owner put a mill on a stream that ran through the property. One day his little girl brought home some sand from the stream in a jar and sifted through it. In the sand were the first shiny nuggets of gold to be found in California.

If the man had stayed put, he could have had all the gold he ever needed. Since that day, $38 million in gold has been taken out of those few acres he sold.

It's better to try and make the most of what you have before trying to find happiness elsewhere. Maybe what can really make you happy is just hidden from your sight, temporarily out of view for a while. So look hard. Dig in where you are before you sell. Study the problems that might be pushing you away from your loved ones before you leave something very important behind. As two songs remind us, don't be "Looking for Love in All the Wrong Places" and "Don't Know What You've Got till It's Gone."

15

LEADERSHIP

DISCIPLINE, ANGER, FEAR

Let each man learn to know himself.
To gain that knowledge, let him labor,
Improve those failings in himself,
Which he condemned so in his neighbor.
How lenient our own faults we view,
We ignore them in hopes they'll smother;
But, oh, how harshly we review
The self-same errors in another.
At moments when you're all alone,
Cannot your deeds be thoughtless?
Look deep within, don't cast that stone,
You, yourself, are not pure and faultless.
Your example is a lesson taught each day
A light which others are apt to borrow.
So first, improve yourself today,
And then improve your friends tomorrow.

—PHILIP DELAMARE

It's
what
you
do

when the coach
isn't around that
makes you a
Champion.

Who Has the Key?

Years ago an old man sat in a cathedral playing the organ. The music was melancholy since the old man was about to be replaced by one much younger.

When the replacement arrived the old man stood, removed the organ key, put it in his pocket and walked toward the door.

"The key, please," said the young man.

The organist handed him the key and quickly walked away. The young man sat down to play and from his hands came the music of a genius. Such harmony had never been heard before. It resounded through the town and over the countryside, filling the hearts of all who heard it with awe.

The old man listened with tears in his eyes as Johann Sebastian Bach ran his magical hands over the keyboard. *What if I hadn't given him the key?* the old man asked himself.

As we go through life, keys can make all the difference between greatness and nothingness. Perhaps someone will hand you the key that will unlock the secrets, or, perhaps, you will give the key to somebody else. It works both ways—keys are given and received—and the world can reap the rewards.

The Key to Strength

Little Jeff was trying unsuccessfully to move a heavy rock. His father stood nearby and finally asked why he wasn't using all his strength. The boy assured his dad that he was.

The father said, "But why aren't you asking me to help?"

Successful leaders use all their strength. That means they ask for help when they need it. Effective rulers delegate authority and utilize all available resources to increase their power.

The key to leadership means getting others around you involved—making them know their efforts are important to the common goal. The more you inspire them to do their part, the better things will turn out for all of you.

He Who Travels the Road Best

Once upon a time a king had a great highway built. Before he opened it to the public, he had a contest to see who could travel the highway best.

On the appointed day the people came. Some had fine chariots, some used their feet. But no matter what vehicle they used, all of them complained that there was a large pile of rocks on the side of the road in one particular spot, which hindered their progress.

At the end of the day a lone traveler crossed the finish line and wearily walked over to the king. He was smudged with dirt but he spoke with respect as he handed the monarch a bag of gold.

"I stopped along the way to clear a pile of rocks," he said. "And under it was a bag of gold. Can you find the rightful owner?"

Solemnly the king replied, "You are the rightful owner. You have earned the gold by winning the contest. For he who travels the road best is he who makes the road smoother for those who follow."

So it is in life. While people scramble to outdo each other, every now and then a leader comes along to pave the way for the rest of us. To these leaders are given the rewards—the sacks of gold called fame and fortune.

Be Honest

Gerhardt, a little German shepherd boy, was extremely poor. One day as he was watching his flock, a hunter came out of the woods and asked him the way to the nearest village. When the boy told him, the hunter said that if the boy would show him the way, he would reward the boy handsomely. When Gerhardt replied that he could not leave his sheep for fear they might be lost, the hunter said, "Well, what of that? They are not your sheep, and the loss of one or two would not matter to your master. I will give you more money than you have earned in a year."

When the boy still declined, the hunter said, "Then will you trust me with your sheep while you go to the village and return with food, drink and a guide for me?"

The boy shook his head saying, "The sheep do not know your voice."

Angrily, the hunter retorted, "Can't you trust me?"

Gerhardt reminded the hunter, "You tried to get me to break faith with my master. How do I know that you would keep your word to me?"

Cornered, the hunter laughed and said, "I see you are a good and faithful boy. I will not forget you. Show me the road and I will try to make it out by myself."

The hunter turned out to be the grand duke, and he was so pleased with Gerhardt's honesty that he later sent for him and sponsored his education. Though Gerhardt became a rich and powerful man, he remained honest and true in all his dealings in life and in his leadership.

Patton on Leadership

General George S. Patton was a master at turning adversity into victory. He could take the worst situation and make it a glorious conquest. Patton boldly proclaimed, "I am a soldier. I fight where I'm told, and I win where I fight."

Patton often said, "May God have mercy on my enemies because I won't."

He knew that we can defeat our competition by being responsible and accountable for our own successes. Rivalry is not a place for the faint of heart. Each of us must take personal responsibility—an I'm-in-charge-of-me mentality.

"Battle is the most magnificent competition in which a human being can indulge," said Patton. "It brings out all that is best. It removes all that is base."

He also observed, "A pint of sweat will save a gallon of blood."

And Patton also wrote: "Never tell people how to do things. Tell what to do and they will surprise you with their ingenuity."

Each of us has the courage and cunning to be successful. Or, as Patton said, "If I do my full duty, the rest will take care of itself."

Great leaders see the organization as a whole. They look for teamwork knowing that turmoil is divisive. They want better communication, for without it soldiers in battle cannot survive. They look for each member of the group to take the initiative.

Patton once said, "If everyone is thinking alike, then somebody isn't thinking."

And he lectured his troops with these brilliant words: "Don't think your job is unimportant. Every single man and woman has a job to do, and it must be done. Every person is a vital link in a great chain. Every department, every unit is important in the vast scheme of this great endeavor. Always remember, victory is the prize and it's worth everything."

What Really Makes a Leader?

During the 1968 Special Olympics—a special competition for mentally and physically handicapped athletes—Kim Peek was in the 50-yard dash.

Kim is brain-damaged and physically-handicapped. He was racing against two other cerebral palsy victims. They were in wheelchairs and Kim was the lone runner. As the gun sounded, Kim moved quickly ahead. Ten yards from the finish line, he turned to see how the others were coming. One girl had turned her wheelchair around and was stuck against the wall. The other boy was pushing his wheelchair with his feet.

Kim stopped and retraced his steps. He pushed the little girl across the finish line. Meanwhile, the boy going backward won the race. The girl took second. Kim lost.

Or did he?

The greatest leader and champion doesn't always win the race but gains recognition by serving others.

Do As I Say

Leading by example is the only way to show that you mean what you say.

I'd rather see a sermon preached than hear one any day.
I'd rather someone walk with me than merely point the way.
The eye's a better pupil, and more willing than the ear.
Fine counsel is confusing, but example is always clear.
The finest preachers are the men who live their creeds,
To see good put into action is what everybody needs.
I can learn to do it if you'll let me see it done.
Your hand I see in action, your tongue too fast may run.
And the lecture you deliver may be very well and true.
But I'd rather get my lesson by observing what you do.
For I might understand you, the high advice you give.
But there's no misunderstanding how you act and how you live.

This poem helps us understand the origin of morale.
What is morale?

It's the mental and emotional condition of a group of people as they face the tasks at hand. It includes confidence, enthusiasm, loyalty and a common purpose.

No team wins if the team members are fighting among themselves.

How about rules? Do you respect the rules or break them? When rules are broken, even by one person, the team suffers.

Relaxing rules only causes morale to drop. We must be taught personal responsibility for our actions. Enthusiasm and purpose initiate morale, rules sustain it. The great leaders in any organization make sure the people under them are following the rules. To do so requires that they lead by example. If you want to improve morale, it's not enough to practice what you preach. Preach only what you practice!

When They Need to Be

Champions may not be great all the time but they are always great when they need to be. The reason they are able to rise to any occasion is twofold. First, crisis does not make or break the man or woman, it merely reveals his or her true character. Champions are cool and consistent in both good times and bad. Second, pressure is not natural, you create it by questioning your own ability. When you know what you can do, there is never any question.

Ever since he was an 18-year-old freshman at the University of North Carolina, Michael Jordan has shown that he fully comprehends this philosophy. Champions know that when tough moments roll around, they can do whatever is needed. There is no reason to worry or waver. You don't wonder *if* you can. Because prior, proper, perfect preparation prevents poor performance, you *know* you can and so at the critical moment you are ready for anything.

When the outcome of a game is on the line, Michael Jordan wants the ball in his hands. There is no pressure, only confidence—no panic, only resolve. Long ago when his 15-foot jump shot soared through the air and into the hoop, netting his college team the NCAA Basketball Tournament victory, we sensed he was a champion. Now that he is a member of the Chicago Bulls, responsible for his team's winning NBA Championship Games at the buzzer, he has confirmed our first impression of him. He has become the standard of excellence we all strive to attain—in and out of sports. You may have asked yourself how he does it. Now you know! Michael Jordan fully comprehends that if you are not training and pushing yourself to your ultimate capacity and potential as a human being, someone else—somewhere else—is. And when you meet that "someone else" in competition, he or she will win. Leaders are not born, they are made. If Jordan can be one, so can the rest of us!

What Motivates Us?

There is a difference between inspiration and motivation. Inspiration affects our attitude—the way we think. Motivation affects our behavior—the way we act. For this reason no one person can motivate another. All we can hope to do is inspire one another to each motivate ourselves. Motivation must come from within. Fear is a common motivator. Think of it as the do-it-or-else method. Reward is another common motivator, thought by many to be the best one of all. Yet, the only motivation that works all the time—regardless of the circumstances—is self-motivation. Self-motivation is self-discipline—which means "minding ourselves." Therefore, *self-disciplined motivation* means doing something simply because we want to do it and doing the right thing simply because it's the right thing to do—both are examples of lasting, top-notch motivation.

Motivation by fear may work temporarily, but only as long as the person instilling the fear in you is there. Motivation by reward doesn't work unless we choose the reward and, even then, the reward eventually loses its luster and charm—no external, material motivator can ever keep us motivated long-term. Enough is never enough.

Self-motivation, on the other hand, forces us to ask the question "Why should I?" The answer can only come from within. Arriving at the answer will help us discover what will satisfy our inner needs—whatever they may be.

Discover the joy of self-motivation, the joy of accomplishing an important goal because you wanted to, not because somebody forced you to do it by threatening dire consequences if you didn't, or coerced you to do it by promising you a reward if you did.

To stay focused, authentic and motivated in all that you do simply check and clean up your motives—be honest with yourself about why you do what you do—and ensure that you replace any actions that are externally motivated with good, pure, powerful, positive self-motivation. Remember that it's what we do when the leader, manager, preacher, parent, coach or teacher is not around that makes us champions!

Input Equals Output

I conducted a leadership experiment with a large group of people in a convention hall. I divided the group down the middle and asked half to close their eyes. The individuals with their eyes open saw an overhead projection of the words: *Oranges, Apples, Bananas.* I asked the group to remember these three words and then I removed the projection.

I now had the groups reverse roles so that open eyes were shut and closed eyes were open. For the individuals in the group that now had their eyes open, I displayed an overhead projection of three different words: *X-Rated, Violence, Sex.* I asked the group to remember these three words and then I removed the projection.

Everyone's eyes were now open. I then displayed an overhead projection of the following: R_PE. I then asked the members of each group to recall the three words they had seen and fill in the appropriate missing letter. Those who had seen *Oranges, Apples, Bananas* filled in the blank with the letter *I.* There could be no other choice for them but *RIPE.* Those who had seen *X-Rated, Violence, Sex* filled in the blank with the letter *A.* There could be no other choice for them but *RAPE.* Think about the far-reaching consequences of this conditioning process. There is a gigantic difference in meaning between *ripe* and *rape*! In the space of 60 seconds I managed to condition their minds so they thought exactly the way I wanted them to think. This scares me—what goes in really does come out. We are the products of our own thought processes. If we think positively, we act positively and positive outcomes result. Conversely, if we think negatively, we act negatively and negative outcomes result. Even the way we visualize others coincides with this input/output formula. A person may not be as good or as bad as you say he or she is now, but will be immediately thereafter. We each rise to the level of expectation that we set, which is far too often the level of expectation that others set for us, and we become what we think we can become. Good leaders are aware of this and, therefore, always input positive information to themselves and others.

You Can If You Think You Can

In December 1982 my dear friend Bob Coyne of Brantford, Ontario, decided to host a junior hockey team from Sweden. In exchange, the members of Bob's Canadian junior team would travel to Sweden the following year as guests of the Swedish team. The team from Sweden arrived in Canada on Boxing Day (December 26). This team was the pride and joy of Stockholm. It consisted of 14- and 15-year-old boys, handpicked from Stockholm and its vicinity, and was reputed to be a notoriously tough hockey club. As hosts, Bob and his team were to provide the Swedish team with a tour of each of the seven different communities where it would play its seven exhibition games. The final game was to be between the Stockholm team and Bob's Brantford team.

Upon arriving in Canada the Stockholm team's hope, of course, was to win all seven games and return home with grand tales of victory. It was the first time away from home for these kids, they were suffering from jet lag to boot and they lost their first game by a dismal 8-1 score. It was a staggering defeat for them. They were a little more prepared for the second game, but again they lost, this time 4-2. They lost the third and fourth games as well. The fifth game was a devastating 9-1 lashing.

At this point in the tour, which was somewhere around New Year's Day, Bob decided they needed a break in the action—a diversion to rally their confidence and rebuild their self-esteem. Bob arranged a visit to Toronto to see the CN Tower, the National Hockey League Hall of Fame and other points of interest. The Swedish team would play no hockey for two entire days, but could swim and play basketball at a local high school for entertainment and exercise.

At the end of the Toronto trip, Bob took them to the student center to sit and relax while they waited for the bus to pick them up and take them back to their sponsoring homes. The coach of the Stockholm team asked Bob if there was something he could say to his team that might psych them up for the next game. Bob was neither prepared nor thinking in those terms but he decided, on the spur of the moment, to see if he could touch their emotions.

Bob started talking to them about home, which got them right up off their chairs. He asked them if they missed their moms and dads, and if the time zone change was bothering them. Bob explained that in Stockholm there were fewer daylight hours during the winter than there were in Canada and surely this change was affecting them. Bob finally steered the conversation towards hockey, reflecting on their five losses in a row, which surely was not typical of the team, and how they all must feel about these losses. Bob concluded by suggesting that what they needed was something to which they could reach out and relate. He told them that all they needed was the confidence to believe in themselves again. So he left them with a phrase he had heard many other times: "You can if you think you can." Bob then repeated this phrase to each kid individually while he looked each one squarely in the eye. When he had repeated the phrase to each one of them he left the room. A few moments later the bus arrived and they all left.

Bob really didn't think he had convinced them, but he went home prepared to reinforce the idea anyway. He made a big sign bearing the phrase YOU CAN IF YOU THINK YOU CAN and took it with him to the next game, which was held at the Six Nations Indian Reservation just south of Francis. Six Nations had a top-notch hockey club and the Stockholm team knew it. Even prior to arriving in Canada, the Stockholm team was prepared that if it lost a game it would be either to Six Nations or to Brantford.

Game time arrived and the Swedish team was still in the locker room. They didn't appear to be coming out, so Bob went in to see what was happening. Most of the team members hung their heads while their coach addressed them, and Bob could see they just weren't up for the game. They turned to look at Bob when he barged in. He smiled broadly and said, "Remember, 'you can if you think you can'!" He waved to the Swedish coach and swiftly exited the locker room.

Bob then hung the sign he had made, unbeknownst to the Swedish team, on the back of their team bench. A minute later the Swedish team emerged and saw the sign. Spontaneously, every member of the team touched the sign.

From there they went out onto the ice, warmed up and then faced off to open the game.

Very early on they took a 1-0 lead and again they all jumped the boards, touched the sign and went back out for the face-off. The game continued. The Swedish team scored another goal and again each member of the team touched the sign. Six Nations came back to tie the game, but for those kids who hadn't won a single game during their entire tour, the tie was as good as a win. The tie put them on top of the world—the noise during the bus ride home was unbelievable!

That brings us to the last day of the tournament. Bob's Brantford team was the Stockholm team's last opponent. He had arranged to pick up the Stockholm team's coach at his hotel room for a pre-game lunch. When Bob entered the coach's room he saw the YOU CAN IF YOU THINK YOU CAN sign propped up on the headboard of the bed. Bob thought it was kind of funny, but he could see that the Stockholm coach really believed it because, as they left for the arena, he grabbed the sign to hang over his bench.

When the Swedish team came onto the ice, they performed the same ritual as they had at Six Nations—each player touched the sign before the start of the game. This final game of the series was a highly competitive, spirited contest and Stockholm beat Brantford by two points. Every time the Swedish team scored they touched the sign and also skated past Bob's bench grinning and triumphantly shaking their fists at him. There was a party for the team after the game ended and the next morning the players flew home to Stockholm.

The following December Bob's team arrived in Stockholm for the exchange tournament. The setup for sports in Sweden is different from the setup in Canada. The Swedes have sports clubs for almost every sport, but all the clubs play in the same arena. The sports building is in downtown Stockholm and Bob and his junior team went there for a reception following their arrival in Sweden. As they entered the main lobby of the huge, city-owned, government-operated arena Bob noticed the YOU CAN IF YOU THINK CAN sign hanging on the wall about 12 feet from the floor.

The sign was nicely framed and beneath it was an inscription of the story of its origin and impact. Bob was surprised, happy and choked up all at the same time.

To this day, that sign still graces the lobby of the Stockholm sports complex, teaching the value of the power of positive thinking leadership to all who enter!

The Kid Who Couldn't Talk

Little Winston was a tongue-tied, pudgy, ugly kid. He stammered when he spoke and he couldn't get his ideas straight enough to say a complete sentence. But he knew he could do better.

While his classmates went out and played sports, Winston began reading biographies of great men and women. He studied quotations collected by Bartlett and committed them to memory.

As he outgrew his childhood stumbling blocks, he became respected for his leadership qualities and his forthright ideas. He was never a slender man, nor could anyone say he was handsome. But Winston Churchill changed the history of the world when he rallied his fellow Englishmen against the tyranny of the Nazis.

Churchill became prime minister of England. He was known and respected throughout the world for his brilliant mind and his command of language.

While his classmates were out playing, Churchill knew he could do better. His quiet hours of dedication and determination proved him right.

16

IT'S NOT WHAT'S ON THE OUTSIDE

Dogs bark at a person whom they do not know.

—HERACLITUS

It's What's Inside That Counts

On a spring day, a balloon salesman was trying to sell his wares to passersby in New York's Central Park. Every now and then he'd let one rise into the sky.

A small African-American girl said, "If you let a black balloon go, will it rise, too?"

"It doesn't matter what color the balloon is," he said. "It's not what's on the outside that makes it soar. It's what's inside."

People are people. We live in different color skins. There's no one right color to be. Think of humanity as different flavored ice creams. The basic ingredients are the same. And when it's hot, we all melt.

Bigotry and racism cause hate. Instead, see people as books with separate covers. Do you judge a book by its cover? If you do, you might be missing a good story.

Remember it's what's inside that counts.

Put Garbage Where It Belongs

Would you allow garbage to be dumped on your head? I think not.

You are the master of what you put into your mind. It is easy to fill your thoughts with vulgar words, filthy jokes, songs and stories, gossip and derogatory comments about minorities and the opposite sex.

When you have a head full of garbage, some of it will spill out. You'll speak garbage, think garbage and drink garbage while you hang out in low-rent places with your garbage-head friends. This poem makes it clear.

> With garbage and junk
> Our can is well fed
> This trash we don't want
> We burn instead
> But what about the dirt
> That you've heard or you've said?
> Oh what can be done
> With a garbage-can head?

If you're a garbage-can head, don't take offense. Just pull your head out and change your ways! If you don't like what you're becoming, make an attitude adjustment. You can select what goes into your mind.

Only you know what's going in. Only you can get it out.

Bird Talk

I once bought a parakeet and promptly started the arduous process of teaching it to talk.

"Danny, Danny," I repeated over and over again—50 repetitions a day for two straight months!

I had given up when it finally happened. I was leaving the room and the parakeet blurted out, "Danny, Danny."

Not one to stop at my first success, I decided to teach him his last name. "Clark, Clark," I said. This time it only took two hundred repetitions before the bird finally said, "Clark, Clark."

Then something very interesting happened. I got sick and spent two days in the house coughing. When I had recovered, I threw a party for some close friends. As I showed off my talking bird, I discovered a great principle about the education process. I put the bird on my finger and, with a little prompting, it said, "Danny Clark." Then, to everyone's amusement the bird coughed.

Of course I didn't teach the bird to cough. He had picked it up the week I was sick. But it did prove that even a bird is a product of its environment. So are human beings. What goes into our minds will eventually come out.

If you grew up with some bad habits, don't be upset at the people who raised you. Just learn this lesson: if you are one way, you can change. You can be different. You can be any which way you want. Just alter your negative environment and hang in there until you get the desired result. Remember, it's not what's on the outside that matters. My buddy owns a dog who only understands French.

Praise for Diversity

America is diverse. More power to us!

We are made up of people from all over the world. That's what makes this such a marvelous place to live. Many of our most successful businesses were started by immigrants. Many of our greatest researchers were born on foreign shores.

The sports world is a wonderful example of people working side-by-side, regardless of nationality. Babe Ruth and Lou Gehrig were sons of German immigrants. Jim Thorpe was a Native American. Joe DiMaggio, Phil Rizzuto, Yogi Berra, Ed Lopat, Vic Raschi—some of the finest Yankees ever to swing a bat—were all first-generation sons of Italian and German parents.

Today we have incredible athletes who are African-American, Oriental and Hispanic. And what about Tiger Woods, the phenomenal young golf pro? His heritage is a blend of many nationalities.

The wonder of America has always been the ability to grow from our differences—to put the parts together for a cohesive and working whole.

Everyone who comes to these shores can live out their dreams. All it takes is fortitude and perseverance.

King for a Day

Dr. Martin Luther King Jr. will always be revered as one of the greatest leaders of all time—regardless of race, country or creed. He was and is a prime example of the beauty of democracy at work, a principle that Dr. King embraced in his soul. Armed with only his convictions, he set out—at the cost of his own life—to change an entire nation.

In the early days of the Civil Rights Movement, his was the lone voice speaking out against the injustice of racial discrimination.

He believed conflicts should be settled peacefully and legally, rather than violently. In the face of physical assault, Dr. King committed himself—and those around him—to non-violent resistance. Who can ever forget the vicious dogs and fire hoses being set against the men, women and children who were asking merely to be treated as human beings?

Dr. King embodies the credo that all Americans should remember: We are created equal. To keep this ideal alive we must all live by its philosophy every day.

From my perspective as a professional speaker committed to touching people's emotions and positively affecting their lives by means of what my words evoke in them, Dr. King is a hero. Many orators have been as good, but none have been better. His powerful words still resonate in the hearts and souls of good, principle-centered people of every race worldwide:

"When evil men plot, good men must plan. When evil men burn and bomb, good men must build and bind. When evil men shout ugly words of hatred, good men commit themselves to the glories of love."

"Most people are thermometers that merely record or register the temperature of majority opinion. We should be thermostats that transform and regulate the temperature of society."

"One day we will learn that the heart can never be totally right if the head is totally wrong. Only through the bringing together of head and heart—intelligence and goodness—shall mankind rise to a fulfillment of his true nature."

"I have a dream that my four little children will one day live in a nation where they will not be judged by the color of their skin, but by the content of their character."

We miss you, Dr. King. The world is better simply because you passed through it. Thanks for fighting for human rights. You had a dream and now it's our turn to keep the dream alive! Oh, that we all could be "King for a day!"

Get Yourself Right

When a father came home from work one afternoon, his son wanted to play. The father had pressing work, but the son was insistent.

On the coffee table lay a magazine which contained a map of the world. The father ripped the map into numerous pieces, gave the pieces to his young son and instructed him to go put the map back together.

The son left the room and the father got to work, thinking it would take a number of hours for the son to put the puzzle together. To his surprise just fifteen minutes later the son was back with the project completed. Amazed, the father asked how he finished so quickly.

"It was easy, on the other side of the map was a picture of a man," said the son. "When I got the man right, the world was right!"

That's how simple it is to make a better world. Start with yourself and make a better you. Only once we each have solved our own problems will we be able to tackle and solve the problems of the world. We can't take care of humanity until we each heal ourselves from within.

The Power of One

We must believe in the Power of One:

- A woman named Rosa Parks changed segregation laws all over the South because she sat in the front of a public bus.
- Ralph Nader started the consumer protection movement when he was in his 20s. The movement has already saved thousands of lives and prevented millions of injuries.
- Rachel Carson activated the environmental movement with her landmark book *Silent Spring.*
- Basketball great Michael Jordan can turn a game around singlehandedly.

In every city, in every state, there are thousands of stories about the Power of One. Look at Microsoft's Bill Gates or Sam Walton who started Wal-Mart. You are one. Why not be one of these "ones," too?

The Real McCoy

Elijah McCoy was a gifted engineer who happened to be the son of slaves. During his lifetime he was awarded 45 patents. In 1872, he invented a device to make steam engines run more smoothly. For a while the market resisted McCoy's invention—no doubt feeling it couldn't work if it was designed by a black man.

But soon buyers recognized the unique design and began asking, "Is this the real McCoy?"

Elijah McCoy's experience was not unusual. Many African-American inventors were denied the opportunities given to white citizens—even though they were just as qualified.

Before the Civil War, African-Americans were not allowed to hold patents. Some were forced to file in a white person's name. Some used aliases. Others saw their precious ideas stolen by unscrupulous wheelers and dealers. Only recently have historians begun to piece together the many sad stories of early black inventors.

Today millions of African-Americans are successful business people. Many own patents and enjoy the prosperity those inventions have brought them. It all started with the real McCoy. And therein lies the lesson.

Land of Opportunity

Some people believe that America, as the "Land of Opportunity," is a thing of the past. They claim that it's too late in our history for anyone to start his or her own business—that every good idea has already been used. They claim it should be easy to be successful. They want instant gratification, to which the products of the marketplace bear witness, from fast food to pain relief to video games with their quick outcomes. When they find out that they have to pay their dues—that success takes time, education, hard work and perseverance—they back off clamoring for quotas and government subsidy. Everybody wants to succeed, but very few of us are willing to prepare to succeed.

Samuel Salter II was different. He didn't dwell on what he didn't have. He didn't harbor angry feelings resulting from the past history of his people and use those feelings as excuses to fail. Samuel saw obstacles not as stumbling blocks, but as stepping stones. He didn't dwell on his character deficits or on the material things that he *didn't* have, but rather on the strengths and assets that he *did* have. He knew that God didn't make "no junk" and didn't respect prisons. Samuel knew God could bless him the same as anybody else. Samuel knew he had a bright mind, enthusiasm and a desire to help others. He studied economics, opportunity cost, scarcity and the fluctuating value of money. He even dabbled in real estate and began to offer his services to others. They were reluctant at first, but the word of his ability spread. Before Samuel knew it, he had an investment firm worth tens of thousands of dollars.

Amazingly, Samuel Salter II was only in high school when he began his firm. He was also an African-American in an industry predominantly run by white men. We all should learn a valuable lesson from Samuel. Instead of waiting for opportunity to knock, we should make things happen. Regardless of our age, gender, race or creed, America is still the "Land of Opportunity." We see people from all walks of life succeeding in business, the arts, entertainment, and sports on a daily basis. Those who sit around whining, "poor me," have nobody to blame but themselves.

The doors to success are never locked—if they are closed we need only turn the knob to open them and walk through. With enough preparation, education and hard work, anybody in America can still get the job of his or her dreams instead of settling for second best. Remember that America's promise is not one of guaranteed security and success, but of life, liberty and the opportunity to pursue happiness.

We All Have the Same

In the simplest sense we are all equal because we each have the same 24 hours every day. Following this line of thought, the way that we become unequal is determined by how we each decide to spend those 24 hours of every day. It's what we do with that time that determines our lot in life. To put it bluntly, if we are not training and pushing ourselves to our ultimate capacity, someone else, somewhere else, is. And when we meet him or her, he or she will win.

Those of us who maximize our days gain steadily on those who fritter away their precious time. Each moment we are either moving forward or backward; there is no such thing as constancy. Time waits for nobody. We go with the flow or against it. We use it or lose it.

The best way to use your time is to plan ahead. It helps increase productivity. There are millions of people trying to capitalize on the time they have. If you don't, you start losing ground. Time is a great equalizer. Hours turn into days, days turn into months and pretty soon those months turn into years. What do you have to account for them?

Time is nothing more than a measurement of change. And if we're not becoming better, we are falling behind. Do you get the picture? There is no going back to try it over. You get one time around. Use your time well.

Inventions from African-Americans

Paper . . . . Africans
Chess . . . . Africans
Alphabet . . . . Africans
Coin changer . . . . James A. Bauer
Rotary engine . . . . Andrew J. Beard
Stainless-steel pads . . . . Alfred Benjamin
Home security system . . . . Marie Brown
Ironing board . . . . Sarah Boone
Street sweepers . . . . C.B. Brooks
Horseshoe . . . . Oscar E. Brown
Lawnmower . . . . John A. Burr
Typewriter . . . . Burridge & Marshman
Peanut butter . . . . George W. Carver
Soap and lotion . . . . George W. Carver
Pressure cooker . . . . Maurice W. Lee
Window cleaner . . . . A.L. Lewis
Pencil sharpener . . . . John L. Love
Fire extinguisher . . . . Tom J. Marshal
Player piano . . . . Joseph Dickinson
Toilet (commode) . . . . T. Elkins
Gas mask . . . . Garrett Morgan
Guitar . . . . Robert Flemming, Jr.
Air conditioner . . . . Frederick M. Jones
Internal combustion
    engine . . . . Frederick M. Jones
Refrigerator . . . . J. Standard
Mop . . . . T.W. Stewart
Elevator . . . . Alexander Miles
Folding chair . . . . Purdy & Sadgwar
Baby buggy . . . . W.H. Richardson
Lawn sprinkler . . . . J.W. Smith

I Will Do More

Passionate determination is the feeling you need to get ahead in life. To make it work for you, try learning this:

I am only one, but I am one.
I cannot do everything, but I can do something.
And what I can do, I ought to do.
And what I ought to do, by the grace of God, I will do.
I will do more than belong—I will participate.
I will do more than care—I will help.
I will do more than believe—I will practice.
I will do more than be fair—I will be kind.
I will do more than dream—I will work.
I will do more than teach—I will inspire.
I will do more than earn—I will enrich.
I will do more than give—I will serve.
I will do more than live—I will grow.
I will do more than talk—I will act.
I will be more than be good—I will be good for
something.

17

SPIRITUAL MOMENTS

Religion is in the heart, not just in the knees.

—DOUGLAS WILLIAM JERROLD

Above all, believe—
in life, love, in yourself.

And if
there is
confusion on your field,
don't be afraid to call
time out and check in
with the Coach.

Love Is a Miracle

One cold evening during the holiday season, a six-year-old boy was standing out in front of a store window. He had no shoes and his clothes were mere rags. A young woman passing by saw the little boy and read the longing in his pale blue eyes. She took him by the hand and led him into the store. There, she bought him new shoes and a complete suit of warm clothing.

When they returned to the street the woman said to the child, "Now you can go home and have a very happy holiday."

The little boy looked up at her and asked, "Are you God, Ma'am?"

She smiled down at him and replied, "No, son, I'm just one of his children."

"I knew you had to be some relation," he said.

We are all related in some way—not only to God, but to each other. Blessed are those that recognize the needs of others and fill them with a simple effort of love and compassion.

Love is a miracle! It can come to any of us at any age, at any time and in any place. All we have to do is reach out and touch someone.

You don't have to wait until the holidays to create your own miracle of love and compassion. Each day can be a holiday, if you show that you care.

Golden Rules

The Golden Rules are universal. There really is one fundamental truth for us all.

The Hindus say the true rule is to guard and do by the things of others as you do by your own.

The Buddhists think one should seek for others the happiness one desires for oneself.

The Jews teach whatsoever you do not wish your neighbor to do to you, do not unto him.

Muslims instruct let none of you treat your brother in a way he himself would dislike to be treated.

Christians admonish all things whatsoever ye would that men should do to you, do ye even so to them.

It all translates into do unto others as you would have others do unto you.

In daily practice people expect as much out of life as you do, so treat them like they deserve it.

As Socrates said, "I am not a Greek or an Athenian. I am a citizen of the world."

We are all citizens of the world and the world will outlive us all. Only our works will leave any lasting impression, as will, of course, the way we treated those around us while we were here. What legacy of leadership are you leaving behind? Will you leave your family, friends, neighbors, community and world in better shape than you found them?

Some of these religions teach that we will be judged and graded on the way we treated those around us when our time on Earth is over.

Are you going to pass the test?

Quarters for Shoes

Every year a television station in a major American city runs a fund-raising activity called Quarters for Shoes. During the holidays the station encourages people to donate quarters for gifts for those members of the community who could use a helping hand.

Here's a letter that it received:

Dear Channel Five,

We are Fred, age 15, Misty, age 12, and B.J., age 9.

Six years ago our father died suddenly. Five months later our mother abandoned us. We have lived with our grandmother ever since. Two years ago grandma adopted us.

Because grandma is a widow and now a single, working parent, she needed help in keeping our home neat. We kids are really messy and didn't keep our things picked up. Grandma gave us an allowance, but we had to pay 25¢ for each item we left laying around. This was okay, but Grandma is a real softy, so she would put our quarters back into our banks, thinking we wouldn't know, but we did. So we remained messy.

Last year, we were watching your station and you were talking about kids who needed shoes and Quarters for Shoes. We decided we wanted to help. The quarters are for being messy and not feeling guilty about it. We like it because we are helping kids not as lucky as we are.

The handwritten letter, signed by Fred, Misty and B.J., included $136. Those three kids might be guilty of having messy rooms, but their hearts are clean and orderly.

Trials

A man who did not believe in God stopped at a black-smith shop to talk to his friend, who was recently converted.

"Do you know what I do with this raw iron?" asked the blacksmith. "I take a piece and heat it in the fire until it is red, almost white. Then I hammer it unmercifully into the shape I desire. When it is formed, I plunge it into a pail of cold water to temper it. Then I heat it again and hammer it some more. And this I do until it is finished."

Before his friend, the nonbeliever, could reply, the black-smith continued.

"But sometimes I find a piece of iron that won't stand this treatment. The heat, the hammering and the cold water are too much and it breaks apart." He pointed to a heap of scrap iron that was near the door of his shop. "Those pieces will never be good for anything."

The blacksmith went on. "Sometimes I have felt God's hammer upon me. But I don't mind, if only he can bring me to what I should be. And so in all these hard times, my prayer is simply this: Try me in any way you wish, Lord, only don't throw me on the scrap heap."

Never Mind, Lord

Only the top of Roger's head was bobbing up and down in the raging river. When the waves lifted him up into view, his arms could be seen thrashing helplessly as he attempted to pull himself toward the distant shore.

Roger had been standing near the fast-moving water when the soft dirt bank crumbled suddenly beneath his feet. He was a strong swimmer, but his strength was no match for the powerful, swift current. When he tried to shout for help, he choked on the water that filled his mouth. Roger struggled for air. The river was racing toward the waterfall and rock-strewn rapids below. It looked as though nothing could save him.

Roger had never believed in God or in the power of prayer, but he had nowhere else to turn. In desperation he sincerely whispered, "God, please bless me. Help me to reach the shore. I don't want to die!"

Roger had hardly finished his prayer when something struck him on his back. A huge log had floated downstream and was pushing against his body. He reached for its branches and grasped them firmly. Then, with a great effort, Roger pulled himself onto the log. Just as he did, one end struck the bank of the stream, causing it to turn toward land. This allowed Roger to quickly—and gratefully—scramble onto the solid earth of the riverbank.

With a sigh of relief Roger said, "Never mind, Lord. I got out by myself. I don't need your help after all."

A Moral Revival

Today's moral revival is a quiet one. It is exemplified by a small book called *Guerrilla Kindness,* written on a whim by a college professor named Gavin Whitsett. The book is a list of small things each of us can do to make life a little more pleasant for others.

You may have heard of them as random acts of kindness.

Much to his surprise, the author has been featured on television talk shows and in magazine articles. Even fellow teachers are talking about the impact of his relatively simple idea.

Who knew this movement would catch on so quickly?

I love the example of the person who stops at a toll booth and pays for the next car in line. It's such a minor, yet meaningful, gesture. It could also be a kind word to someone, a thank-you card, a small gift, an extra tip where none is expected.

Individuals might not be able to save the world, but by doing small deeds we can make living in the world a more pleasant experience. If everyone set a goal of achieving a few of those random acts of kindness each and every day, not only would the people around them feel better, but they would find the true meaning of those sacred words, "It's better to give than receive."

Boomers Turn to Religion

Between the years of 1946 and 1966, about 78 million Americans were born. They are affectionately known as the baby boomers.

Many of these baby boomers rejected traditional American values, including religion and respect for others. They thought it clever to say "Never trust anyone over 30."

Now the baby boomers are over 30. They have children of their own, and they don't want their children to make the same mistakes they made. As a result, the boomers have turned to religion.

One study shows that church attendance by baby boomers climbed steadily between 1975 and 1990—the time when boomers were raising families of their own. A recent Gallup Poll shows a significant increase in the percentage of Americans who say religion plays an important role in their lives. In 1993 Bible sales doubled.

The baby boomers are returning to traditional American values. I find it comforting that spiritual humility, mutual respect, family values and responsible citizenship—which sustained the nation for two centuries—are alive and well.

Hanukkah

It lasts for eight days and it is called Hanukkah.

The Jewish tradition of lighting candles for eight days has survived for 2,000 years. It began when Judah Maccabee recaptured the temple in 165 B.C. It took eight days to cleanse the temple; hence, the eight days of Hanukkah.

Tradition is a powerful unifying force. When the Jews were forced from their homeland, they were allowed to take few possessions. But they did not forget their traditions. Every year in Jewish homes all over the world, the menorah appears at Hanukkah time. Each evening at sundown the family lights candles and remembers its roots.

Sadly, there are some misguided individuals who want to stifle the holiday tradition. They want to drive it from public view because it has a religious base. They are seeking to ban displays of religious symbols—the menorah and the crèche—from public property.

One of the wonderful aspects of living in America is that every group of people can readily exercise its national and religious traditions. Instead of looking to ban such displays, we should add to them. Let the Moslems and Hindus add their religious symbols. Let us learn from one another and broaden our spiritual and religious horizons.

The Easter Egg

Each child in a classroom of eight-year-olds was asked to bring something to school that symbolized life.

Johnny brought a smooth stone he had collected in a nearby stream. He showed everyone the moss on its underside and explained green-growing moss is alive.

Sally brought her grandfather's oxygen tank and explained that the air we breathe allows us to live. There is no more significant symbol of life than air.

Danny proudly presented a large plastic Easter egg. When the teacher opened it, she found it empty. Baffled by its imagery, she asked why this symbolized life. "It's like the tomb at Easter," he explained. "You know, the sepulcher that Jesus was put in. When they came to get his dead body, the tomb was empty. Jesus was not dead. He had risen. The empty tomb is about everlasting life!"

Recognize Life's Opportunities

A large neighborhood was flooded and all the homes were destroyed. There was only one hope for survival—rescue by boat. At last the boat came by to pick up a man stranded on his roof. He told the rescuers, "I'm a religious man and God will save me. No thanks. I don't need a ride."

An hour later another boat came by to rescue the man. The water was up to his waist. The man said, "I'm a religious man and God will save me. No thanks, I don't need a ride."

Finally, a helicopter came by to rescue the man. The water was up to his chest. But again the man replied, "I'm a religious man. I've done everything God required. He will save me."

The man drowned. Naturally he wanted to talk to God about why he wasn't saved, so he set up an appointment. When he finally got to see God, he asked, "How could you let this happen? Why didn't you save me?"

God answered, "I sent two rowboats and a helicopter, what more did you want? In life you will have many opportunities to succeed. But you must take action. It's up to you to accept or reject the opportunities. You must take responsibility for yourself. I will force no one to do right, team up or come back home to me."

God then sent the man back to earth for one more chance. God's words of encouragement to the man before he departed were simple words the man had heard before: "Straight is the gate and narrow the way that leads to eternal life, and few there be that find it. Faith without works is dead!"

18

GOOD LUCK AND BE HAPPY

Luck is not chance—it's toil.
Fortune's expensive smile is earned!

—EMILY DICKINSON

Happiness lies in the fulfillment of the spirit
through the body.
Thus, we possess only the happiness we are able
to understand.

—MAURICE MAETERLINCK

Practice doesn't make perfect— perfect practice makes perfect! And even though we may never reach perfection, in the process we attain excellence!

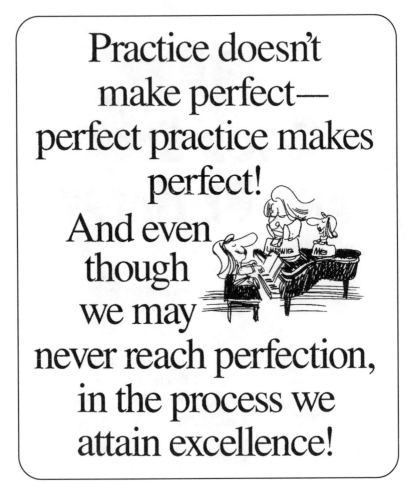

Non Illigetemum Carborundum

Have you ever had a tough day? How about a rough month? Can you imagine 12 months of pure hell? The next time you think you have it bad, remember that neither success nor failure means anything in and of itself—the meaning of both emerges only in comparison to something or someone else. For this reason, I want to introduce you to one of the greatest men who ever lived.

Donald C. Sansom graduated high school at the age of 17. On his 18th birthday, February 25, 1943, he was eligible to enlist in the United States Army Air Corps. The United States was up to her eyeballs in World War II and Don wanted to do his part and serve his country. On April 7 Don left on a troop train headed for preflight officer training school in Santa Ana, California.

That December Don graduated third in his class of 130 servicemen and at 18 years of age, he was the youngest second lieutenant in the United States Army Air Corps.

Overseas training took place in Sioux City, Iowa and by April 1944 Don left for North Africa. On the morning of D-day, when the Allied forces stormed the Normandy beaches, Don boarded a troop ship bound for Italy. Don still recalls the message broadcast over the ship's public address system instructing every soldier to meet on deck in 15 minutes. Over 4,000 soldiers stood at attention as the commander addressed them. "Men, we are headed into war," he said solemnly. "Right now the Allies are flying 1,000 plane raids into Germany every single day. The enemy is shooting down between 50 and 100 planes a day." He then continued, "Using simple arithmetic we can calculate that with 10 crewmen aboard each of these bombers, we are losing between 500 and 1,000 men every day. This means that within the week more than one-third of you could either be dead or captured. I don't know about you, but I think we should change these odds. Look around. Let's commit to one another right here and now to never say "never." We shall change the odds. We shall win this conflict. We shall win it for our families, for our country, for the free world! God bless each of you for standing up for what's right. God bless America!" He then concluded with the Latin words, "Non illigetemum carborundum."

Don couldn't hold back the tears that welled up as he felt for the first time the true meaning of *duty, pride* and *honor.* The loud cheers of the soldiers echoed in his mind and heart for days afterwards. Finally they arrived in Italy and Don was assigned to fly with the squadron commander. Because of his exceptional skill and proven leadership abilities, Don was named the lead bombardier in a B-17 flown by Deke Davies.

Don felt great about his chances for survival, for Deke's reputation was legendary. Deke had already flown 49 missions, returning with his planes shot-up, ripped apart, missing its engines and on fire, but somehow he always found a way to bring his plane and crew back safely.

The next morning would be Don's first bombing mission and Deke's last prior to being rotated home to receive a true hero's welcome. They took off and were flying over Budapest, Hungary. Don was sitting in the bombardier's seat under the nose of the aircraft when they were severely hit by enemy fire. Engine number one was blown apart and engine number two was on fire. With only two of four engines functioning they finished the mission, successfully hit their target and turned around to head back to the base. Halfway back to base they lost fuel and altitude and crash-landed in a wheat field in Yugoslavia.

(Before I continue, it's important to interrupt and remind you to try to feel the emotions Don's family must have felt upon receiving the news that he was missing-in-action. The news of his being alive and of his whereabouts wasn't released for another six months and his friends and loved ones wondered whether he would ever come home).

Back to the story. German soldiers immediately pulled up in trucks and opened machine-gun fire on the wreckage. Don ignited the plane in order to destroy the equipment and documents, and he and his nine fellow crewmembers scattered for cover. The Germans quickly captured the entire crew except for Don and two others, who managed to elude the enemy for over two hours by crawling on their bellies through the field. Finally they made it to a road at the end of the farmland and the peasants working alongside it pointed to a small, nearby bridge underneath which Don and his comrades could hide. When Don heard the *clomp* of the soldiers as they marched across the bridge he thought he and his two comrades were safe—the enemy soldiers had suspended their search and were heading back to base. But wouldn't you know it? The last soldier needed to relieve his bladder and stepped down the embankment for some privacy. He inadvertently looked under the bridge and saw the American airmen crouched in the shadows. He started screaming and within seconds Don and his comrades were surrounded with enemy machine guns pointed at their heads. Don's co-pilot pulled out a white handkerchief, waved it in surrender and reminded his fellow airmen of their commander's words, "Non illigetemum carborundum."

Don and the others were immediately stripped and put in a local farmer's pigpen together with the pigs, mud and muck. They were guarded for two weeks until they were transferred by train to Frankfurt, Germany for interrogation. After one week in solitary confinement, they were transferred to Stalag Luft 3, a German prison camp for airmen of the Allies. The day prior to the arrival of Don and his comrades, the Germans had captured and brutally executed 50 prisoners attempting to escape. It was this prisoner-of-war camp that inspired the film *The Great Escape* and the television series *Hogan's Heroes.*

When winter came, Don and his fellow prisoners were forced on death marches in 15- to 20-degrees-below-0 temperatures and blizzard conditions. These death marches spanned 85 miles and lasted 3 days. The cold was so fierce that many prisoners froze to death, literally dying as they marched. They eventually left this camp in northeastern Germany on the Baltic Sea and marched one last time across Germany to its southwestern corner, where they stopped at a huge installation called Stalag 7A. Ten thousand soldiers were incarcerated at this single location. Enduring torture and starvation while sustaining motivation and personal dignity would have been nearly impossible except for the tiny inspirational reminder Don's co-pilot had carved in the latrine door: NON ILLIGETEMUM CARBORUNDUM.

Don and his fellow prisoners remained in this camp until it was finally liberated on April 29, 1945 by Patton's Seventh Army Tank Battalion, which had just won a battle in a small village next to the camp. Don was sent to France for the rehabilitation of his sickly and weakened 129-pound body. He was released at a healthier 170 pounds and allowed to return home to the States. During the three weeks of his rehabilitation Don had time to focus on his dreams and set personal and educational goals to attain them. It was during that time that he set his professional sights on becoming a dentist.

In 1946, while attending the University of Utah as a student in the predentistry program, he fell in love with the beautiful, talented and artistic Barbara Sims. They married and headed for Kansas City in 1947 for Don to attend dental school. Over the years they became the proud parents of six children and settled in Utah to raise their family. Today Dr. Donald C. Sansom, affectionately known to family and hundreds of admiring friends as "Doc," not only has one of the largest and most successful dental practices in the intermountain West, but is especially appreciated for his amazing love of life. Don, even at the age of 72, is the legendary "Silver Fox" of the Snowbird Ski Resort—guaranteed to out snow ski anyone else on the mountain. He is an amazing water skier as well, and he can shoot his age in golf. Most important to him, though, are the scores of people young and old that he has *taught* how to snow ski, water ski, golf, mountain bike, hike and be fully alive!

A lot of people only look forward to Friday instead of Monday. They hate their jobs and think they are paid for attendance instead of productivity. Not Don. Many of them have stopped dreaming and when you lose your dreams you die. They are dead and don't even know it. They are missing-in-action and don't know how to make their way back home. Not Don. And why not Don? His glass has never been half-empty. His work ethic has never been one of half measure. His love of freedom and respect for America has never been halfhearted and his ability to bounce back has never been half-cocked. Since the day he heard the Latin phrase on the troop ship, and again underneath the enemy bridge when he was captured in war—and ever since he saw it on a daily basis at the prison camp latrine door—that phrase has served as Don's his rallying cry, helping him to persevere and helping him to help others do the same. In fact, he has claimed the phrase as the official dental motto. Regardless of whether he's dealing with a negative patient, moguls on a black diamond ski run, a cold mountain lake during a weekend of waterskiing, or a deep sand trap in the golf course rough, Don "Doc" Sansom grins and wins by understanding: "Non Illigetemum Carborundum—Don't Let the Bastards Grind You Down!"

Do You Shun Competition?

Competition is the economic system America is based on. If you shun it, you shouldn't.

Mr. Ling owned a dry cleaning store that had been in the family for years. Then a developer came along and wanted to push Mr. Ling out of his spot. Mr. Ling did not know how to do anything else for a living. He didn't want to lose this store and he made it clear to the developer he was going to stay put.

The conflict escalated as the developer built the shopping mall around Mr. Ling's establishment. To get even, the developer put cleaning shops on both sides of Mr. Ling to drive him out of business. Most would have quit, but not Mr. Ling.

The Ling family hadn't been in business for so many years without knowing how to compete and survive. To combat the competition, Mr. Ling made a giant sign and hung it above his front door. As a matter of fact, after he hung the sign, Mr. Ling had more business than ever. What did the sign say? THIS WAY TO MAIN ENTRANCE.

There is always a way to survive. We always rise to the level of our competition and become better as a result.

Like Mr. Ling, you might find it hard, but only those who compete are going to survive, thrive and succeed.

Would You Tell Them?

If you sat down to write a letter that would be opened after you're gone, what would you write? How about:

- Nothing is known positively and completely—keep searching.
- The world is full of things to do over and sort out—practice makes perfect.
- Every government could be better—vote.
- The best picture has not yet been painted—paint it.
- The greatest novel has not yet been written—write it.
- The most inspirational music is yet to come—listen.
- The study of space is in its infancy—imagine.
- Only 2 percent of all knowledge is known—study.
- The greatest sports records have yet to be broken—dream.
- Live each day as if it were your last—do it now.
- The regrets you'll have when you die are not regarding the things you did, but the things you wish you had done—leave no regrets.

I would conclude my letter by confessing that atoms never made much sense to me. The thought of my body being composed of tiny particles spinning in space is too abstract for me to comprehend. What I do understand is that through the make-up of cells, chromosomes and genes, somehow all those atoms have combined in distinct forms to make every human being completely unique. That means each of us is here for a specific purpose—we each would most definitely be lousy as someone else, yet we are awesome as the person each of us is meant to be—when our time on earth is through, no one else will ever fit the space left behind by the removal of each of our jigsaw-puzzle-piece selves.

Think about your protons, neutrons and electrons spinning around in space with the rest of us. You, and only you, have the God-given right and ability to make something of them—you are so extremely unique. What will it be?

Perseverance

Two frogs fell in a bowl of cream.
One had an optimistic gleam,
But the other took the gloomy view.
"We'll drown," he cried, and without adieu
He gave a last despairing cry,
Flung up his legs and said good-bye.
Said the other frog with a steady grin,
"I can't get out, but I won't give in;
I'll just swim around till my strength is spent,
Then will I die the more content."
Bravely he swam till it would seem
His struggles began to churn the cream.
On top of the butter at last he stopped,
And out of the bowl he gaily hopped.
What of the moral? It's easily found:
If you can't get out, keep swimming around.

The Pearl

There once was an oyster, whose story I tell
Who found that some sand had got under his shell;
Just one little grain, but it gave him a pain
For oysters have feelings for all sorts of things.

How did he berate the working of fate
Which had led him to such a deplorable state?
Did he curse the government and cry for an election?
And cry that the seas should have given protection?

No. He said to himself as he lay on the shelf,
Since I cannot remove it, I'll try to improve it.

The years rolled around as years always do.
And he came to his ultimate destiny—stew!
And the small grain of sand that had bothered him so
Was a beautiful pearl, all richly aglow.

The tale has a moral, for isn't it grand
What an oyster can do with a morsel of sand?
What couldn't we do if we'd only begin
With all the things that get under our skin.

How Bad Do You Want It?

If you want a thing bad enough,
To go out and fight for it,
Work day and night for it,
Give up your time and your peace and your sleep for it,
If only the desire of it,
Makes you mad enough,
Never to tire of it,
Makes you hold all things tawdry and cheap for it,
If life seems all empty and useless without it,
And all that you scheme and dream is about it,
If you'll gladly sweat for it,
Fret for it,
Plan for it,
Lose all terror of God and man for it,
If you'll simply go after the thing that you want,
With all your capacity,
Strength and tenacity,
Faith, hope and confidence, stern pertinacity,
If neither cold, poverty, famished and haunt,
Nor sickness, nor pain
Of body, or brain,
Can turn you away from the thing that you want,
If dogged and grim you besiege and beset it,
You'll get it.

Does It Show on Your Face?

The next time you study yourself in the mirror, don't look at how your face looks, look at what it shows. Is happiness reflected back?

You don't have to tell how you live each day
You don't have to say if you work or play
A tried, true barometer serves in this place
However you live, it will show in your face.
The deceit that you bear in your heart
Will not stay inside when it first gets a start
For sinew and blood are a thin veil of lace
What you wear in your heart you wear on your face.
If your life is unselfish, if for others you live
For not what you get, but how much you give
If you live close to God in his infinite grace
You don't have to tell it, it shows in your face.

If happiness does not show on your face, seek it out. It isn't only found by doing what one likes, but in liking what one does. No one has ever injured their eyesight by looking on the bright side of things.

Playing the Game

The best way to play any game in life is to give it your best shot. Many people miss out because they don't carry through to the end. So whenever you play a game or commit to a project, try and remember these words:

Whatever the game, and whatever the odds,
The winning is all up to you;
For it isn't the score, and it isn't the prize,
That counts when the playing is through!
In the great game of Life, it's the purpose to win,
And the courage to fight to the end
That determines for you what degree of success
Will be scored to your credit, my friend.
The best you can do may not be quite enough
To defeat your opponents today;
But you never can lose, and you never can fail,
If you put all you've got in your play;
And the greatest reward that your efforts can bring,
Is the fact that you stood to the test—
That you played a clean game, and fought a good fight,
And you always were doing your best!
Anyone who gives their best, never really loses.

Parable of the Eagle

The bald eagle is the most magnificent bird—the ultimate symbol of freedom, strength, loyalty, honor, majesty and grace. When our founding fathers were selecting a national symbol, John Adams pushed for the dove as the symbol of peace. Benjamin Franklin wanted the turkey for its cunning. Thank God they agreed on Thomas Jefferson's suggestion of the mighty eagle—it represents:

Freedom—soaring upwards of hundreds of feet in the sky, its eyesight is nine times greater than that of any human, and when hunting it folds back its wings to dive straight down at speeds of 100 miles an hour.

Strength—the female weighs between 12 and 14 pounds with a wingspan of 6 feet and is larger than the 9-pound male. Its talons have the gripping strength of 3-4 times that of a very strong muscle-bound man. They build the largest nests of any bird, some weighing 2,000 pounds.

Loyalty—they mate for life and return to the same nest year after year to hatch their young.

Honor—the parents teach their offspring everything they know about flying, hunting, building a nest, selecting the right nesting sight and even choosing the perfect lifelong mate. Only then do the adults send the baby birds out into the world to soar on their own.

Majesty and *Grace*—eagles have no natural enemies, are respected by man and beast, go where they want to go and soar and glide and fly in the clouds above the highest cliffs for hours at a time without any rest.

If only we could fully comprehend the "Parable of the Eagle":

A farmer in Wyoming was walking through the forest and found a newborn eagle that had fallen from its nest. He took it home, nursed it back to full strength and put it in the chicken coop to raise it. A few years later a Native American naturalist stopped by the farmer's house and noticed the full-grown bird. "What is that eagle doing in the chicken coop? It isn't right that an eagle should be kept with chickens." The Native American picked up the bird and said,

"Thou hast the heart of an eagle. Thou dost belong to the sky and not to the earth. Stretch forth thy wings and fly."

The bird looked around outside its comfort zone but quickly saw the chickens and dropped to the ground. "See, I told you it was a chicken," the farmer bragged. "I have trained it as a chicken and it thinks and pecks and walks like a chicken."

The naturalist exclaimed, "No, no, it is a mighty eagle." He took the bird and stood on top of the farmer's shed. "Stretch forth thy wings and fly," he said. But once again the eagle saw its chicken friends below and jumped down to peck with them.

Early the next morning the naturalist revisited the farm and took the bird from the chicken coop to the base of a great mountain. In classic Native American tradition, he held the bird high over his head and bellowed loud enough for his voice to echo and bounce off the cliff walls. "Thou art an eagle. Thou hast the heart of an eagle. Thou dost belong to the wind and the sky and not unto the earth. Stretch forth thy wings and fly." The eagle looked down uncomfortably, but the naturalist forced it to look directly into the sun. A moment passed and then, with the screech of an eagle, it stretched forth its wings and flew.

Sometimes we fail to dream mighty dreams and fail to soar to the heights that the eagle in each of us can attain because we have our eyes down with the chickens. We are pecking and grabbing about because we lack self-confidence and self-esteem and so we minimize our own worth. We are groping because we're missing the link that connects us from where we are to where we want to be. Don't you think it is now time to start seeing yourself as you really are, an eagle soaring above the average, negative crowd? You were born to succeed. Stretch forth *your* wings and fly!

Clark's Credo

- I'm smart, talented and I never say "never."
- I'm wanted, important, lovable, capable and I can succeed.
- I have pride, class, flexibility, grace, discipline and balance.
- I'm a good athlete, I love music and I get good grades in school.
- I never say "I can't"—I always say "I can, I will."
- If I fall down or fail, I just get back up and go again.
- If I spill or make a mistake, I learn why, clean it up and say "no big deal."
- I treat others as I want to be treated.
- I always tell the truth and play by the rules.
- I dream mighty dreams. If I don't dream, how can I make a dream come true?
- I love God and will do the right thing simply because it's the right thing to do!
- Therefore I leave no regrets by always leaving my family, friends, job, neighborhood, country and world in better shape than I found them. I'm somebody very special. No one can ever take my place. Whenever I leave, everybody says, "I like me best when I'm with you, I want to see you again."

About the Author

Dan Clark, CSP, is one of the "hottest" speakers on the platform today. Since 1982, Dan has spoken to over 2.5 million people in all 50 states, throughout Canada, and in 13 other countries in Europe and Asia, including the former Soviet Union.

Dan is the author of seven highly acclaimed books including *Getting High—How to Really Do It*, *One Minute Messages* and *Internal Excavations*. Dan is also a primary contributing author to the *New York Times* bestselling *Chicken Soup for the Soul* series.

Dan is a successful businessman, actor, songwriter/recording artist, creator of over 40 audio and video training programs, and an award-winning athlete who fought back from a paralyzing injury that cut short his football career.

Dan's client list is a Who's Who of the best organizations in the world, including Meeting Professionals International, GE Capital, Republic Mortgage Insurance Co., IBM, 3M, AT&T-Lucent Technologies, Boeing, ServiceMaster, Marriott Hotels, Nations Bank, Nordstrom, Prudential Insurance, Intermountain Health Care, Footlocker, the NCAA, American School Counselors Association, American Vocation Association, the United Nations and hundreds more.

You can contact Dan Clark for speaking engagements seminars and a full products catalog at:

Dan Clark
Dan Clark Associates
P.O. Box 8689
Salt Lake City, UT 84108
(800) 676-1121 • fax (801) 485-5789
e-mail sdanclarkp@aol.com